Sal Mineo

Also by H. Paul Jeffers

An Honest President: The Life and Presidencies of Grover Cleveland
'21': Every Day Was New Year's Eve
Where There's Smoke, There's Murder: A Nicholas Chase Mystery
Bully Pulpit: A Teddy Roosevelt Book of Quotations
Corpus Corpus
The Perfect Pipe
The Good Cigar: A Celebration of the Art of Cigar Smoking
High Spirits
What Mommy Said: An Arlene Flynn Mystery
Colonel Roosevelt: Theodore Roosevelt Goes to War, 1897–1898
Commissioner Roosevelt: The Story of Theodore Roosevelt &
the New York City Police
Reader's Guide to Murder
A Spy in Canaan: My Secret Life as a Jewish-American Businessman,
with Howard Schack
Hollywood Mother of the Year: Sheila MacRae's Own Story,
with Sheila MacRae
Blood on the Nueces
Morgan
Owlboot Trail
Santa Claus
Secret Orders
Texas Bounty
The Adventure of the Stalwart Companions
Bloody Business: Scotland Yard's Most Famous and Shocking Cases
The CIA: A Close Look at the Central Intelligence Agency
Gentleman Gerald: The Crimes and Times of Gerald Chapman, America's First
"Public Enemy No. 1"
Gods and Lovers
A Grand Night for Murder
Murder Along the Way: A Prosecutor's Personal Account of Fighting Violent
Crime in the Suburbs, with Kenneth Gribetz
Murder on Mike
Tombstone Revenge
Who Killed Precious? How FBI Special Agents Combine High Technology and
Psychology to Identify Violent Criminals

Sal Mineo

His Life, Murder, and Mystery

———

H. Paul Jeffers

CARROLL & GRAF PUBLISHERS, INC.
NEW YORK

First Carroll & Graf edition 2000

Carroll & Graf Publishers, Inc.
A Division of Avalon Publishing Group
19 West 21st Street
New York, NY 10010-6805

Library of Congress Cataloging-In-Publication Data is available.
ISBN: 0-7867-0777-1

Manufactured in the United States of America

To the memory of Jim Kershner and high school days.

When in disgrace with fortune and men's eyes
I all alone beweep my outcast fate,
And trouble deaf heaven with my bootless cries.
              —William Shakespeare, *Sonnet* 29

Contents

Prologue

Invitation to Brunch
in Boys Town

That a quarter of a century has gone by since the last time I saw Sal Mineo is as difficult for me to believe as is the cruel reality that he has been dead all this time, murdered in a West Hollywood alleyway. He died at the very moment he seemed poised for a deserved and brilliant new career. Yet I can hear him now as clearly as on a Saturday morning in January 1976 when he phoned me at my house in Huntington Beach, California.

"Hey, Paulie. It's me, and I'm back in L.A."

There was no mistaking the voice. Not *that* voice. Hollywood had taken the boy out of the Bronx years ago, but there'd been no way of taking the Bronx out of Sal Mineo. It was there when he played Tony Curtis as a boy in *Six Bridges to Cross,* then opposite Paul Newman in *Somebody Up There Likes Me,* and again a few years later in *Exodus.* And despite *Rebel Without a Cause* being set in Los Angeles, New York had been written all over the young doe-eyed, pouty-lipped actor who created the first homosexual teenager in a movie in Hollywood history, in the character of rich, sad, lonely, desperately love-seeking Plato.

Because 1950s American morality required it, he was doomed to die at the movie's end, but as I watched the film in my Pennsylvania hometown I was astonished to see a homosexual character depicted on the screen, however timidly. I use "homosexual" because the popularizing of the term "gay" was a decade and a half away, as were my meeting Sal Mineo in New York City and my unexpected confirmation of Sal's sexual preference.

How I achieved both the same night was a result of curiosity, coupled with the happy accident of geography. Having settled in New York in 1964 to pursue a career in broadcast journalism at ABC News and then at all-news radio station WINS, I was also struggling to carve out a second career as an author of books. By 1969, at age 34, I'd published four nonfiction titles for young adults and a paperback novel with so much sex, perversion, and violence that my friends and family were shocked and embarrassed. My apartment was at 75th Street and York Avenue, and Sal was directing a play just two blocks away at an off-Broadway theater on East 73rd, logically named Stage 73.

The name of the play was *Fortune and Men's Eyes*. Written by John Herbert, it was set in a prison. Featuring frontal nudity, its most dramatic moment, I'd heard, was a homosexual rape in a shower room right on stage.

The most powerful of New York's drama critics, Clive Barnes, had scathingly written, "How far can you go? Or, if you think it more pertinent, how far are we going? In the theater, that is. And in the business of breaking old taboos, and all that nonsense."

Of Sal, he wrote, "I'm not sure what kind of reputation Mr. Mineo has—he is a minor Hollywood player, I believe—but I am perfectly certain what reputation Mr. Mineo deserves."

Ordinarily, a Clive Barnes blast would close a show. But the result in this case was outrage in New York's gay community in the immediate aftermath of what's become known as the Stonewall Rebellion, in which gays launched the Gay Pride Movement by fighting back against police who had raided a gay bar in Greenwich Village. The Barnes review provoked a boost in patronage at the box office.

Being a fan of Sal, I settled into my seat in the middle of the small theater wishing he were acting in the play. Opening the program to pages listing Who's Who in the Cast, I went directly to his name: "SAL MINEO (Director)."

I read, "Mr. Mineo is an erotic politician."

This certainly intrigued me.

The biography warned, "When you meet him, he scares you."

The edge was taken off that admonition with, "The man is warm, mysterious, sensuous, playfully evil, artistic, detached, and often times, brilliantly sardonic."

Possessing some of those character traits myself, I was determined to meet him no matter how scary he might be at first. Thanks to the press pass I carried in my wallet, after the show I managed not only to insinuate myself backstage but right up to him. After blurting my name and identifying myself as a newsman, I asked, "Just what is an *erotic politician?*"

"Stick around until I take care of some show business," he replied, smiling sardonically. "You can buy me a drink and I'll show you."

Half an hour or so later, I could hardly believe I was in a booth at the rear of a small bar on First Avenue drinking Scotch with Sal Mineo and everyone I'd seen him play in movies. I was looking at him and seeing the curly-haired, dark-eyed, sinewy juvenile delinquent in *Six Bridges to Cross;* Paul Newman's friend in *Somebody Up There Likes Me;* vulnerable Plato in *Rebel;* the teenage toughs in *Crime in the Streets, The Young Don't Cry,* and *Dino,* who'd saddled him with the nickname "switchblade kid" that he had tried to throw off in *The Gene Krupa Story.* Nursing drinks with me were Dov Landau, the tormented victim of rape in a Nazi concentration camp who became an Israeli freedom fighter in *Exodus;* and barechested American Indian youths from *Tonka* and *Cheyenne Autumn.* Present from *Who Killed Teddy Bear?* was a busboy named Lawrence, a Peeping Tom, stalking, sexual predator whose exquisitely muscular torso was seen sheathed in form-fitting T-shirts, snug white briefs and in a swimming pool scene, clad in a skintight bikini that flaunted his rampant sexuality.

"What did you think of the play?" he asked. "Were you shocked by the subject?"

"Not really. I knew it was about guys in prison. I expected it to be grim."

"I meant were you shocked by the sex?"

"I've always assumed that guys in prison have sex with one another."

"What do you think in general of guys who swing with guys?"

"To each his own."

"What about you?"

"What *about* me?"

He leaned across the table. "Would you ever have sex with a guy?"

I laughed nervously. "Is that a proposition?"

"What if it is?"

I was starting to grasp the meaning of *erotic politician* and to appreciate that he was very good at being one.

He reared back and chuckled. "What are you nervous about?"

"I've never had a sexual proposition from a movie star."

"I've never propositioned a newsman and I'm not nervous."

"But you're . . . *Sal Mineo*."

"Just think of me as a wop from the Bronx."

"Yeah, right."

He looked at his watch. "Will it be your place or mine? We can just talk if you like."

Mine was only two blocks away.

On the way, he asked me about myself. When I told him I hoped to have a career writing books, he exclaimed, "That's great. You can write my life story."

"I'd be honored."

With a shrug, he said, "What the hell's it matter? Nobody would want to read a book about me anyway. I'm just what Clive Barnes said. I used to be a minor Hollywood player."

"Two Academy Award nominations is not a minor player."

"*Rebel Without a Cause* was almost 15 years ago and *Exodus* nine. It's been downhill for me ever since."

"That's bullshit and you know it."

"Anyway, about you writing my life story," he said as we arrived at my apartment house, "since I'm only 30 years old I'm probably too young to have a book written about me, right?"

Minutes later when I found myself in my living room with the Sal Mineo who had created on screen the characters that had shaped my image of him, I discovered that he was none of them.

Wondering who was the true Sal Mineo as he left in the morning, I asked, "Were you serious about me writing your life story someday?"

Giving a thumbs-up, he replied, "Absolutely!"

Thereafter, whenever our divergent paths happened to cross, or in sporadic phone calls, he'd sooner or later get around to the idea and tease me with stories he wanted in the book and a few he did not. But that was as far as it ever went.

Although thrilled to hear from Sal on a Saturday seven years after curiosity and geography first brought us together for what ranked as one of the most astonishing experiences of my life, I was surprised to learn he was in Los Angeles. "I thought you were in San Francisco in a play," I said. "Something about a cat."

"It's called *P.S. Your Cat Is Dead*. I play a bisexual burglar who gets caught in the act and gets tied up and tormented by his victim. We're bringing it to L.A. I moved back to town a couple of days ago."

"That's great. When can I see you?"

"Whatcha doin' tuhmaruh? We could have brunch and then hang out together for a couple of hours, if you get my meaning, which I'm sure you do."

We met at a restaurant near the Westwood Playhouse. Sal lived nearby in a neighborhood of West Hollywood known as Boys Town, so named because of its population of gay men.

He was as handsome as ever. Basking in the sight of his unruly black hair, the bedroom eyes, imperfect nose, muscled arms and torso, narrow hips, and bewitching smile, I blurted out, "You're looking fit and very sexy."

"Since I'm half naked in the play," he said, flexing, "I thought I'd better get into shape."

He went on to tell me more about the play and spoke proudly of getting good reviews, but after a few minutes he said, "To hell with wasting time eating. Let's go to my place."

It was a modest, almost shabby apartment on Holloway Drive, just below Sunset.

That afternoon, as he had each time I saw him during the seven years of our much-too-intermittent meetings, he fulfilled all the enticing promises I'd found in the biographical sketch in the Stage 73 program.

Alas, that was my last time with him. A couple of weeks later as he returned home from rehearsing his play he was accosted by a man with a knife, stabbed once in the chest, and left to bleed to death.

But Sal isn't really gone. As you will read, a quarter of a century later he remains as alive, vibrant, and exciting as ever in the memories and hearts of a lot of people like me who loved him. Yet, except for one novel published in 1982 and brief passages about him in film histories and a handful of Hollywood true-crime books, he has been shockingly unappreciated as a gifted actor and a man of dauntless tenacity with the honesty to recognize and embrace who he was and the bravery to declare himself proudly to a mostly hostile world.

Believing his story deserved to be recorded and having no idea how many seasons of life were left for me, I decided to do it myself.

one

"The Kid's Got a Glow"

When 13-year-old Sal Mineo hurried along the block of West 44th Street toward the St. James Theater for an audition, he'd already been in two Broadway shows. In a bit part in *The Rose Tattoo* by Tennessee Williams, he was a scrawny Italian kid with one line: "The goat is in the yard." He'd played a shoeshine boy in *Dinosaur Wharf*, but it closed after only four performances. There was also a small role in *The Little Screwball*, in a summer stock production at Connecticut's Westbury Country Playhouse starring comedy veteran Walter Abel. None of these had called on the actor listed in the programs as Salvatore Mineo, Jr., to sing. Yet after a performance of *Screwball*, a talent scout had asked him to come to New York to try out as an understudy for the role of Chulalongkorn, the Crown Prince of Siam, in the smash hit heralded on the St. James marquee:

RODGERS and HAMMERSTEIN
present
GERTRUDE LAWRENCE
and
YUL BRYNNER
In a New Musical Play
THE KING AND I

The show had been running for more than a year. Commissioned by Miss Lawrence as a vehicle for herself and based on Margaret Landon's novel *Anna and the King of Siam*, it was the story of Anna Leonowens, an English widow with a young son who, in the 1860s, had been hired to teach English to the children of the King of Siam. The part of the scary, overbearing, bald-headed, muscular monarch who was tamed by a headstrong teacher had made Yul Brynner a star.

Directed by John van Druten and choreographed by Jerome Robbins, the lavish production offered a beautifully soaring score with several songs that were on their way to becoming pop standards, including "Getting to Know You," "We Kiss in a Shadow," "I Have Dreamed," and the romantic "Hello, Young Lovers." The role of the prince who becomes king at the end of the show called for the prince to reprise a number about life's contradictions titled "A Puzzlement." But the sheet music clasped in Sal's hand as other boys took to the stage ahead of him was for none of these. While the other auditioners all performed numbers from the show, he'd chosen to do a novelty tune, *Down Yonder*, a hillbilly song elevated by a Doris Day recording to the heady heights of the "Your Hit Parade" radio program.

Spotlighted as he sang the lively ditty, Sal heard whispers and giggles coming out of the black depths of the theater.

"Everybody was in hysterics, and I knew that was it," Sal would say of the restlessness he detected in the people out there in the dark. "I had goofed."

What he couldn't observe or hear from the stage as sweat beaded on his brow was casting director John Fearnley turning to his assistant, Barbara Wolferman, and whispering, "He's the one. The kid's got a glow."

No one had to convince Josephine Mineo that her child was special.

Her third son, the black-haired, brown-eyed boy with a captivating smile had been born on January 10, 1939, seven years, 11 months and two days after Josephine Alvisi had married Salvatore Mineo. A skilled woodworker and sculptor who'd emigrated from Sicily, Salvatore, Sr., earned a living in the Great Depression by starting a coffin-making company. The family lived in a small walk-up apartment in New York City's East Harlem, a polyglot neighbor-hood of Italians and Puerto Ricans. Little Salvatore was nicknamed Junior. His brother Victor had been born in 1936 and Michael had come into the world in 1937.

On the day Sal was born, glimpses into the future of that world were taking shape a couple of miles beyond the East River on a huge tract of reclaimed marshy land that had been the city's main garbage dump. In his 1925 novel *The Great Gatsby,* F. Scott Fitzgerald saw it as "a valley of ashes—a fantastic farm where ashes grow like wheat into ridges and hills and grotesque gardens bounded on one side by a small foul river." In 1939 the nations of the world had erected grand exhibition halls to show "the world of tomorrow." Mayor Fiorello LaGuardia was to fling open the gates of the New York World's Fair in a ceremony on April 30.

Had the Mineos wanted to take in the exposition, admission would cost 75 cents each for Salvatore and Josephine and a quarter for three-year-old Victor. Michael and Junior would get in free. But for a coffin-maker with a wife and three kids to support, a buck and a half plus subway fares to Flushing Meadow in Queens was a princely sum. Neither was there spare money to go downtown to take in a movie with a stage show at Radio City Music Hall or the Roxy, Capitol, or Paramount theaters. And even as attractive as were the prices of men's shoes advertised in the papers as on sale at Macy's for $3.89 to $6.94 and a bargain for ladies' corsets at Bergdorf-Goodman ($5 to $32), the Mineos would have to make do with what they had and try to put away enough money little by little to buy a house for a growing family.

Need for additional living space became even more imperative in 1943 with the birth of a girl, Sarina. But it would be another five years before the Mineos were able to afford to buy an old house in a Bronx neighborhood that still boasted trees and open spaces. Lo-cated on East 217th Street within walking distance (through Wood-lawn Cemetery) to Van Courtlandt Park, the three-story house was readily convertible into a two-family home. The Mineos rented out the basement to help defray the mortgage.

Sal's upstairs room had been a kitchen. It still had a sink and a stove.

Any new boy in a neighborhood is likely to have trouble being

accepted by kids who have lived in the area all their lives, but in
Sal's move to the Bronx he found himself shunned because word
was out that his father made coffins.

"They wouldn't have anything to do with me," Sal would recall.
"So late one afternoon I thought I'd get on their good side and have
some fun. I told them to come over to the back door of my father's
shop and look in the big coffin just inside the door. I promised them
it would be full of bags of candy. I got home from school just before
they arrived, climbed into the coffin, and shut the lid. When the kids
showed up and opened it, I jumped up and yelled, 'Boo.' Their eyes
almost fell out of their heads. Were they scared! They ran like hell,
screaming for their mothers."

Learning of this escapade, Salvatore Mineo ordered Sal to give
candy to each of the boys he'd terrified, to be paid for out of his
allowance.

"The kids took the candy," Sal noted, "but they didn't take me.
I still didn't belong."

Acceptance came three months later when Sal saw the gang of
kids ducking behind a fence. They had a stolen a pack of cigarettes
and a couple of cigars. As they started to puff away, one of them
told Sal that if he wanted to join the gang he'd have to smoke an
entire cigar. Not wanting to be shunned again, Sal lit up the stogie.
As the others coughed and choked on their cigarettes, he willed himself to smoke the cigar down to a stub. Impressed, the gang elected
him vice president.

When Sal was nine and attending the neighborhood parochial
school, St. Mary's, the nuns of the Dominican order astonished him
by telling him he was to be in a play about Jesus. He was to portray
the Savior.

"I was struck dumb," Sal would recall for an interviewer eight
years later. "I had been to movies and I knew there was such a thing
as acting. But to have these nuns, who had dedicated their lives to
God, ask *me* to portray Jesus—well, that was something beyond my
understanding. I was afraid that it would be wrong. The sisters kept
telling me it was all right, I had nothing to be afraid of. That afternoon I took the script home. It was handwritten. I studied it as
though my life depended on it."

He returned to school confident that he could play the role.

When he found a drawing of Christ in a religious book and noted that He was carrying a staff, he informed the nuns that he should have one in the play. The sisters replied that it wasn't necessary. When he persisted in his desire for a staff, someone proposed that he carry a sawed-off broomstick.

"What an idea! I wouldn't hear of it," Sal recalled. But by the afternoon of the play, he still had no staff. After putting on his costume in a classroom, he walked disconsolately toward the room where the play was to be presented. Waiting for the drama to begin, he found a solution to the problem of Jesus's staff. On a wall beneath a sign declaring FOR EMERGENCY ONLY hung a large fire hook. He grabbed the hook off the wall, tied a blue ribbon from his costume to its top, heard his cue, and happily made his entrance.

Years later, he said that it had been a sacred moment of revelation that he had been born to be an actor, and more than that, a star.

Although the nuns had spotted young Salvatore Mineo as a personification of the Lord Jesus, the nine-year-old soon disappointed them by getting involved in a schoolyard brawl that left him with a bloody and broken nose. Other misdeeds soon confirmed the nuns' fears that Salvatore was "a natural troublemaker." He was booted out of school.

At age ten he was the leader of a group of gamin would-be gangsters. After one daring caper, they stashed the loot in one of Salvatore Mineo, Sr.'s caskets. Their cache was discovered almost immediately.

With Josephine at her wits' end and fearing that her youngest son could be destined for a reformatory, fate took a hand in the form of the owner of a school of dancing who earned his money by persuading mothers like Josephine that their kids had real talent, which, with a little training, could land them lucrative work in the theater and in the new and rapidly growing field of television. After spotting Sal playing sandlot baseball, he tracked down Josephine, told her, "The kid's graceful," and urged her to sign him up for classes.

Sal was thrilled with the prospect of being on television. Josephine was skeptical.

The man persisted. Her youngest son was not only good-looking, he argued, he positively radiated charm.

Josephine looked at the man warily. His true goal, she suspected, was to collect tuition. Dubious about his promise of Sal making a lot of money on TV, she hoped dancing classes would get Sal off the streets for a few hours a week. She asked the man to leave his card.

When the pitchman was gone, Sal pleaded to be signed up.

In this he was supported by his brothers, Vic and Mike, and sister, Sarina, each of whom hoped to benefit from Josephine's rule regarding her children: what one got, they all got. Vic and Mike wanted clarinet lessons. Sarina wanted to learn to dance, too.

Josephine agreed to enroll Sal in the school along with Sarina because Sarina would let her know if Sal actually went to classes. She needn't have worried. With the possibility of being on TV as motivation, Sal took to dancing enthusiastically and discovered he not only enjoyed it, he was good.

When it became obvious to Josephine, and even to Sal, that the dancing-school proprietor had no connections to anyone in theater and television, but convinced that the boy had promise, Josephine placed him in a different school, one with a record of placing worthy students on TV programs. To Sal's delight, he found himself performing occasionally on local TV on *The Ted Steele Show*.

Being a dancer on television came at a price, however. He found himself ostracized from the gang. When the president called him a sissy, a fistfight ensued. This resulted in both being summoned to the office of the principal of Sal's new public school, P.S. 72. He asked Sal why he'd been in a fight. Sal explained. The principal demanded proof that Sal was a dancer. Sal tapped a few bars. The principal declared, "Son, you're a pretty good hoofer."

One day in the fall of 1950, as 11-year-old Sal and seven-year-old Sarina were clogging and tapping away in class, a smartly dressed woman appeared in the dance studio. Sal assumed she was a suspicious mother checking to see if her kid was there.

After a few minutes, she walked over to him and in a demanding tone said, "Boy, let me hear you say, 'The goat is in the yard.' "

Sal said the words.

The woman commanded, "Say the line again."

When Sal complied, she introduced herself. She was Cheryl Crawford, a Broadway producer with offices on West 45th Street. She was producing a new play by Tennessee Williams, *The Rose Tattoo*.

Starring Eli Wallach and Maureen Stapleton and directed by Daniel Mann, it was scheduled to open at the Martin Beck Theater in February, after a tryout run in Chicago. If Sal *was* interested and his parents approved, she said, she would offer him a contract to say the line in the play six nights a week and on Wednesday and Saturday afternoons for $65 a week. Sal gasped in amazement. He signed two days later and was given a date and time to meet the play's company at Grand Central Terminal to catch a train for Chicago.

Having never been away from home, he cried so much as the train departed that the play's author, Tennessee Williams, astonished everyone in the car by plunking Sal onto his lap until the sobbing stopped.

When *Madame Pompadour* opened the new Martin Beck Theater at 302 West 45th Street on November 11, 1924, cynics said the play would soon have to close because theatergoers would not cross Eighth Avenue. In the span of the next 27 years, they eagerly did so to take in Ruth Gordon in *Hotel Universe*, Lunt and Fontanne in *Reunion in Vienna*, Katherine Cornell in *The Barrets of Wimpole Street*, Orson Welles and Basil Rathbone with Edith Evans in *Romeo and Juliet*, and Paul Lukas in *Watch on the Rhine*. On February 3, 1951 they gladly crossed Eighth for *The Rose Tattoo*. Seconds after the curtain went up, a slight, black-haired kid who'd just turned 12 walked on stage to declare in a New York accent so thick you could cut it with a knife, "The goat is in the yard."

Catching the Broadway debut of a Salvatore Mineo, cited in the Playbill's biographical sketches as "Master Mineo," was not, of course, the audience's purpose. They were drawn by the reputation of playwright Williams and the talents of the stars, Maureen Stapleton and Eli Wallach. She had come to Broadway from Troy, New York, in 1943 with no training, no cash and no stage experience; only an ambition to be an actress. Talent put her on stage and kept her there. Eli had been at war for four years as a soldier, only to be discharged and land a part as a sailor in the hit *Mr. Roberts*. He'd been in an off-Broadway production of Tennessee Williams's *This Property is Condemned*. His amazing career would continue in theater and on screen into the 21st century.

Also in the cast of *The Rose Tattoo* was a young actor making his second Broadway appearance, Don Murray. Martin Balsam, as "Man," was so new to the stage that he did not merit a biographical note in the program. Both would forge lasting success on stage and in films.

In order to join this cast and speak his line on the Martin Beck stage a few seconds after 8:30 six nights a week, Master Mineo had to leave the house on East 217th Street no later than 6:30. This allowed for delays in the running times of the two subway lines that carried him from the Bronx to Times Square station three blocks from the theater. Because he had to be on hand for curtain calls, he rarely returned home before one in the morning. On matinee days he left home at noon. The hours between afternoon and evening performances on Wednesdays and Saturdays were whiled away in Times Square's game arcades and pool halls. "All of a sudden I was on Broadway," Sal recalled. "A million miles of colored neon, ear-splitting whistles, and those head-piercing police sirens. I thought the world had gone mad."

In a *Saturday Evening Post* profile of Sal Mineo the movie star, titled "The Boy Called Sal," published on October 31, 1959, Sal told writer Dean Jennings of being alone and waylaid in the subway by midtown hoodlums who saw him as an intruder on their turf.

"I felt like a hunted animal," he said of switching trains half a dozen times and scuttling through the labyrinth of subway stairs and levels, up to the street and down again, to shake off the young switchblade thugs.

Sal also found himself a target of bellicose guys close to home.

"With his delicate features and sensuous lips and a make-up kit clutched in his hand," the *Post* article noted, "Sal was a natural fall guy for the Bronx gangs. Many a night he showed up at the theater with torn clothes or a bloody nose."

A few individuals who noticed the pretty young boy riding subways or as he walked the blocks of Times Square alone eyed him as a different sort of prey. That a man wanted to have sex with a boy came as a shock. That men wanted it with him was scary. Sal had seen his favorite actor, John Garfield, in the movie *Castle on the Hudson,* in which Garfield as a youth carried a pistol to protect himself against street thugs. Sal bought a realistic toy pistol and successfully wielded it to ward off advances.

None of this was told to his parents and brothers. Their reaction, he feared, would put an end to what he saw as the beginning of an acting career.

In wandering around the Broadway theater district, Sal had dis- covered what he wanted and needed in life. Looking up at one of the theater marquees, he counted the letters to see if his name would fit. Salvatore was too long. If the day came when his name was going up on a sign or marquee, he decided, it would be short and sweet— SAL MINEO. "To be an actor was a brand new challenge," he recalled of his start, from the heights he achieved in only a few years. Ob- serving Stapleton and Wallach, he said, "I was learning something new every night."

Their lessons in acting ended when the play closed. Having said his one line for more than a year at $65 a week, Sal was out of work and the youngest person standing in line to pick up a check at the New York State Unemployment Office. But being on the dole did not last long. That summer he played Candido in *The Little Screwball* and in the fall he found himself the backup for the boy playing the Crown Prince of Siam.

He was also informed that he might have to fill in for one of the other children who made up the King's large brood, none of whom had a speaking part. Consequently, it was when one of these boys got sick that Sal first set foot on the St. James stage with an audience out front. The boy who was ill was slightly smaller than Sal, so Sal had to squeeze into the costume. It was so tight he could barely breathe. At one point in the scene he had to bow low for Miss Lawrence. As he did so, the belt holding up his satin pants broke and the britches dropped to his feet to reveal what Sal called "the craziest-colored pair of shorts a prince ever wore." The audience roared with laughter. Gertrude Lawrence got him out of his misery with an ad-lib and a pat on the rump.

Still ahead of Sal, however, loomed an inevitable moment when he would be called upon to step onto the stage of the St. James Theater with Gertrude Lawrence and Yul Brynner in the part he'd been understudying—the Crown Prince, who had lines to speak and a song to do. While acting with the genial and considerate Gertrude Lawrence did not worry him, Sal was terrified of playing scenes with her costar.

"I had watched him from the wings for over a year," Sal would later write for a movie fan magazine. "He was so very stern as the King with his Oriental makeup, his broad, unrestrained gestures, his very loud voice, that I thought he must be that way off stage, too. I had heard he had a good sense of humor but I couldn't believe it. I couldn't see how anyone who played the King as ruthlessly as Yul Brynner *could* have a sense of humor!"

The dreaded moment arrived in August 1952 when the boy who played Chulalongkorn went on vacation. Until that moment, Sal had not dared to speak to the man everyone referred to as "Mr. B." and the star had not spoken to him. Quite likely, Sal supposed, Brynner had not even noticed the understudy.

"I was so shy of him, so completely awed," Sal wrote, "that I never dared approach him, though I very much wanted to. But now that I was to play opposite him, I was more afraid of the man than ever."

Realizing he had never been shown how to apply the Prince's makeup, Sal sought help from Don Lawson, Brynner's makeup man. "Why don't you ask Mr. B.?" asked Lawson. "I'm sure he'll be glad to teach you."

Sal hesitated. "An important actor like Mr. Brynner," he reported thinking, "wouldn't want to be bothered with such trifles as telling a 13-year-old kid how to put on greasepaint."

With no one else to turn to, Sal went to Brynner's dressing room and stood at the closed door, knees shaking, trying to summon courage to knock.

He did so weakly, but was heard and answered.

"Come in!"

. Trembling, Sal opened the door and saw Brynner seated on a bench in front of his makeup table, back to the door and looking into a mirror. Seeing Sal's reflection, he boomed, "Hiya, Sal!"

So stunned was Sal that Brynner knew his name that "a very polite apologetic speech" he had planned went right out of his head.

"I hear you're going on tonight," Brynner said, beckoning him into the dressing room. "I'm sure you'll be terrific."

Sal blurted, "I don't know how to do my makeup. Mr. Lawson told me to ask you. I want my makeup to be right."

Brynner rose from the bench.

"Sit, sit," he said, ordering Sal onto the bench with all the force he exhibited so intimidatingly on stage. He handed Sal a stick of greasepaint. "I'll tell you how to put on the makeup, but I won't do it for you. You must learn to do it yourself." Studying Sal's face in the mirror, he added with a scowl, "Frankly, I don't see how makeup can help you."

Sal needed a moment to realize a joke had been cracked.

Made up and in costume, Sal waited anxiously in the wings for the moment in Act One during "March of the Siamese Children" when Prince Chulalongkorn makes his entrance. Arms crossed on his chest, chin high, and barefooted, he strode boldly to center stage and bowed his head to his father, the King.

As Sal lowered his head, Brynner whispered, "Relax, kid."

Of the night of his debut in a Broadway musical that became a classic of the theater Sal wrote, "All I remember was that Yul's voice was so loud, so clear, and carried so far, that it made my own voice seem very small. After the show, he was the first to shake my hand. 'Nice job,' he said. That was all."

Presently, Sal inherited the part of the prince permanently. In writing about his experiences in a charming magazine article titled. "The King and Me," published seven years after he took over as Chulalongkorn, he drew aside the veil that separated the audience in a theater and the actors on stage. He wrote, "If you have seen *The King and I* either on the stage or in the movies, you'll recall the scene at the very end where the King is dying and is giving final instructions to his son. The King lies on a divan and the two keep whispering to each other, while other stage business is going on. To make it appear that he was really giving me final instructions he told me jokes. When the jokes began to pall, he started to play 'knock-knock' and expected me to come prepared with my own. In the midst of my grief at seeing my 'father' in his death throes. I had to think up a good 'knock-knock' joke. It's a wonder we ever kept sad faces."

A professional relationship developed in which the veteran actor mentored the beginner.

"Every night, we would meet in the wings before we went on. He would talk to a 13-year-old boy as an equal. We discussed acting and one day he presented me with several books on the subject," Sal recalled. "At one point during the play's run, I was beginning to have trouble with my part. I was getting mechanical and I wasn't getting what I thought were enough good laughs. One night, I told the King about it. He suggested that we get together and rehearse it again. Immediately, I began getting laughs."

Yul Brynner taught Sal acting technique, timing, how to play comedy, and most importantly, how to listen to the other actor's lines and react to them.

When *The King and I* closed in 1954, after 1,246 performances, Sal had played the Prince nearly 900 times. No less an expert than Richard Rodgers told an interviewer, "Sal Mineo is the finest young actor I know."

Now 15, the boy whom nuns once picked to portray Jesus looked like an angel in a Michelangelo fresco. With jet-black hair tumbling over his forehead, full black eyebrows over alluring eyes, sensuous lips and dimpled cheeks, and a wistful laughter that seemed to pour out of him, he did, indeed, have a glow.

In show business that's called "star quality."

But now actor Sal Mineo found himself confronting the player's timeless question: "What do I do next?"

two

Wrong for the Part

For scores of ambitious and hungry young actors in New York in the early 1950s the big chance was in television. The medium had existed in the experimental stage for decades, but it had burst upon Americans as a means of entertainment in 1948. In acknowledging its arrival, *Time* magazine's May 24, 1948, issue inaugurated a section devoted to TV, saying "chances are that it will change the American way of life more than anything since the Model T." Proving *Time* correct, rooftops within reach of television broadcasting stations sprouted antennas to grab from the air a rapidly expanding menu of offerings—news, sports, weather forecasts, and entertainment ranging from programs for edification (and diversion from mischief-making) of children to comedies and dramas for adults.

Regarded as a means of bringing the riches of culture to the masses, television attracted to the New York City studios of ABC, CBS, NBC, and the DuMont networks a stellar roster of men and women to produce, write, and direct an astonishing array of dramas on such programs as *The Hallmark Hall of Fame*.

Making his network television debut on that program on May 5, 1952, Sal Mineo played a character named Charles in a drama titled "A Woman for the Ages." It capsulized the life of Abigail Adams, wife of the second president of the United States. Narrated by Sarah Churchill, actress-daughter of Winston Churchill, it was written by

Jean Holloway and starred Sylvia Field as Abigail, John Boruff as
John Adams, and Bill Daniels as John Quincy Adams. Unfortunately, reviews of the production by the new but growing breed of
"television critics" made no mention of Sal's performance.

Eighteen months later, however, Sal's work in his second network
TV show could not be overlooked. He appeared on an ambitious
and extravagantly praised Sunday afternoon series on the CBS network called *Omnibus*. Supported by the TV-Radio Workshop of the
Ford Foundation, it was hosted by the erudite British Broadcasting
Corporation commentator Alistair Cook. Sal played an aspiring
young matador named Paco in a 33-minute-long adaptation of an
Ernest Hemingway short story, "The Capital of the World." The
cast included Anne Bancroft and Leslie Nielsen. The play was directed by Sal's newfound friend and mentor, Yul Brynner.

The production would require Sal to put in hours practicing the
moves of a bullfighter and the wearing of a matador's form-fitting
"suit of lights."

When he learned he was to be directed on *Omnibus* by Brynner,
Sal was "delighted." "As a director, Yul gives the actor a feeling of
security," he said. "You know you're going to be good if he's guid-
ing you."

However, garnering praise from the man who was still the King
of Siam, who had swapped knock-knock jokes with Sal on stage
eight times a week at the St. James Theater, was hard to do.

"It was typical of him not to compliment an actor while he was
directing him," Sal noted. "One day after rehearsing a scene in
which I thought I had done a darned good job, Yul said coolly, 'It
was good.' After the show was over, he told me I was wonderful.
Thanks to his direction, I received many compliments on my performance. Our friendship became stronger."

In the course of their deepening professional and personal collaboration during the run of *The King and I*, Brynner had mentioned
that one of his favorite pastimes was waterskiing. Asked if he par-
took of the sport, Sal replied that while he enjoyed the water and
was a good swimmer, he'd never been on water skis. A few days
later, Brynner called Sal into his dressing room and showed him a
set of skis that Brynner had made himself. When Sal expressed admiration for them, Brynner gave them to him, then invited Sal to

learn how to use them during a weekend with Brynner and his wife and several others from the production at Brynner's waterfront house in Connecticut.

Brynner provided the lessons, Sal wrote of that weekend, patiently coaching until he felt Sal had caught onto it.

"All the while he watched me carefully to see that I wouldn't get hurt. He was so cautious that he kept the motorboat going at a very slow pace. I remember yelling to him, 'Faster, faster! Go faster! faster!' "

Invited for a second weekend of learning how to waterski, Sal was disappointed by the weather. Kept ashore by rain, a strong wind, and choppy waters, he spent much of the weekend in Brynner's basement workshop where Brynner made his skis. When Sal said that his father was a carpenter and suggested that he could supply wood for Brynner's skis, Yul accepted the offer.

Asked what his father built from wood, Sal answered, "Coffins."

Yul blared, "Fantastic!"

From time to time after that, Salvatore Mineo arrived at the St. James Theater stage door with a load of lumber. As the Bronx coffin-maker and the King of Siam discussed the fine art of carpentry, a Crown Prince called Sal beamed.

Shortly after the closing of *The King and I,* Sal got a picture postcard of a bullfight from Mexico, where Brynner was vacationing. Unsigned, the card bore only "Knock-knock," leaving no doubt who'd sent it.

Because of the abundance of available roles in television, Sal did not remain out of work long after his stage run in *The King and I.* He landed a one-day part on TV's *Janet Dean, Registered Nurse.* A medical drama about an earnest young nurse, played by Ella Raines, its theme was Janet Dean's belief that it was as important to treat patients' hopes and fears as their cuts, bruises, illnesses, and broken bones. Sal, as Jose Garcia in an emergency room, was asked what was wrong with him. He replied, "Jose Garcia is strong as a bull."

On *Omnibus* on October 16, 1955, he was in "A Few Scenes Out of the California Boyhood of William Saroyan," written and narrated by Saroyan himself. Sal was "Señor Cortez."

On December 4 that year he appeared on *Philco Playhouse* in a drama titled "The Trees."

While Sal added these jobs to his résumé, his mother grew concerned about him getting an education. Looking for a school that would permit him the freedom to act, she found the Lodge Professional Children's School, which offered tutors and flexible schedules. In keeping with her rule on treating her children evenhandedly, she allowed Mike to pursue his expressed desire to try to emulate his little brother's success as an actor.

The Lodge School also served as a kind of clearinghouse for information regarding which shows, producers, and movie studios were looking for actors. The most exciting of these reports going around in 1954 was a casting call for a movie loosely inspired by a daring robbery in Boston four years earlier.

On January 17, 1950, 11 armed men wearing Halloween masks, visored caps, gloves, rubber-soled shoes, and Navy pea coats had barged into the money-storage rooms of the Brink's armored car company. They gang coolly spent 17 minutes pillaging the vaults and got away with nearly $3 million in coins and currency. A *Collier's* magazine article about the caper by *Boston Globe* crime reporter Joseph F. Dinneen had been purchased by Universal-International Pictures for $150,000.

To be directed by a veteran of Universal's B film factory, Joseph Pevney, *Six Bridges to Cross* would be shot in Boston and would star Jeff Chandler as the robbery's mastermind. Producers were in New York searching for a youth to play the Chandler character as a boy.

Word that auditions were being held was conveyed to Mike Mineo by a friend and another aspiring actor from the Bronx, Barry ZeVan. After reading for the part and being turned down, he had been asked by the casting director if he knew other actors who might be interested in reading. Barry named Mike. Because it was Mike's first time at auditioning, Sal went along to provide him moral support.

After Mike had read, the casting director turned to Sal and looked him up and down. The slender, five-feet-six-or-thereabouts, 105-pounds-soaking-wet kid with dark eyes and olive skin was the right age. With a nose that seemed to have been broken at last once, probably in a collision with another boy's fist, he certainly looked believable as a tough Boston street kid. But he was nothing like anyone's idea of Chandler as a youth.

"You don't resemble Jeff a bit," said the casting director, "but what the hell, since you're here, you might as well read."

According to Hollywood legends, on such whims movie careers were launched, the most famous of which was Lana Turner being spotted while seated at the soda fountain of Schwab's Drug Store on Sunset Boulevard. Rock Hudson, the story went, had been a truck driver when his good looks just happened to have been glimpsed by an agent who was passing by. The theme of "being discovered" had been made into a 1937 movie, *A Star is Born,* with Janet Gaynor as naive Esther Blodgett. The film had been remade in 1954 as a Cinemascope-extravaganza-musical starring Judy Garland as the girl whom Hollywood transformed into superstar Vickie Lester.

Not a believer in such "lightning strikes" yarns and with no expectation of landing the job, but believing in the time-tested actors' maxim that an audition is a learning experience and so is never a waste of time, Sal auditioned.

A week or so later, the telephone rang in the house on East 217th Street in the Bronx. Is this the residence of Sal Mineo? Yes. Is he in? No, this is his mother. When do you expect him to be home? Any minute now. Will you please have him contact this number as soon as possible?

Returning the call, Sal was informed that Jeff Chandler had changed his mind about *Six Bridges to Cross.* The lead role would now be played by Tony Curtis.

A few years later, a writer for a movie fan magazine who related this turn of events in an article about Sal posed the question that had been asked by the casting director who'd auditioned kids for an actor who could play Jeff Chandler as a youth: "Who looks like Tony Curtis as a kid?"

Sal Mineo, of course.

Presently, wearing a soft cap, long-sleeved sweater over a T-shirt, baggy pants, and canvas sneakers, he found himself with four teenage boys and one girl in a trash-littered Boston back alley. He faced a battery of lights and reflectors and a movie camera as somebody yelled, "Quiet on the set!" Joseph Pevney followed with the shout "Action!"

The caption on a publicity photo said of the scene, "Young Boston hoodlums meet in a slum alley to discuss a market heist." This involved Sal leading his gang in pirating apples and pears from crates in an open-air market.

Because several such scenes were shot in rough neighborhoods of Boston, Sal quickly found himself the focus of attention by authentic teenage gang members. They looked at a boy with makeup on his face and waited for an opportunity to express how they felt about it. The difference between Sal's confrontation with them and with the tough guys in the Bronx and Manhattan was that in Boston he was not alone. Alerted to the threat to Sal from the gang, members of the film crew whisked him away to the safety of a hotel.

And so Sal Mineo, the kid who'd begged his mother to pay for dancing lessons in order to get on television, had attained the dream of numberless actors: He'd broken into the movies.

When shooting ended, he returned to the Bronx with no job and no idea what (or when) the next one might be. That he get back to work was imperative because he had become a source of income for the family. And he had reached a point at which he did not feel content without a role to prepare. More than once he'd heard other actors say that an actor was only as good as his last performance and that if you didn't keep working, you were quickly forgotten. He was determined not to let that happen to him.

To his surprise, however, he learned that his work on *Six Bridges to Cross* was not quite finished. He was advised that he would have to go out to the Universal Studios in Hollywood to fix some problems with the soundtrack. Some of his lines had not been picked up properly by the microphone and portions of the audio contained extraneous sounds. He would have to go into a recording studio and re-do some dialogue in a process called "looping."

Having acted in his first movie, Sal now found himself experiencing other "firsts" in his life: first time being so far away from his family, first trip across the country, and first time in a Hollywood motion-picture studio.

Asked if she was worried about her boy being on his own in Hollywood, Josephine replied, "Nobody's going to turn Sal's head. He's been a grown-up for years."

Located in Universal City, across the Hollywood hills in the San Fernando Valley, the sound stages and back lots of the film company that had been started in 1912 by Carl Laemmle had felt the tread of the feet of Rudolph Valentino, Boris Karloff as the Frankenstein monster, Bela Lugosi's Dracula, the zany Abbott and Costello, Doris Day, Rock Hudson, Jeff Chandler, and the young man who'd replaced him in *Six Bridges,* Tony Curtis.

Now, fresh from the Bronx had come an unknown 15-year-old Curtis look-alike by the name of Sal Mineo. Put up in a hotel, he traveled from Hollywood proper through the gaps in the hills that the maps called "canyons" to the U-I studios and quickly completed the required loopings. He entertained fantasies about someone in authority spotting him and signing him to a long-term contract, but he knew in his heart that such things happened only in movie scripts.

Contracts were proffered and deals were made with actors who had track records. And agents. Sal claimed neither.

All that aside, he *was* in the capital of the movie business, he'd made *one* movie, and he was young, good-looking, ambitious, and *talented,* so what was the big hurry? If he had to go back to New York without a deal for a second film, there was plenty of work for him in TV and maybe on Broadway again, where he did have a track record.

No one knows exactly how, where, when, and from whom he heard that U-I was looking for a boy to fill a featured role in a picture being made with Charlton Heston as a reluctant commander · of cadets at a religious military academy.

Sal later said, "I just talked my way into it."

Filmed almost entirely at St. Catherine's Military School, some 40 miles from Hollywood, the movie was *The Private War of Major Benson.* Heston played a battle-scarred army officer whose inappropriate remarks in a magazine result in him being assigned as far away from the press in Washington, D.C., as possible. Upon his arrival at "Sheridan Military Academy" in California, he is horrified to discover he's in charge of 300 boys—and expected to coach their football team. The boys range in ages from six (Tim Hovey as Tiger, a tot who has trouble saluting properly and keeping his uniform pants up) to 16 (Sal as Cadet Colonel Sylvester Dusik, as sharp a teenage soldier as any regular army officer could want to execute his orders).

Perplexed at being in a school run by nuns, and confronted with

boys who are not used to having such a demanding and unsym-
pathetic commander, Benson turns for help to Kay Lambert, played
by Julie Adams, a school nurse whom the boys adore. Complicating
matters, one of the cadets (Tim Considine), whose father is a Washington big shot, persuades the students to sign a petition demanding
that Benson be removed. The only cadet who does not sign is Sylvester.

Sal appeared in a dozen scenes with Heston but was required to
do little more than look serious and soldierly, count cadence during
drills, salute smartly, and deliver lines that included, "Pass in review!
Harch!" "Jeepers, sir, no kidding?" "Does everybody in this school
have two left feet?" and "There's this girl I kind of like."

It was a film of its time. Families still went to movies together.
Eisenhower was president and the country enjoyed prosperity and
peace. Made one year after a truce stopped the Korean War and a
decade before all things military began to come into disrepute as the
nation got deeper and deeper in a war in Vietnam, its only distinc-
tion 50 years later is that it marked Sal Mineo's second appearance
in a feature film. Near the end of the picture, the girl whom Sylvester
"kind of" liked voiced a sentiment about Sal Mineo that soon would
be echoed by millions of teenage girls: "Isn't he a dream?"

Expecting to go back to New York after completing *Major Benson,* Sal picked up talk among young actors on the U-I lot that
Warner Bros. Studios intended to follow up on the success of a hit
film about juvenile delinquency, *Blackboard Jungle,* with a B picture
about troubled teenagers, to be called *Rebel Without a Cause.*

The director of the film was Nicholas Ray. Forty-three years of
age, he was born in Galesville, Wisconsin, as Raymond Nicholas
Kienzle. The son of a builder of Norwegian descent, he'd studied
architecture in college but fell in love with acting. Moving to New
York City in 1931, he changed his name to Nick Ray and soon had
roles in politically and socially conscious plays of the Group and
Federal theaters. In 1936 he'd acted in *The Young Go First,* the
directorial debut of Elia Kazan. On the film *A Tree Grows in Brooklyn* he'd been Kazan's assistant. Having gone to Hollywood in 1948,
he gained a reputation for making movies with dual themes of violence and the outsider. One of these, *Knock on Any Door,* had
dealt with a deprived adolescent who drifted into a life of crime.

In *Rebel Without a Cause,* the lead role of tormented and confused teen Jim Stark was to be played by James Dean, a young New York stage and television actor and a Kazan protégé whose film work in the yet-unreleased Kazan version of the John Steinbeck classic *East of Eden* was the talk of Hollywood.

When a casting call was put out for members of a school gang and for the role of Jim Stark's worshipful friend, a troubled character named Plato, Sal postponed returning home.

He joined a throng of young hopefuls at Warner Bros., auditioning for Ray.

"I was almost sick, I wanted that part so badly," Sal would recall.

Looking over the assembled actors, Ray spotted "this kid in the back who looked like my son except he was prettier." Ray called Sal over and asked what he'd done. Sal recited his résumé and blurted that he didn't want to be just a gang member, he was dying to be Plato.

"Frankly, you're not at all the kind of boy I have in mind, but as long as you're here," Ray said, "let's see how you do." He led Sal to a taller, brawnier actor, Corey Allen, cast as the leader of a high-school gang. "Take off your jacket," said Ray to Sal, "and improvise a scene with him."

Although impressed with what he saw, Ray remained doubtful about Sal as Plato, thanked Sal, and told him he'd be in touch, but not to get his hopes up.

The next day, Sal got a phone call from Ray. "I'd like you to come in for another scene," he said, "this one with Jimmy."

Although Sal and Dean had worked in television in New York at the same time, they had never crossed paths. Sal was familiar with—and awed by—Dean's résumé. Dean had racked up a list of credits that in 1952 and '53 included 22 roles, ranging from bit parts on TV in *Treasury Men in Action, Martin Kane, Danger,* and other action shows to the prestigious *Kraft Theater, U.S. Steel Hour, Studio One,* and *Omnibus.* On stage he'd been in *See the Jaguar,* and as Bachir he'd provided a tour de force performance in *The Immoralist.*

Sal would write of auditioning with him, "I thought I dressed pretty sharp for those days in pegged pants, skinny tie, jacket—until Jimmy Dean walked in with his tee shirt and blue jeans. We went through a scene and nothing happened between us. Nick Ray finally walked over and suggested we sit and talk for a while. When Jimmy found out I was from the Bronx, we started gabbing about New York and then progressed to cars, and before we knew it, we were buddies. Then we went back to the script, and this time it went off like clockwork. When we reached a part where we were to laugh hysterically, Jimmy let out with a giggle, and I couldn't help but follow along. Pretty soon we just couldn't stop laughing."

At the end of the scene Ray again thanked Sal and told him he'd be in touch.

The call came the next day and again Sal was asked to come to the Warners' lot, this time to Ray's office.

"He had a deep frown when I walked in," Sal said of the meeting. "Finally, after looking at me for a few minutes, he said, 'Sal, every once in a while a director has to gamble. I'm going to take a chance. You're Plato.' "

three

Will the World End at Night?

Postwar American moviegoers had been shocked in 1949 by the
theme of two films. One was Nick Ray's *Knock on Any Door*, with
Humphrey Bogart and newcomer John Derek. As the title warned,
its point was that any American parent might discover one day that
one or all of his or her children had gone wrong. The other, *City
Across the River*, written by Irving Shulman and based on his novel
The Amboy Dukes, had put on screen a youth gang in the slums of
Brooklyn. It starred Stephen McNally and had introduced a handsome youth who would soon change his screen name. Anthony Curtis would become just plain Tony.

How kids could wind up as criminals also had been the cautionary message of *Six Bridges to Cross* in 1954, in which Sal portrayed
Curtis's character's start along the road to prison.

Not since the 1937 film production of Sidney Kingsley's grim
Broadway play *Dead End* had Hollywood cameras focused seriously
on the subject of juvenile delinquency.

The alarming subject was also at the heart of another picture in
1954. It starred Glenn Ford as an idealistic new high-school teacher
terrorized by his students. *Blackboard Jungle* broke new cinematic
ground by featuring the hot new music of America's youth, rock
and roll, in the form of Bill Haley and the Comets performing "Rock

Around the Clock." The film was also the second for a remarkable young black actor named Sidney Poitier.

Keenly aware of the money-making possibilities of films on the subject of delinquent kids, Warner Bros. looked for such a property and realized that in 1946 it had optioned a scholarly book on the very topic. Published in 1944 by Robert M. Lindner, a prison psychiatrist, the book had an intriguing title: *Rebel Without a Cause.* Executives hoped that a script with that name would be a successful vehicle for Marlon Brando. But the star of the movie that Warner Bros. had just made of Tennessee Williams's hit play *A Streetcar Named Desire* was not interested.

For a screenplay using the Lindner title the studio turned to a story that had been written by Nicholas Ray. Called *The Blind Run,* its topic was juvenile delinquency in Los Angeles. With Ray signed to direct the picture, the studio rejected his request that it be written by Clifford Odets and hired novelist Leon Uris to develop a script. He was soon replaced by the master of juvenile-delinquency films, Irving Shulman. When the personalities of the writer and James Dean failed to click, Ray turned to scenarist Stewart Stern to develop the treatment created by Shulman.

Being replaced did not concern Shulman. With the permission of Warner Bros. he went off to write a novel using the same theme and characters. In *Children of the Dark,* published in 1956, Shulman declared in an author's note "that the subject matter with which I was concerned [in the film treatment] is of such national significance" that he felt he had to deal with it at greater length. In a preface to the book, he predicted that if effective controls and solutions were not found soon for juvenile delinquency "the epidemic may become a national disaster."

National alarm over kids growing up to be bad became as widespread in 1950s America as the threat from Soviet Communism and the belief that Earth was being observed by flying saucers, piloted by creatures from outer space.

Shulman's adaption of Ray's *The Blind Run* involved three main characters, Steve Stark (later renamed Jim), Judy Phillips, and Richard Crawford (changed in the film to John), a kid who was so smart and studious that he was known around school as Plato.

No explanation is given for the nickname in the film, but in his novel Shulman depicted Plato as a brainy boy reading *Gods, Graves, and Scholars* for the third time and wondering if he ought to dedicate himself to archaeology. There were so many things he liked, so many things he was good at, but he had no one to talk things over with. Plato wanted a brother who was bright and capable and who recognized Plato's genius. Too bad, Plato thought, that he didn't have a brother or even a friend, a really *close* friend.

Stewart Stern wrote Plato as an enigmatic and sexually ambiguous youth with an absent father. On a school outing to the Griffith Observatory planetarium, when the universe displayed in lights on the ceiling explodes and the lecturer asserts that "man" is alone in an uncaring cosmos, Plato asks, "What does *he* know about man alone?"

Plato asks Jim, "Do you think the end of the world will come at night time?"

Jim thought it would happen during the day.

Completing Nicholas Ray's trio of costars was a young woman who had appeared in her first movie at age five. Seven years younger than James Dean and eight months older than Sal, she was born Natasha Gurdin. As Natalie Wood she became a star with a beguiling role as a girl who didn't believe in Santa Claus in 1947's *Miracle on 34th Street*. With 20 movies in her credits, she had just made *The Silver Chalice* with Paul Newman.

But it was not this illustrious career that Hollywood cynics and gossips cited as Ray's reason for casting her as Judy. The word around town was that Ray was having an affair with the 16-year-old beauty.

To see how well Natalie Wood, James Dean, and Sal Mineo would perform together on the screen, Ray chose to test their chemistry by shooting a scene from Stern's script. It was enacted on a portion of the set that had been built for *A Streetcar Named Desire*. (The film of that test has survived, and is now appended to a special home-video edition of *Rebel*.) Jim, Judy, and Plato have taken refuge from their teenage angst in an abandoned mansion. The scene begins with a two-shot of Jim and Plato standing, facing each other close enough to be dancing. Dean suddenly grabs Sal and lifts him as if he were a doll. He twirls him several times as they both giggle madly.

Dean lets Sal go and settles beside Natalie on cushions on the floor while Sal kneels behind Judy. Scripted lines are spoken until Dean reaches up to clasp Sal at the back of the neck and somersault him across Natalie onto the floor.

Anyone who watches the horseplay forgets that Natalie Wood is present. She's a witness to what is unquestionably a love scene between a couple of guys who can't keep their hands off each other.

When the time came to shoot Sal's first scene with Dean, Ray's directorial advice to Sal was that he not to try to *act* Plato, but to be himself. He asked Sal what Sal wanted as much as Plato wanted a friend.

Sal replied, "My driver's license."

"Fine," said Ray. "Look at Jimmy as if he is your driver's license."

Throughout the movie the attraction and affection between Sal and Dean are obvious. As author John Howlett noted in a Dean biography, "Plato's adoring eyes established the love of the younger boy for his hero."

What the camera captured in Sal's eyes all through the film was love for Dean that rose to the level of intense sexual desire, which Dean encouraged. Discussing Plato's relationship to Jim Stark, Dean said to Sal, "You know how I am with Natalie. Well, why don't you pretend I'm her and you're me? Pretend you want to touch my hair, but you're shy. I'm not shy like you. I love you. I'll touch your hair."

Nick Ray said of the effect of Jimmy's words on Sal, "He was transcendent, the feeling coming out of him. I tiptoed away. The next scene, Sal broke the sound barrier."

Dean's encouragement of Sal to cultivate homoerotic thoughts toward him was fine with Nick Ray because it helped the film and because everything about Sal led him to suppose that Sal was entertaining such thoughts anyway, at least subconsciously. The moment Ray had spotted the pretty boy at the back of the crowd during auditions for gang members he'd sensed that Sal Mineo was homosexual, but that Sal probably had not yet realized it.

That Dean would immediately grasp that Sal was in love with him came as no surprise to Ray. He was well acquainted with Dean's sexual history.

As an actor looking for the big break in New York when Sal Mineo was commuting to jobs while living comfortably at home in the Bronx with his parents, brothers, and sister, Jimmy was fresh from a farm in Indiana, living in a YMCA and struggling to make it in the toughest city in the nation for someone who wanted to act. Sal had been shocked to discover that men wanted to have sex with him. When Jimmy discovered men wanted to have sex with him, he had happily accommodated them.

"James Dean was not straight, he was not gay, he was bisexual," Nick Ray would later declare. "That seems to confuse people, or they just ignore the facts. Some—most—will say he was heterosexual, and there's some proof for that, apart from the usual dating of actresses his age. Others will say no, he was gay, and there's some proof for that too, keeping in mind that it's always tougher to get that kind of proof. But Jimmy himself said more than once that he swung both ways, so why all the mystery or confusion?"

Regarding Dean's easygoing attitude toward using sex to help him in his career, an actor who knew Dean in New York recalled Jimmy saying, "I'm certainly not going to go through life with one hand tied behind my back."

In *Laid Bare, A Memoir of Wrecked Lives and the Hollywood Death Trip*, John Gilmore wrote that in Hollywood Jimmy had told him, "I've had my cock sucked by five of the big names in Hollywood, and I think it's pretty funny because I wanted more than anything to just get some little part, something to do, and they'd invite me to fancy dinners overlooking the blue Pacific, and we'd have a few drinks, and how long could I go on? That's what I wanted to know, and the answer was it could go on until they had what they wanted and there was nothing left."

Another Dean friend once remarked of Dean's ambition, "Jimmy would fuck a snake to get ahead."

Barely three years before Dean enticed Sal to think of him erotically, Sal had bought a toy gun to scare off men who'd wanted to have sex with him. In Hollywood in 1955 he left behind forever the innocent boy riding alone on subway trains or killing time in Times Square between performances. In addition to all he had been taught about acting by Maureen Stapleton, Eli Wallach, Gertrude Lawrence, and Yul Brynner, he'd learned that in the business he'd chosen to pursue as a career there was a population of boys and men who sought love with members of their own sex. Since arriving in Hollywood, he had heard stories that some of the biggest male movie stars were homosexual, that everyone in Hollywood knew it, that the movie studios were aware of it, and that they did all they could to keep that knowledge from the public.

Soon after arriving in town to do the looping for *Six Bridges to Cross*, he'd been told a joke about Tab Hunter saying to Anthony Perkins, "Someday you'll make a fine actor," to which Perkins retorted, "I already have. Several of them."

He'd been amazed to hear that an icon of wholesome manliness, Rock Hudson, was having a love affair with George Nader, another he-man with whom Sal had scenes in *Six Bridges*.

Sal also heard that Jimmy Dean was romantically involved with a young man who had a small part in *Rebel*. His name was Jack Simmons. The gossip columnist Sidney Skolsky, whose daughter Steffi played a gang member in the film, did not state that Jimmy and Jack were lovers, but he noted that Jack was always around Dean's house and the movie set. The item continued, "He gets Jimmy coffee or a sandwich or whatever Jimmy wants. Jack also runs interference for him when there are people Jimmy doesn't want to see." Skolsky's meaning was clear.

While Sal could not avoid hearing such tales, he was also counseled by movie veterans not to pay attention to them. There had never been a movie made, he was told, that did not at some point become a subject of gossip concerning who was sleeping with whom and which actress or actor had gotten a role by putting out sexually for a studio boss, a producer, a director, and even a writer. In the lore and legend of the place known as Tinsel Town, every leading man fell in love with the leading lady.

Once in a while an actor did so with another actor. As long as the public didn't know of it, so what if a couple of guys went to bed together?

As work on *Rebel* got underway Sal heard gossip that Natalie Wood was head over heels in love with Dean, so much so that she saw *East of Eden* 20 times. That one member of the movie's gang had fallen for Natalie was not gossip, however. Sal noticed that Dennis Hopper was constantly loitering near a trailer where Sal and

Natalie were being tutored. Hopper had hopes of starting a romance with Natalie, notwithstanding widespread knowledge that she was having an affair with Nick Ray at his bungalow at a Hollywood hotel, the exclusive Chateau Marmont.

Dean biographer Paul Alexander, in *Boulevard of Broken Dreams: The Life, Times, and Legend of James Dean,* wrote that regardless of what Natalie Wood might have felt for him, Jimmy did not have a fling with her. "Nor did he have an affair with Sal," he wrote, noting that Dean was involved at the time with Jack Simmons.

But in a 1991 book about Dean, Marlon Brando, and Montgomery Clift, *Rebel Males,* Graham McCann stated flatly that "during the making of the movie [James Dean] had affairs with Natalie Wood *and* Sal Mineo."

Another author contended that Sal had a homosexual affair during the making of *Rebel,* but *not* with Dean. In a 1994 memoir, *Palimpsest,* Gore Vidal described being in residence at the Chateau Marmont in the spring of 1955. Noting that there were several bungalows around the pool, he wrote, "Nick Ray lived in one, preparing *Rebel Without a Cause,* and rather openly having an affair with the adolescent Sal Mineo, while the sallow Jimmy Dean skulked in and out, unrecognizable behind thick glasses that distorted myopic eyes."

Convinced that Sal Mineo had tumbled head over heels in love with Jimmy Dean, Nick Ray expected it wouldn't be long until Sal offered Jimmy something more tangible in the way of love than a transcendent look.

Many thought it had already happened. A story buzzed along the Hollywood gossip grapevine that Dean and Sal were lovers. Despite no evidence of an affair, the assumption that it had happened persisted years later. When Dean biographer Joe Hyams asked Sal if he and Jimmy had made love, Sal denied it. "But we could have," he added, snapping his fingers, "just like that."

Hyams wrote of the denial, "I took what Sal said with a grain of salt."

When the question was posed in 1973 during a night-long conversation in a Horn and Hardart automat between Sal and the author who would eventually write this book, Sal answered in the same manner, adding with the smile that never failed to warm hearts as it lit up a movie screen, "If I'd understood back then that a guy could be in love with another one, it would have happened. But I didn't come to that realization for a few more years, and then it was too late for Jimmy and me."

Regardless of what was being noised away from the *Rebel* sound stages and location sets about what might have been going on between them, Sal and Jimmy's on-screen homoeroticism was astonishing, not just because of their obvious mutual sexual desire, but because it was permitted in a motion picture in the 1950s.

Stewart Stern saw in Plato "the kid in school who would have been tagged a faggot. He hadn't shaved yet, and he had a picture of Alan Ladd in his locker at school."

If Stern and Nick Ray had been allowed to have their way in making the film, the sexual attraction between Plato and Jim Stark would have been explicit.

A working draft of the screenplay called for Plato and Jim to kiss.

When a studio censor read it, he immediately blue-penciled it and shot off a memo: "It is of course vital that there be no inference of a questionable or homosexual relationship between Plato and Jim."

The kiss could be cut from the film, but not the adoring look for James Dean shining in Sal Mineo's big brown eyes.

Regarding Dean's talents as an actor, Sal was initially dubious. Years later, he ruminated, "Rehearsing with him kept us all on our toes. Without warning he'd throw in different lines and improvise through scenes. I hadn't seen the rushes and frankly, from what I'd seen of Jimmy on the set, I didn't know what the fuss was about. I didn't think he was very good. Then I saw a screening and he was great."

When cameraman Ted McCord's Cinemascope camera rolled on *Rebel Without a Cause* on March 28, 1955, the film in the magazine was black-and-white because this was a low-budget picture from which Warner Bros. expected to rake in a substantial profit, based on the calculation that release of *East of Eden* would result in making James Dean a huge box-office draw for this, his second film. The script didn't require expensive sets. There were no lavish costumes, no hordes of extras. The cast had been signed up at bargain prices.

But two days into shooting, someone in the studio front office remembered that the contract with the inventor of Cinemascope required that a Cinemascope picture be shot in color. Nick Ray was summoned and told to junk the scenes that had been shot and start over.

In the B&W version Dean wore a black leather jacket. For Warnercolor he donned a light red windbreaker that would become an icon of the film and James Dean's hallmark. Nick Ray saw it as a symbol of the film's message. "When you first see Jimmy in his red jacket against his black Mercury, it's not a pose," he said. "It's a warning."

The audience's first look at Dean is under the title and credits. (Sal is listed as a featured player after the word "with"). Jim Stark falls to the ground, drunk, and discovers a toy monkey. He plays with it like a child, then curls into a fetal position.

Hauled in by the cops to a police station, Jim is interviewed by a detective assigned to cases involving juveniles.

An anguished Jim delivers a line that Nick Ray considered "the spine" of Jim Stark's dilemma, and the theme of the film: "If I could have just one day when I wasn't all confused . . . I wasn't ashamed of everything. If I felt I belonged some place."

It's in the station that Jim observes two other kids in trouble, a pretty girl and a pretty boy, both looking as lost and confused as himself.

The main story line deals with Jim's attempt to handle his problems—a henpecked father, played by Jim Backus in his first dramatic role; a mother (Ann Doran) whose answer to any crisis is to move from one town to another; and fitting in with the kids at school.

Having noticed Judy and Plato at the police station, Jim encounters them the next day. At Griffith Observatory planetarium Jim learns that Judy is the girlfriend of the leader of the school gang, Buzz, played by Corey Allen. Plato advises Jim that Buzz is "a wheel" and the gang is dangerous. After Jim and Buzz clash in an inconclusive knife fight, they agree to meet again to test each other's bravery that night by racing cars toward a cliff. The *Blind Run* of Nick Ray's original story becomes a "chickie run" in which the one who "bails out" of his car first is "chicken." Jim asks Buzz, "Why do we do this?"

Buzz replies, "We have to do something."

As Jim hurtles toward the cliff in a stolen car, Plato crosses his fingers and shuts his eyes. When he opens them, he is relieved to see that Jim has bailed out of the car and is safe. Buzz flies over the cliff to his death, trapped in his car when a strap of his leather jacket caught on the door handle. Jim reaches out a hand to Judy with Plato watching. A romantic triangle is formed.

Learning that Buzz's gang believes Jim is about to tell the police details of the chickie run and that the gang plans to prevent this, Plato races home and into his bedroom, where he's hidden a .45-caliber automatic pistol under his pillow. (How and why the gun has been put there goes unexplained in the film. But in Irving Shulman's novelization of his screen treatment, Plato's father was a gun collector.) Dashing out of his house, Plato heads for a derelict mansion that he'd pointed out to Jim from a plaza at the Griffith Observatory as the place Plato often used as a haven from his problems.

The sequence that follows was Sal's favorite in the movie. It included the scene he'd played with Dean and Wood in the screen test shot on the set of A Streetcar Named Desire. Now it was performed in a villa that had been the real-life Getty mansion and, on screen, Norma Desmond's palatial home in Sunset Boulevard. Jim and Judy find Plato in the mansion. Plato says, "We're safe here, I hope."

Carrying a candlestick, he pretends he's an agent for exclusive real estate showing the house to newlyweds. As the subject of children is raised, Plato says, "We really don't encourage them. They're so noisy and troublesome."

"Here in the romantic ruins of a past world," observed Dean biographer David Dalton in James Dean: The Mutant King, "they dream of a new society reconstructed from their own intense imaginings, and a generation comes of age."

This was Stewart Stern's intent. "The purpose of the film," he said, "was to tell the story of a generation growing up—in one night."

Stern saw something mythic, a night journey, that was also "a magic world, but it was magic built on the armature of Jim's unfulfilled wishes about his parents. He created an idealized family in which he was the father, Judy the mother, and Plato the child. He could act out all those things he wished his father could have been able to do—defend him against his own rage, disarm his anger with understanding, risk his life for him."

In Stern's vision, Plato regards Jim as a father figure. After the chickie run, Plato says to Jim, "Hey, do you want to come home with me? I mean, there's nobody home at my house and, heck, I'm not tired, are you? You see, I don't have too many people I can talk to."

"Who does?" Jim asks.

"If you want to come, we can talk and in the morning we can talk like my dad used to. Gee, if only you could have been my dad."

Looking at each other, Plato and Jim are as hesitant and awkward as a boy and girl after a date, wondering if they should kiss.

Analyzing *Rebel* in a landmark examination of homosexuality in films, Vito Russo agreed in *The Celluloid Closet* that in Plato's admiration of Jim Stark he seeks a father figure more than a lover. "But because Dean returns [Sal's] feelings so blatantly, sparks fly. Dean's rebellious youth in crisis, a tender and courageous figure, is as loving toward Plato as he is toward Natalie Wood, and the three form a family relationship. Dean's Jim Stark is torn between society's guidelines for masculine behavior and his own natural feelings of affection for men and women. To act upon them in the case of Plato or any other man was forbidden, of course."

In the film, Plato accepts Judy because she is important to Jim. Irving Shulman's concept of Plato's view of her was dramatically different. In the novel *Children of the Dark* Plato hated Judy for coming between him and Jim. Judy recognized this. "The way Plato looked at her was different," Shulman wrote. "He looked at her as a problem which must be understood, solved, and eliminated."

In the mansion in the film Judy hums a lullaby as Plato falls asleep on the floor, content to be with his family. The idyllic moment is shattered by the arrival of the gang.

Terrified and believing he has been abandoned by Jim, Plato cowers alone with a gun in his hand that seems too large for him to hold. "Save me," he cries. "Save me. Save me."

He shoots one of the gang and takes a shot at Jim. Shouting

"You're not my father," he flees the mansion. After firing at a policeman who'd been sent to investigate gunfire in the old house, he breaks into the Griffith Observatory and hides in the planetarium.

Moments later, after Jim believes he has persuaded Plato to give himself up to the police, Plato lies dead, shot by the cops. He wears Jim's borrowed red jacket.

Tenderly zipping it closed, Jim sobs, "Poor kid, he was always cold."

"In Plato's death scene," Sal said of James Dean's performance, "I understood what being loved meant. Here was the chance for me to feel what it would be like for someone close, someone that I idolized, to be grieving for me. It was an opportunity to experience what kind of grief that would be—what would he be like, what he would sound like, what would he be thinking?"

Immediately after Plato's death scene, Sal noticed a change in his relationship with Dean. "He was very protective," Sal said, "and for the whole day he'd never let me out of his sight. He was always there."

Later, Sal would proudly claim that in Plato he had created the first gay teenager in films.

"You watch it now, you know he had the hots for James Dean," he said. "You watch it now, and everyone knows about Jimmy [being bisexual], so it's like *he* had the hots for Natalie *and* me. Ergo, I had to be bumped off, out of the way."

Nick Ray's strategy in making a movie with a large cast of actors who were mostly in their teens (James Dean was 24) was to encourage them to bond.

"Nick's whole thing," said Steffi Skolsky, "was to make us family and to make the movie come from *us,* rather than from his direction."

Sal remembered the experience the same way. He said, "Working in *Rebel* was like being part of a close-knit family. Everybody became very tight, and Jimmy was the focus of it. We all grew around him, and as a result, we all tended to idolize him."

Sal's hero-worship and love for Dean did not spare him from Dean's unpredictable moods, however. "There were mornings when he really was awful to people," Sal recalled. "He'd totally disregard them and not say anything the whole day, and I'd feel rejected and end up saying to myself, 'What did I do wrong?' I was only 16, and if he didn't say good morning to me I'd be a wreck the whole day. If he put his arm around me, that was fabulous, because I knew he meant it."

Dennis Hopper noticed that Dean was closer to Sal than any actor on the film, except for Natalie. "On the set Sal seemed always to be under Jimmy's protective arm," said Hopper, "which was the relationship that Jimmy created and that their parts demanded."

The triangle of Dean, Wood, and Mineo (some in Hollywood saw a ménage à trois) continued off the set with the elder Dean picking up still-too-young-to drive Sal at the house at 4918 Rhodes Avenue in North Hollywood where Sal lived with his tutor, Mrs. Bernard Hoene, and her husband, 18-year-old daughter Lorie, and 20-year-old son Frank. Dean drove Sal and Natalie to the studio and to locations at breathtaking speeds in Dean's 1955 Ford station wagon. When Ray learned that his three co-stars were hurtling along highways at perilous speeds, he put a stop to the practice. Knowing that Dean was passionate about fast cars and loved racing them, Ray understood that he had no chance of keeping Dean from speeding around in a car that he'd bought along with the Ford station wagon. It was a Porsche Spyder convertible.

"Jimmy liked speed, thrills, excitement, and being in control of his life," Sal remembered. "He didn't fear death. He really believed he was immortal."

"Death can't be considered," Dean told a friend about Dean's participating in auto races, "because if you're afraid to die there's no room in your life to make discoveries."

Having obtained a driver's license in the course of making *Rebel,* Sal bought a used car, a 1949 Mercury like Jim's in *Rebel.* One evening in March he drove down Hollywood Boulevard. Approaching the Pantages Theater, he saw a crowd and a line of limousines. The marquee noted that the occasion was the annual presentation of Oscars by the Academy of Motion Picture Arts and Sciences. Wondering what it would be like to get Hollywood's highest honor, he continued on his way.

Two events in the final weeks of shooting *Rebel* signaled Sal that his movie career was on the right track. For the first time his name appeared in a movie magazine. A letter to *Photoplay* asked, "Could you please tell me about the young man who played Sylvester in *The Private War of Major Benson?*" The magazine's answer noted that he was 16 years old, five-foot-five, and weighed 120 pounds. The item concluded, "You can catch him next in *Rebel Without a Cause* costarring with James Dean and Natalie Wood."

That the item had probably been planted by the Warner Bros. publicity office to boost one of its forthcoming pictures did not occur to him.

The second event was signing a contract for his fourth movie and James Dean's third. Based on Edna Ferber's mammoth bestselling novel about Texas, *Giant* was to costar Dean with Rock Hudson and Elizabeth Taylor. The epic production would be produced and directed by one of Hollywood's greatest directors, George Stevens. In the cast were Mercedes McCambridge, Chill Wills, Carroll Baker, Elsa Cardenas, and Dennis Hopper.

At the urging of James Dean, who told Stevens that Sal "had the look of the angels," Sal was signed to a featured role as Angel Obregon II, the son of dirt-poor Mexican workers on a vast cattle ranch owned by Hudson's character. The Obregons and the boy are taken under the wing of Hudson's wife (Elizabeth Taylor).

Stevens did not have to be sold on the idea of Sal Mineo being in the film. Talk around Hollywood about Sal's performance in *Rebel* was being voiced in superlatives—"a new teenage idol," "rising star," "a name that will be a hot ticket."

When production concluded on *Rebel* on May 26, 1955, Sal had a few weeks on his hands before he was needed for *Giant*. He went back to New York City to see his family as a far more successful actor—and a good deal wealthier—than when he'd left to take care of some looping for *Six Bridges*. There would be no more being called a sissy, no need to defend himself from toughs in the neighborhood who saw him as an easy target.

The third child of Josephine and Salvatore Mineo, coffin-maker, was a bona fide movie actor; though not yet the star he envisioned on a future Academy Awards night being called to the stage to accept his Oscar.

*   *   *

Most of the filming of *Giant* would be done on location at Marfa, a speck of a town on the map of West Texas. The centers of production were the Worth Evans ranch, renamed in the film as Reata (Rock Hudson's mansion), and at the Ben Avant ranch, which became Dean's oil-rich property known in the film as Little Reata. The town of Marfa was a deadly dull spot and the heat was scorching. But the burn of a Texas sun could not compare to the blazing temperature of the relationships that developed between James Dean and both the movie's star and director.

Throughout production of *Rebel,* Dean had been virtually co-director with Nick Ray, who believed in allowing actors to express themselves regarding how they played their parts. George Stevens was not that kind of director. Working in films since 1921, he'd been directing features since 1933. He had an Oscar for 1951's *A Place in the Sun* and in 1953 was given the Motion Picture Academy's Irving Thalberg Memorial Award for "high quality production." On *Giant,* Stevens became so fed up with James Dean's unconventionality and moodiness that he vowed never to work with him again.

Dean's problem with Rock Hudson was partly rooted in the actors' different approaches to acting. Hudson was old-time Hollywood: learn your lines, hit your mark, stay in your light, and don't bump into the furniture. Dean was Method Acting and improvisation.

The other cause of the strain between the superstar and the quirky newcomer was rooted in a generational difference in how Hudson and Dean viewed homosexuality. The stress between the two was exacerbated by their sharing living quarters, along with character actor Chill Wills, who played Hudson's uncle.

Biographer Paul Alexander wrote in *Boulevard of Broken Dreams* that Dean had no taste for the "old" homosexual set's "fey ways" and "penchant for drag." Hudson felt threatened by Dean's "edgy and unconventional personality even as [Hudson] was attracted by [Dean's] sweet boyish looks."

Sal's attitude toward Hudson was properly deferential. Despite all the stories he'd heard about Hudson being homosexual, he had difficulty in accepting as fact that the actor who had a reputation as a great lover of women and all-around he-man really preferred making love to young men. He'd also heard that Hudson preferred having sex with guys who were tall and blond and muscular. Being a five-eight, black-haired, 120-pound Italian with no build at all to brag about, he felt confident that he was not Rock Hudson's cup of tea. And he was certain that Hudson would not dare to make a move on a minor.

In the film, Sal and Dean shared no scenes. Sal's main moments on the screen are in the big house on Hudson's Reata ranch when he arrives to say goodbye to Hudson and others because he has entered the Army. In this second film in which he wears a uniform, he is only a year older than he was in *The Private War of Major Benson*, but Angel appears more mature. It's a sequence in which he has no lines. After making his entrance at a party in progress, Angel is relegated to the background in a scene involving Hudson and his son (Dennis Hopper).

The explanation for this minuscule amount of screen time in a finished film that would run 201 minutes was that Stevens had to trim the total footage from the more than five hours shot to a length that would keep audiences in their seats. While cutting was necessary, Stevens was more than a little disingenuous in offering this rationale for Sal's tiny part. The director/producer had known all along that the role of Angel would be slashed and end up on the cutting room floor.

This deception was keyed to the marketing of *Giant*. With everyone in the motion-picture industry predicting that *Rebel* would make Sal Mineo a star and that audiences would flock to see James Dean and Sal Mineo together again, Stevens was committed to featuring Sal prominently in the advertising of *Giant*—but not on the Cinemascope screen.

Sal was resigned to having his part decimated. "Somebody had to be cut out," he said. "I was one of the somebodies."

Yet there would be some consolation for Sal. His character gets one of the most dramatic moments, although Sal is not seen. It is one of the two most memorable scenes in *Giant*. (The other is the reaction of Dean's character, Jett Rink, when he strikes oil.) Cutting from Angel's goodbyes to the people of Reata, the film reveals Angel's family standing on a railroad platform. A train, which the audience expects is bringing Angel home departs, revealing a luggage wagon bearing Angel's flag-draped casket.

"Stevens was a good director," Sal told journalist Boze Hadleigh in 1972, "but a tough old buzzard. The best directors are usually tough nuts to crack, but the result's usually worth it."

While working with Stevens on *Giant* Sal signed a contract for his next picture and was thrilled to find out he would be in his third film with James Dean. Warner Bros. would be making *Somebody Up There Likes Me,* based on the bestselling autobiography of boxer Rocky Graziano. Sal would be playing Rocky's best friend, Romolo. He was also delighted to learn that most of the movie would be made in New York.

Shooting of *Giant* was scheduled to be completed in mid-September 1955. One day as Sal left the commissary on the Warner lot he passed a small man with hunched shoulders, gray hair, and a mustache. When the old man startled him by smiling and saying, "Hi, how's it goin'?" Sal recognized Dean on his way to do a scene as an aged Jett Rink.

Sal's work on the picture was completed. He was about to go back to New York to spend time with his family and promote *Rebel,* scheduled to open at the Astor Theater in Times Square on October 3. Joining him in New York to do publicity for *Rebel* were Natalie Wood and Nick Adams, who played a gang member in *Rebel.* Natalie was also to appear with Jo Van Fleet in an ABC-TV special of *Heidi.*

On the night of September 30, 1955, the three of them—Sal, Natalie, and Nick—went to see Arthur Miller's *A View from the Bridge.* Its star was Dean's brother in *East of Eden,* Richard Davalos. After the performance, they and Davalos and his wife decided to eat at the China Doll restaurant at Sixth Avenue and 54th Street, opposite the Warwick Hotel, where Natalie and Nick were staying. (Natalie had been accompanied to New York by a chaperone hired by Warner Bros. because she was under age.)

Eventually, the conversation turned to the person they had in common.

Someone asked if anyone knew what Jimmy Dean was up to.

Sal said, "I think he's racing this weekend."

Natalie looked at Sal with a worried expression and said, "I wish he weren't."

Nick said, "If he doesn't stop this crazy thing he has for speed he won't live to see 30."

Davalos said, "Jimmy knows what he's doing."

The quintet finished dinner around 11:30 and went their separate ways: the Davaloses to their apartment, Natalie and Nick across the street to the Warwick, and Sal to the Bronx.

When he reached home Sal would learn that at the time he'd been enjoying *A View from the Bridge,* at 5:45 P.M. California time at the intersection of routes 466 and 41 east of the town of Cholame, a young man named Donald Gene Turnupseed had turned his black-and-white Ford into the path of a speeding low-slung silver Porsche Spyder.

Its driver, James Dean, was D.O.A. at Paso Robles War Memorial hospital.

In *Rebel Without a Cause* Plato had asked Jim Stark if the world would end at night. Jim thought it would be in the daytime. James Dean's world ended in a moment of crushing metal in the half-dark, half-light of dusk.

four

A Giraffe for the Mantel

Four days after James Dean was killed, thousands of movie fans, celebrity watchers, and the morbidly curious stood on Broadway in spaces designated by New York Police Department barricades. Between 44th and 45th streets, they gawked as limousines drew up in front of the Astor Theater to bring privileged people with invitations issued by Warner Bros. to the most anticipated movie premiere of the year.

The death of the 24-year-old star of the film, whose debut in *East of Eden* had been hailed by critics who'd praised James Dean as brilliant, made this first screening of *Rebel Without a Cause* a major event. It was covered not only by the New York and Hollywood press, but by reporters from across the country and Europe.

For Sal Mineo it was at the same time a melancholy and exciting moment.

He'd come down from 217th Street in the Bronx in the kind of long black limousine that had always been associated in Josephine and Salvatore Mineo's minds with funerals. Now here they were with Victor, Michael, and Sarina, dressed to the nines as if they were on their way to a Sicilian wedding. When the limousine stopped, a young man in a tuxedo opened the door.

As Sal stepped out onto a red carpet, flashbulbs went off in cameras held by dozens of news photographers. Several yelled, "Hey, Sal, look this way," as if they knew him personally.

To the New York press the opening of *Rebel Without a Cause* was more than just another assignment to cover a movie that was being pushed by a studio publicity department, only to be forgotten when the studio's next movie was released. This was a picture providing two unbeatable angles: its star was dead and one of the costars was a Bronx boy who had made good in the two toughest places in the country—Broadway and Hollywood. And he was only 16.

Although the premier of the film was held on October 3, reviews did not appear until the wider opening of the picture on October 29.

The New York Times film critic Bosley Crowther's review began, "It is a violent, brutal and disturbing picture of modern teenagers that Warner Brothers presents in its new melodrama at the Astor. Young people neglected by their parents or given no understanding and moral support by fathers and mothers who are themselves unable to achieve balance and security in their homes are the bristling heroes and heroines of this excessively graphic exercise. Like *Blackboard Jungle* before it, it is a picture to make the hair stand on end."

Sal found his name listed seventh in the credits, behind Dean, Wood, Backus, Ann Doran (Jim's mother), Rochelle Hudson (Judy's mother), and William Hopper (Judy's father). The only mention of his name in the review was found in the fourth paragraph. Crowther described Jim, Judy, and Plato as "several social cuts above the vocational high-school hoodlums in that previous film." The review continued, "As for Mr. Mineo, he is a thoroughly lost and hero-searching lad because his parents have left him completely in the care of a maid."

Regarding whether Sal played Plato convincingly Crowther offered no opinion, except to include him in a generalized "wish" that the young actors "had not been so intent on imitating Marlon Brando in varying degrees."

What Crowther found resembling Brando in Sal's Plato is mystifying.

Crowther's disappointment in the film extended to Stewart Stern's script. His "proposal that these youngsters would be the way they are for the skimpy reasons he shows us," he said, "may be a little hard to believe." And he faulted "a pictorial slickness about the whole thing in color and Cinemascope that battles at times with the realism in the direction of Nicholas Ray."

In Crowther's view the film might have been better if it had been shot in black and white as originally planned.

William Zinsser of the *New York Herald Tribune* swiped at screenplay and direction as so sluggish that he did not name Stern and Ray, or anyone in the picture except James Dean. "His rare talent and appealing personality," he wrote, "even shine through this turgid melodrama."

Perhaps obeying the rule that one should not speak ill of the dead, most reviews brimmed with praise for Dean. Arthur Knight of *Saturday Review* thought Dean projected "the wildness, the torment, the crude tenderness of a rootless generation."

The majority of the reviews referred to Dean's death.

Typical was the notice in *Newsweek*: "In this movie he wins an auto race with death. Only four weeks ago, at the age of twenty-four, he lost one." The magazine *America* found that the "chickie race" in the picture and the "tragic coincidence that Dean lost his life in an automobile accident a few weeks ago, gives this sequence an almost *unbearable* morbid ring."

Film critics and social commentators took a condemnatory view of what they saw as the message of the movie—the mythologizing of youthful violence as represented by the switchblades and fast cars. While there were instances in which teenagers emulated the chickie run and toted switchblade knives, the icon of the film turned out to be quite different.

James Dean's red jacket became the enduring emblem of a James Dean cult, defined by David Dalton in *James Dean: The Mutant King* as "a community in which youth could recognize itself as a separate and vital force."

"From the first news of the crash," Dalton noted, "countless rites were performed to preserve the bond between this force and its inspiration."

*   *   *

No one performed rites of remembrance for Dean more personally than Sal. Because Dean had owned an MG sportcar before he acquired the Porsche Spyder, Sal disposed of his 1949 Mercury and bought a similar MG, then emulated his idol by driving it fast. Because James Dean enjoyed playing drums, especially bongos, Sal acquired a set of drums. Dean had been interested in bullfighting, primarily for its graceful movements. Sal began lessons in the art of the bullring.

Taking to heart Dean's advice that an actor must pay attention to his body, and being sensitive about his height (five foot eight) and weight (120 pounds, with a 23-inch waist), Sal plunged into a regimen of weight lifting, shadowboxing, swimming, and other exercises, including continuing dancing, to improve his physique.

But no Dean influence proved more important to Sal than Dean's approach to acting. In the tide of mournful tributes following Dean's death was this from the youth who idolized him: "Working with James Dean was one of the greatest experiences of my life. I learned a lot from Jimmy as a person and as an actor."

As a protégé of Elia Kazan, Dean had employed techniques taught at New York's Actors' Studio, cofounded by Kazan with Lee Strasberg. Known as "The Method," the system stressed the need for actors to find the core of their performances by reaching into their own life experiences. Method acting also stressed actors observing people in their everyday pursuits and using what they learned to instill naturalism into performances.

Before Sal met Dean on the set of *Rebel,* Sal had not brought anyone to a role but himself. In *A Rose Tattoo* he'd been the same young Italian boy who lived on 217th Street. In *The King and I* he was Sal Mineo in Oriental makeup. The Boston street kid in *Somebody Up There Likes Me* was Sal Mineo of the Bronx. Sylvester in *The Private War of Major Benson* was Sal Mineo in a military cadet uniform. But on the set of *Rebel* James Dean had shown him that acting was more than simply knowing lines and remembering stage movements. Nick Ray had told Sal to think of Jim Stark as a driver's license. Dean had shown him that the key to Plato's character was rooted in Plato's love for Jim and a desire to express it sexually.

What appeared in every scene between Plato and Jim was the love for Dean that Sal found in himself.

"When the script called for us to have close scenes," he told an interviewer ten years after *Rebel*, "they always worked."

One can only imagine the deleted kiss.

Having discovered from Dean what acting should be, Sal sought training with one of the best acting teachers in New York, Claudia Franck, a proponent of The Method.

Assuming that Dean's death had spelled doom for the plans to make *Somebody Up There Likes Me,* Sal continued his classes with a tutor from the Lodge school and looked forward to his high-school diploma in June and possibly going on to college.

Two things occurred to put pursing a higher education on hold.

He learned that the film biography of Rocky Graziano would proceed as planned, but with Paul Newman in the starring role.

And he learned that his performance in *Rebel* had been recognized by the Motion Picture Academy with a nomination for an Oscar for Actor in a Supporting Role. The 28th annual awards were to be presented on March 21, 1956, and televised from the Pantages Theater in Los Angeles and NBC's Century Theater in New York.

With breathtaking suddenness, he found himself included on a roster of Hollywood's most illustrious names: Spencer Tracy, Katharine Hepburn, Susan Hayward, Anna Magnani, Frank Sinatra, James Cagney, Ernest Borgnine, and James Dean (nominated posthumously for best actor for *East of Eden*).

Aware that the person favored to claim the Oscar in his own category was Jack Lemmon, nominated for his antic performance as Ensign Frank Pulver in *Mr. Roberts*, Sal learned that his sister, Sarina, had cleared a place on the mantel for her brother's golden statuette. He advised her not to set her heart on it.

"The whole month before, I was in a daze," Sal said of being nominated.

He knew the awards were significant enough to want to share the honor with the person who had done more than anyone to make his acting career possible. So he brought Josephine out to Hollywood to accompany him to the ceremony.

Recalling that night, he said, "People kept asking me, 'Who's your

date?' And when I told them, 'My mother,' they all thought this was
the most wonderful thing. Mother was so excited. I thought any
minute she would cry. When I didn't get it [the Oscar went to Lem-
mon] each of us thought the other needed comforting. I didn't mind
for myself, I just thought she did. And Mother didn't mind for herself, she thought I did. But then people came up and started con-
gratulating us. They said it was an honor just being nominated.
'Look forward to the next movie,' they told me. 'That's the important thing.' "

Although Sal did not take home an Oscar, he got a consolation
prize from a fan named Marcie who'd watched the telecast and was
disappointed that he hadn't won the Oscar. Having recently grad-
uated from high school and planning to go to college in the fall, she
was working at the J. L. Hudson store in Detroit, Michigan. When
she went to work the morning after the Oscars, she saw a display
of small stuffed animals. She bought a giraffe and sent it to Sal.
Although he could have displayed the gift in the space Sarina had
made for an Oscar, he kept it in his MG.

Two and a half months after the Academy Awards, on June 2,
1956, Sal appeared on CBS-TV's prestigious weekly drama program
Studio One. The play was by one of television's most prolific and
brilliant writers, Reginald Rose. Titled "Dino," the story was that
of a teenager named Dino Minetta. He has just been released from
a reformatory after serving time for taking part in a robbery in
which an old man had been killed. A psychiatrist in a settlement
house, played by Brian Keith, struggles to keep Dino from returning
to his errant ways.

Watching the program at her home was actress Elaine Stritch.
With her were Maureen Stapleton, Jason Robards, and several other
actors. More than 40 years later, Stritch recalled Sal's performance
as Dino. "We all saw this kid. We absolutely flipped out. It was rare
to see that kind of reality in an actor that age. It scared me a little,
it was so good. There was an element of danger in it, and what's
he going to do next? You didn't know which direction this kid was
going to take."

Stapleton, of course, remembered Sal from *The Rose Tattoo.* He'd
come a long way from saying, "The goat is in the yard."

Sal's performance as yet another delinquent, but in this case a redeemed one, won him an Emmy Award nomination. It would not be the last time Sal found himself involved with Dino.

Exactly what being nominated for an Academy Award could mean to an actor's career Sal discovered with the release of *Giant*. He found his name on posters and in advertising that gave the impression that he had a major role in the film. George Stevens's calculation that having Sal Mineo in *Giant* would be a box-office draw proved correct, although fans of Sal who went to the movie primarily to see him were cruelly tricked.

The Oscar nomination prompted *The New York Times* to note that in only six years Sal Mineo had gone from the Bronx "to the crest of the Hollywood wave."

five

————

Mineo Mania

When Sal Mineo went west in 1954 to do the looping required for
Six Bridges to Cross he arrived in a Hollywood in the throes of a
wrenching transition. Television had rocked the movie capital of the
world with the force of a magnitude-seven earthquake. Studios were
scrambling to find ways to lure people out of their homes and into
the theaters. To compete with "the tube" they introduced wide-
screen technologies such as Cinemascope and VistaVision. An advertising campaign exhorted, "Get more out of life, go out to a
movie."

The film industry also found itself dealing with a new breed of
young, independent-minded, and quirky actors such as Marlon
Brando, Montgomery Clift, and James Dean, of whom the columnist
Hedda Hopper wrote, "They've brought out from New York another dirty-shirt-tail actor. If this is the kind of talent they're im-
porting, they can send it right back again so far as I am concerned."

Of course, they couldn't. This new generation of actors appealed
mightily to the only age group in the country that still went to movies regularly. The young not only flocked to theaters, but also piled
into cars to see pictures in drive-ins. Between 1946 and 1951, more
than 3,000 of these outdoor "passion pits" had sprung up.

The importance of this younger audience evidenced itself in the

by SAL MINEO

the king and me

I'll never forget my first meeting with Yul Brynner. He

was a big star. I was a thirteen-year-old kid, and

I was scared to death! But that was only the beginning . . .

One hot summer night in August, 1952, I appeared backstage of the theater where the stage version of "The King and I" was playing. For more than a year I had been acting as understudy for the boy who was playing the part of the Crown Prince but I had never had a chance to go on for him. Now he was leaving for his vacation and I was taking over his role for the first time that night.

Despite the fact that this was my big opportunity—or maybe because of it—I was scared. For one thing, I was only thirteen years old and had been in only one production before. For another, I would be playing with Yul Brynner, and though I had never met him, there was something about the man that terrified me.

I had seen "The King and I" several times from the audience. I had watched Yul from the wings for over a year. He was so very stern as the King with his Oriental makeup, his broad, unrestrained gestures, his very loud voice, that I thought he must be that way off the stage too. I had heard he had a good sense of humor but I couldn't believe it. I couldn't see how anyone who played the King as ruthlessly as Yul Brunner, *could* have a sense of humor!

Looking back, I don't know why I should have been so afraid of him, (*Continued on page* 100)

"By the time Yul directed me on NBC-TV's 'Omnibus' I'd learned he's really a very kind person"

Sal's first head shot. This photo was sent to casting directors and producers along with a résum
that included two Broadway shows, six network TV programs, and the movie *Six Bridges to Cro*
Sal was 14 years old.   AUTHOR'S COLLECTION.

l with the neighborhood kids in his first film, *Six Bridges to Cross*. Sal would grow up on
reen to be Tony Curtis.

Sal as Plato in *Rebel Without a Cause*, the role that earned him his first Academy Award nomination and won him instant movie stardom. WARNER BROS. PICTURES.

l with James Dean and Natalie Wood in *Rebel Without a Cause*. Rumors spread though llywood that Dean was having an affair with Sal (as well as Natalie), but Sal always nied them.

e fan photo cards from Sal's early movie career.

One of Sal's numerous publicity portraits.

success of films dealing with their age group. Impressive box office receipts for *Blackboard Jungle* and *Rebel Without a Cause* had come primarily from adolescents. And most of the audience for *Giant* was attracted by James Dean, not Rock Hudson. Bosley Crowther of *The New York Times,* who had scorned Dean in *Rebel,* said his performance in *Giant* was "the most tangy" in the film.

Like television, the arrival in Hollywood of James Dean and other actors of his generation and style, both personal and professional, was mega-seismic in its impact on movies and the town where most were produced. Of this younger generation of moviegoers Elia Kazan said, "There was a genuine feeling that the moral standards of the old generation were hollow, that they no longer meant anything and weren't valid for us anymore."

Whether teenage Sal Mineo fit this portrait remained to be seen. He was, after all, the son of a Sicilian and had been raised in strict accordance with the rules laid down by Josephine and Salvatore and the Roman Catholic church. Although he was wise to the ways of the New York streets and the vagaries and challenges of the Broadway theater, he came to Hollywood a boy who was every bit as innocent as Sylvester in *The Private War of Major Benson.* He was as starstruck and awed by Hollywood as a tourist buying a map that purported to pinpoint homes of stars and places where they met, dined, and danced: the Coconut Grove, the Brown Derby, Romanoff's, Chasen's, the Bel-Air, and Beverly Hills hotels. Even Schwab's Drug Store remained on a corner opposite the Garden of Allah, a hotel with bungalows on Sunset Boulevard where Erroll Flynn had skinny-dipped in the pool and justified the phrase "in like Flynn" by romancing women in his bungalow.

When Sal found himself admitted without challenge to the Universal-International lot in 1954, most of the pre-TV old Hollywood was still in place and still ruled by the movie moguls. Jack L. Warner lorded over James Dean, as he'd reigned over James Cagney, Bette Davis, and all others who had signed their names to Warner Bros. contracts. Similar moguls still held sway at the other studios. Directors made the movies the bosses wanted them to make, and if the studio censor vetoed two high-school boys kissing, the kiss was out of the picture.

People who made movies, on-screen and behind the cameras, were divided into A list and B list. Some were invited to Academy Awards parties and others weren't.

Just as rigid was what author John Howlett called "the sexing of Hollywood" in the mid-1950s. "Stars had to be seen to date, boys with girls, girls with boys—whatever they might choose to do between the sheets," he wrote in his biography of James Dean. Homosexual Hollywood was largely left to its own devices in a protected environment. "While publicity machines worked to manicure their heterosexual images, Tab Hunter and Anthony Perkins remained relatively unscathed by rumor and Rock Hudson could openly date George Nader—even turn up at parties in drag [without the public finding out]."

In 1956, just two years after he'd first arrived in Hollywood, Sal Mineo had an Academy Award nomination on his résumé and five films under his belt, and was subject of a profile in *The New York Times,* which noted that despite a "boyish face that belies his acting maturity" he'd "zoomed into cinematic prominence."

Concerning the Oscar nomination, Sal had told the interviewer, with a modesty that in retrospect crossed over to disrespectful flippancy, "Actually, I got a bigger thrill when I won a swimming medal in school than when I was notified of my nomination. The medal I could hold in my hand and know I had accomplished something."

Seemingly exhibiting exactly the attitude that old Hollywood found so dismaying in the fresh crop of actors coming to town to make movies for a new audience of juveniles, he had also told the *Times* that making movies "interfered" with his remodeling of a car as a member of a hot-rod club in Westwood known as the "Kerb Krushers."

Expounding on the club for a fan magazine, he explained, "We meet Wednesday nights to talk about cars and tear them apart or put them together again. Sometimes we add a new exhaust pipe. Other nights we hop up the engine or jazz up the paint job. Anything mechanical goes at the Kerb Krushers' meetings."

Returning to work after the death of James Dean and the opening of *Giant,* Sal was under contract to Metro-Goldwyn-Mayer to play Rocky Graziano's friend Romolo in *Somebody Up There Likes Me.* Its star was another young newcomer to Hollywood.

Fourteen years older than Sal, Paul Newman came to movies by way of the drama school at Yale University, the Actors' Studio, and Broadway. His success in *Picnic* in 1953 led to a Warner Bros. contract and a miscast role in a Biblical epic, *The Silver Chalice*.

The film's director would be a veteran of Warner Bros. B movies, Robert Wise. In 1949 he had made what many students of film considered the finest boxing film ever made to that time, *The Set Up*. It was followed by other successes, including the science-fiction *The Day the Earth Stood Still* and *Executive Suite*.

Based on Graziano's autobiographical book, *Somebody*'s screenplay would be written by Wise's writer on *Executive Suite*, Ernest Lehman. A former financial editor and short-story writer, he was a native of New York City.

MGM originally intended the film to be shot in color. Without James Dean, the studio elected to save money by making it in black-and-white and filming it on a back-lot set representing New York's Lower East Side tenements. Deciding the sets looked phony in daylight, Wise chose to use them for night exteriors and shoot the daytime sequences on location in New York. It was there, while scouting sites and looking for someone to play a street tough, that he discovered a curly-haired young actor named Steve McQueen. The future star of such pictures as *The Great Escape, The Sand Pebbles, Nevada Smith, The Thomas Crown Affair (1968)*, and *Bullit* would not get a screen credit.

Also in the *Somebody* cast were Pier Angeli as Rocky's wife, Everett Sloane as a fight trainer, Eileen Heckart as Rocky's long-suffering mother, Harold J. Stone as Rocky's abusive father, and Robert Loggia (in his first movie) as a hood named Frankie Peppo.

The film is a tour de force for Newman. After studying Graziano's fidgety movements and mumbling New York accent, he re-created them perfectly. He also learned to box and became so good in the ring that he feared what might happen in a climactic scene in which Rocky defeats his arch rival in the middleweight class, Tony Zale, who was signed to play himself in the film. Wise noticed that Newman seemed "a little gun-shy" in the ring with Zale.

"Paul was afraid that if he actually clipped Zale," Wise recalled, "Tony, in just a fighter's reflex reaction, would cold-cock him."

Zale was replaced by an actor.

Sal made working with Newman a learning experience. He especially studied Newman's use of the eyes and facial expressions to convey emotions.

However, while Newman had to adopt a believable New York City accent, Sal came to the role of Romolo with no need for mimicry to create a convincing youth, whom the audience first meets as a shoeshine boy. As he abandons the chore with only one of his customer's shoes cleaned to follow Rocky, the irate customer yells, "What about my other shoe?"

Romolo replies, "Eat it."

Pleading with Rocky to join him in an illegal venture, Romolo admits to Rocky, "Without you I'm nickels and dimes."

Following a heist for which a fence pays $75 to a gang of four, Romolo protests, "How can you split 75 four ways? It don't come out even."

Later, lounging on a subway bench and reading a newspaper with a cigarette dangling from a corner of his mouth, he asks Rocky, "What's the program for today?"

The program begins with rifling a gum machine. Spotted and chased by a cop, Rocky and Romolo barely make it onto a departing train. As it pulls away, a triumphant and exultant Romolo taunts the law by sticking out his tongue.

Later, fleeing the police across a rooftop, Romolo and Rocky find themselves collared. In a courtroom scene, while his lawyer pleads Romolo's youth as a defense and implores the judge for leniency, Romolo fakes tears and wails. He gets probation. Rocky is sent to jail.

Sal disappears for much of the film but returns as Rocky, now a professional boxer and a married man, finds Romolo hiding out from the police.

"We ain't got a chance, guys like us, do we, Rocky?" he asks. "Do we?"

Looking fuller and even taller, Sal provides no hint of Sylvester or Plato.

In what is Sal's most memorable scene, on-the-run Rocky tells Romolo to get him a suit.

Romolo replies, "I got no dough."

"So?"

Sal's reply is wide-eyed and knowing, with an impish grin.

The close-up of Sal turning on that winning smile is repeated in the credits at the end of the film as his name is superimposed.

Sal believed Paul Newman deserved an Oscar for his role as Rocky and was surprised that he was not even nominated. "I thought he was wonderful," he said. "I loved working with him."

While making *Somebody Up There Likes Me,* Sal signed for his next two films.

The first was titled *Crime in the Streets.* Originally a television drama, it was adapted for the big screen by its author, Reginald Rose. Remembering Sal's stunning performance in "Dino," Rose recommended him to Allied Artists for this film, to be directed by Donald Siegel. Like Nick Ray, Siegel made action pictures dealing with young social outcasts.

Starring in *Crime in the Streets* would be James Whitmore as an idealistic social worker. A member of the Yale Drama School players, he served in the Marines during the war and had made a memorable debut on Broadway in 1949 playing a wise-cracking sergeant in *Command Decision.* He'd been nominated for an Academy Award as supporting player in *Battleground.* His most recent work was as a protective farmer-father of Ado Annie in the film of *Oklahoma!*

Signed to costar with Whitmore was John Cassavetes as an alienated teenager who plans to commit a murder but backs out. Although this would be his third film, the opening credits said "introducing John Cassavetes."

Sal received costar billing, but because of his Oscar nomination for *Rebel* he found that he was featured more prominently in posters and advertising than Whitmore and Cassavetes.

The press book sent out by Allied Artists to assist theater owners in advertising and promoting the film asked on its cover, "Rebels *with* a cause?"

Beneath a picture of Sal was a box declaring:

SAL MINEO, sensation of
"Rebel Without a Cause"
rages to stardom!

A sample newspaper story presented in the press book carried the headline:

17-YEAR OLD SAL MINEO IS

ASSURED A BRILLIANT FUTURE

The caption of a composite photo of scenes from the film stated, "Stark terror, vicious brutality, despondency and warm love are the ingredients that make up the powerful drama in Allied Artists' production, *Crime in the Streets,* the tense screen story of tenement district kids living on twisted pleasures they call 'kicks.' "

Theater-owners exhibiting *Crime in the Streets* were asked to order a supply of glossy 8-by-10 and 5-by-7 fan photos at "low-cost prices" so that the theaters could offer a free photo of Sal to "the first 100 teenagers attending a particular performance."

The photo was a head-and-shoulders shot of Sal from the right side in jacket and tie, eyes averted rightward.

Other enticements included *Crime in the Streets* lapel badges for ushers, and banners for display on marquees.

Theaters also received tags to be placed on windshields of parked cars that said:

POLICE WARNING

Please Lock Your Car

If you don't

you'll encourage

"Crime in the Streets"

In this film Sal played the "meanest" of all his film characters, a 16-year-old psychopath named Baby Giola, who pretends to cry in order to lure a man to his death at the hands of a knife-wielding accomplice.

The producer of the picture, Vincent M. Fennelly, declared in a proposed newspaper story included in the press book, "I made *Crime in the Streets* because I believed it was a very powerful piece of dramatic entertainment, which will hold audiences rapt and spellbound. But while the picture is a compelling excitment-packed drama, there is no question that many fathers and mothers can derive benefit from seeing it, because it definitely points out the reason many adolescent boys and girls go astray is that they suffered from a lack of love."

It's the theme of *Rebel Without a Cause,* but the audience for which the film was intended was not parents. It was a movie made for teenagers and it offered that audience the same young actor who'd made such a compelling impression in *Rebel Without a Cause* that he'd been nominated for an Oscar. The promotion for *Crime in the Streets* exploited Sal's emergence as an actor who could draw teenagers into theaters with such statements as, "Somebody's got to love him or he'll explode," "The picture that isn't 'chicken,' " and "It dares to tell WHY the rock 'n' roll generation is loose on a thrill binge that shakes and shocks you!"

Baby Giola is depicted in ads as "16 and seething with all the pent-up fury of today's adolescents, hungry for 'kicks' and ready to go, Go, GO all the way." Sal provided a chilling performance that would contribute significantly to a nickname that soon would be pinned on him: "The Switchblade Kid."

His next film would be heralded by Universal-International as "the whole wonderful story of today's tempestuous teenagers told the way they want it told, with all the excitement of rock and roll, with all the laughter and heartache of growing up!" As with *Crime in the Streets* and *Giant,* Sal would be promoted as having a much bigger role in the film than proved to be the case. In *Rock Pretty Baby* the leading character is not portrayed by Sal, but by John Saxon. Yet when it was released it was Sal who got top billing and promotion for being "as great as he was in *Rebel Without a Cause* and *Giant!*"

In fact, Sal's role was secondary to Saxon's as the leader of a rock band who'd rather see his group win a battle of bands than go to medical school. Sal plays Nino Barrato, the rock band's drummer, with lines such as, "You should have heard my old man. Why you got to be a drummer? If you want to beat skins, be practical. Be a masseur."

Looking at another character's shapely girl who's in a bathing suit, Nino groans, "Mama mia! Maybe I'm chasing the wrong girl."

Sal rightly judged the movie as "campy" and was reluctant to help promote it. However, it did afford him the opportunity to demonstrate his growing competence as a drummer.

His next job in 1956—his fifth in a year—was *The Young Don't Cry*. A Columbia film, it was written by Phillip Jessup, based on his novel. Once again opposite James Whitmore, Sal was Leslie Henderson, an orphan in search of his true identity. Whitmore is a convicted murderer who befriends him, then compels Sal to help him escape.

Directed by Alfred L. Werker, who'd started his career in the silent era and for whom this would be the last picture, and co-starring veteran character actor J. Carrol Nash, it was filmed in and around Savannah, Georgia. Sal claimed to have spent his time off drinking mint juleps and being chased by "southern belles."

Sal's account of the movie's opening at the Victoria Theater in New York's Times Square depicted a manifestation of the phenomenon of Mineo Mania. "I was supposed to appear at eight o'clock and arrived at the theater about half an hour early. When I got there the streets were empty and I was wondering whether people would show up at all. At eight, I looked out and almost fainted. There was no longer a street, just a mass of eight thousand people waiting—for me! It was finally midnight before the police cleared a path for me."

A reporter covering the premiere observed "hysterical teenagers, banked ten deep." As they broke through police lines and surged toward Sal's taxi, a police captain said, "What do you say we lift you up on top of the marquee? That way you can wave to the whole crowd and you won't run the risk of being trampled to death." Sal replied, "Gosh, no. It's a good idea, but I just couldn't stand on top of a Broadway theater marquee. I'm not important enough for that."

The police found another solution. "They put me on a stand," Sal recalled. "I was crying and couldn't control my emotions. I started mumbling about my gratitude, and then the police lines broke. My clothes were ripped and after it was all over you couldn't recognize me. It was just wonderful."

Reporter Martin Abramson saw in Sal an actor who violated all the rules for big-time Hollywood success. "He is neither tall nor conventionally handsome," he wrote, "and is usually cast in the unappetizing role of a delinquent." Yet before Abramson's eyes were "frenzied hands clutching his thick mane of jet-black hair" and tearing at his sleeves.

Sal understood why they did this. He told Abramson, "When they want to idolize someone they see on the screen, they pick someone who looks like them, acts like them, talks like them. It's my good luck that they found that they can identify themselves with me."

Observing the skyrocketing of Sal Mineo into movie stardom, studio executives, producers, directors, other actors, agents, professional managers, and the Hollywood press were amazed that the teenager's astonishing rise to such heady heights in show business had not been the result of professional management. Martin Abramson noted, in his story about Sal being mobbed by fans at the opening of *The Young Don't Cry,* "Sal has no press agent, and never had the usual Hollywood publicity build up. He has no show-wise brain trust behind him. He clings to his real name—no 'Rory' or 'Rock' or 'Tab' for him. He has the same friends, the same habits, the same unaffected, warm personality he had before the golden Heavens opened up for him. He stays in Hollywood just long enough to finish a picture, then it is back to his native Bronx."

Sal said he did this because he feared that in living in Hollywood he might lose contact with the vital things, the real people in life. "If I lived in Hollywood and my career went on the skids it would be a disaster," he said. "In the Bronx, on the other hand, my neighbors tell me, 'So your job didn't turn out? So get yourself another job.' "

Rather than being handled by a talent agency, Sal's career was a Mineo family enterprise headed by his mother. Opportunities were discussed around the dinner table. Brother Victor handled contract negotiations and, along with Michael, often traveled with Sal to act as assistant and sometimes bodyguard. In handling Sal's affairs the family agreed that offers of long-term contracts should be turned down. Sal would be a freelancer. The result was better parts and more money. The same strategy was applied to television. An offer of a three-year contract for Sal by Kraft was turned down. The family wanted to see how Sal did in his first appearance on *Kraft Television Theater.* When he did well, the contract offer was accepted, but on much better terms for Sal.

The effect of treating Sal's career as a family business had resulted in stardom for Sal and income of $200,000 a year.

As thousands of fan letters began pouring in, Josephine enlisted neighborhood girls to help answer them. Eventually, the cost came to thousands a year. Nor was professional help brought in to look after Sal's publicity. Josephine asked, "Who needs a press agent to make up stories? We want the public to know the real Sal, the one we love, not a character."

While well-intentioned, Sal's decision to place his career and finances in the hands of his family and not in the care and keeping of Hollywood professionals would eventually come back to haunt him.

But for the moment, his acting career was taking off and was the wonder of the lions and sages of the old Hollywood. Between 1954 and the autumn of 1956 Sal had made seven films with some of the biggest names in the business and earned an Academy Award nomination. His name had become a box-office draw for exactly the audience the industry needed to attract into theaters. And he'd proved that he could bring more to the screen than a pretty face and a winning personality. He'd shown that he was an outstanding actor.

As the busy year of 1956 drew to a close, Sal also demonstrated that he could be more than a movie star. The opportunity was offered by a new NBC television show called *Can Do,* hosted by Robert Alda. It was an audience participation program in which contestants could win up to $50,000 for correctly guessing whether celebrities could successfully perform certain stunts. The first round was worth $1,500. The prize doubled with each correct guess. One of the contestants was asked whether Sal Mineo could operate a construction crane. The contestant guessed he could. Sal proved the contestant right. (The show proved short-lived; it debuted on November 26 and went off the air on December 31.)

Sal spent that New Year's Eve with his family.

While Sal was making movies almost nonstop in 1956, the year had witnessed what one historian of American popular music called "the fruition" of the rock-and-roll music that had been introduced to the movies in *Blackboard Jungle* by Bill Haley and the Comets and which had been at the heart of *Rock Pretty Baby.* Throughout

1956 Bill Haley flooded the market with new rock-and-roll songs, including "See You Later Alligator." Little Richard had stormed the pop music charts with "Long Tall Sally" and Chuck Berry had weighed in with "Roll Over Beethoven." And RCA Victor records had released a record that had been recorded in Nashville, Tennessee, by a kid from Tupelo, Mississippi, named Elvis Presley. The record was "Heartbreak Hotel" and it had hit and held the No. 1 spot on *Billboard* magazine's pop charts for two months. It was followed by Presley's "Hound Dog" and "Don't Be Cruel." Any doubts that rock and roll could be a commercial success had been laid to rest.

As movie studios had recognized that the future of motion pictures lay in the wallets and purses of teenagers, executives of the music and recording industries were quick to realize that a historic shift was underway in the demographics of the audience for popular music. Teenagers with money to spend from allowances or wages earned on after-school jobs were plunking it down to buy records by the new artists riding the wave of interest in rock and roll. Recording companies were scrambling to find and develop young stars. For Epic records at the start of 1957 just such a personality seemed to be Sal Mineo. The question was, could he sing? When the company learned that he'd had singing lessons and had sung in *The King and I* on Broadway, Sal was asked to cut a song titled "Start Movin'."

When Sal appeared on *Kraft Television Theater* on May 1, 1957, in a production titled "Drummer Man," he introduced the song. Three days later, he appeared on ABC-TV to promote the record on Alan Freed's *Rock 'n' Roll Review*. Teenage fans of Sal Mineo who found it on sale in their local stores bought more than 1,200,000 copies, boosting the record to number nine on the charts and keeping it in the Top 40 for 13 weeks. A second release, "Lasting Love," got to number 27 and remained in the Top 40 for three weeks.

Thrilled by Sal's success as a rock singer, Epic produced an album simply called *Sal* on which Sal performed a dozen songs. The album's liner notes observed, "Time was when actors acted and singers sang, but nowadays the line between the two has grown very dim indeed." After summarizing Sal's acting career, the notes concluded, "With stage, screen and television credits to spare, Sal moved into his recording career with consummate ease. It is rare enough when a young singer scores a hit with his first record, rarer still when his second eclipses the first. It was a natural outcome of such success that Sal should make a collection of songs for his fans, and this is the result."

Sal's choices ranged from the familiar ("Too Young") to the old standard "Down by the River Side" to a song that was expected of an Italian singer, "Oh Marie." The last number on the album was an old tune aimed at teenage girls who no doubt listened to it and dreamed of Sal crooning it to them—"Baby Face." His voice sounded as young as he was. The lyrics were delivered with feeling and he had no problem staying on key. The chief attraction to buyers of the album, mostly teenage girls, was that it sounded as though Sal were singing directly to each of them. His face dominated the front of the album. With curly black hair tumbling forward and gazing over his left shoulder he offered an expression somewhere between innocence and seductive.

The most unusual number was titled "Tattoo." Sal sings about his body being adorned with pictures of women he's met and loved around the world. Rangoon Rosie was on his arm. If you wanted to see Rose bustle and rustle he'd roll up his sleeve and make a muscle. Tangiers Tessie adorned his chest. If you wanted to see Tess wiggle and wriggle he'd take off his shirt and you'd see her jiggle. But Boston Betsy was tattooed in his heart. (The performance compares favorably to those by Burl Ives and Groucho Marx concerning "Lydia, the tattooed lady.")

Later that year and into 1958 Epic released "Love Affair," "Party Time," "Little Pigeon," and "You Shouldn't Do That." They were in the Top 50 for more than ten weeks.

Although the records proved very successful and lucrative, Sal recognized that his future did not lie in being a singer. He quipped, "Nobody is going to mistake me for Pat Boone." He quit making records in 1959.

With no film obligations at hand in 1957, Sal returned to television. On *Kraft Televison Theater* he was in a production of Bruce Bassett's teleplay "Barefoot Soldier," costarring Nancy Marchand and Collin Wilcox. Two weeks later, he did *The Alcoa Hour*.

Then Reginald Rose asked Sal to become Dino Minetta again. This time Americans would meet Sal as The Switchblade Kid on the big screen.

six

The Switchblade Kid

When Dwight David Eisenhower took the oath of office on January 20, 1957, to begin his second term as president of the United States, critics of his Republican administration referred to him as "chairman of the bored." Automobiles (and there were plenty of them in Ike's nation of "peace and prosperity") were huge and comfortable and sported tail fins as they plied the growing network of red-light–free interstate highways, built because Ike wanted a system of highways for moving tanks, trucks, and troops in the event of war. Homes without a TV set had become the exception. Watching the tube was so ingrained in the American family's daily life that the Swanson food company had invented the "TV dinner." Just pop it into an oven and in minutes you had a hot meal of meat and vegetables and no dishes to wash.

The Russians were a problem, and there was the ugly shadow of possible nuclear war, but Ike seemed to be handling the world so well that he'd just been elected to four more years.

But in the late 1950s there was another America. Ike was in charge of an adult population that had come of age in the era of the big bands and movies that starred Clark Gable, Spencer Tracy, and Katharine Hepburn. The figurehead of the country's adolescents was a Philadelphia disc jockey named Dick Clark. He had a television show called *American Bandstand* on which kids danced to rock and roll. Boys wore pegged pants and their slicked-back hairstyle was called the D.A., short for "duck's ass." The supreme fantasy of these boys was Marilyn Monroe.

The idols of teenage girls dancing in bobby socks were Elvis Presley (so famous that he had reached the point where he need be identified only by his first name), Rick Nelson (no longer cute "little Ricky" of the Ozzie and Harriet program), David Nelson (although nowhere near the status of his younger brother), Pat Boone in signature white buck shoes, Frankie Avalon, John Saxon, Edd "Kookie" Byrnes of the TV show 77 Sunset Strip, Tommy Sands, Tab Hunter (although he was slipping), Jeffrey Hunter, and Robert Wagner (romantically linked to Natalie Wood).

Among these teen icons in 1957 none surpassed the popularity of Sal Mineo.

"As a Hollywood movie star, fabulously successful recording star and TV star," said one fan magazine, "this teenager has a glamour and appeal which most full-grown men scarcely attain."

Recognizing a way to sell magazines to teenage girls, periodicals rushed to print articles about his romantic life. Typical was the July 1957 issue of Behind the Scene. An article entitled "The Women in Sal Mineo's Life" declared in a headline, "Hollywood's junior Casanova has learned that most gals are ready and willing—if he's able."

It began, "You're a handsome 18-year-old fellow with dark curly hair and velvety brown eyes. What's more, you've got fame and fortune, and ahead of you lies a brilliant movie career. Your biggest problem is the swarm of teenage gals who keep pitching their best curves at you. Can you fight them off? If you're Sal Mineo, it's not easy."

Writer John Sansoni devoted most of the article to describing how "the talented youth whose stock-in-trade is a wide-eyed stare of innocence" had so many females pursuing him that he had "to grow up in a hurry." But Sansoni's story also attempted to reveal the Sal Mineo known by kids who had grown up with him. Visiting Sal's neighborhood, he repeatedly heard, "Sal's an all-right guy." He also discovered that the anchor in Sal's life was his family.

A writer for Movie Life magazine who also traveled to the Bronx in search of the real Sal Mineo wrote, "His family, warm, loving, solidly understanding, is his haven."

The person overseeing that haven was his mother.

"Sal always had a spark, a talent," said Josephine to yet another magazine reporter. "I saw it way back."

Accompanying the resulting article were photos of Sal at all stages of his life. On the day of his first communion, at age eight, he was dressed in a white suit with short pants. For a formal portrait on the day he was confirmed in the Roman Catholic church he looks properly serious and thoughtful, holding an open Bible. There was a schoolboy picture with jacket and bow tie.

"On the days when he went from school to his dancing lessons, of course he had to dress up more than the other boys," Josephine explained, "so he was always in fights. When he'd come out all messed up I didn't say much. I wanted him to be a real boy. I knew he had to fight."

A Christmas snapshot at age 11 caught him and sister Sarina posing before the tree with Sal's present, a boxer dog he named El Bimbo. When he was 12 he posed with Sarina, Michael, and Victor in a row according to height. In his first tuxedo he was on his way to a party in honor of Rodgers and Hammerstein. At age 15 he was photographed as a guest on the TV show of talk-show pioneer Joe Franklin. And the entire family was photographed gathered at a piano being played by Sal and Sarina, accompanied by Victor on saxophone and Michael on clarinet, while Josephine and "Big Sal" look on admiringly.

"They gave him the rich security of love—plus a respect for his ability to make his own adult decisions," the article concluded. "They nurtured the spark till it became a light, not only for them, but for all of us."

Sal's relationships with his older siblings was typical of brothers. Victor and Mike were guardians and teachers in the ways of boys on their way to manhood. Sal's attitude toward Sarina was that of most older brothers. He considered her a pest, a nuisance. "She was a bother to me," he recalled at a time when fame and fortune were his. "I had to watch out for her on the street, feed her, do all the chores."

One day he came home from school and found the house empty. A note told him to go to a hospital about half a mile from the Mineo home, to the children's ward. He ran all the way. He found the family standing around a room with fear on their faces.

"There on the bed," Sal remembered, "was the little figure of my sister. My mother told me Sarina had polio. In that instant I hated myself for every moment I had not loved her and protected her."

Sarina recovered, but that moment in the children's ward was one Sal could never forget.

Less than a decade later Sarina's brother Sal was a movie star making $300,000 a year and in a position to buy his family a new home. It was a rambling house (some called it a mansion) in a decidedly upscale suburb of New York. Located in Mamaronek, it was the former home of the silent-film star Mary Pickford. It stood on the shore of Long Island Sound and afforded Sal the opportunity to indulge his love of swimming and the waterskiing he'd learned from Yul Brynner, and to dash over the water in another indulgence, a trim little speedboat also named El Bimbo.

Another journalistic sojourner to Mamaronek concentrated on discovering Sal's likes and hobbies. They were "jazz, companions his own age, steak, malted milks, art exhibits, walking alone at night, movies, TV, good clothes and sleeping late." The reporter noted, "Sal is a talented painter in oils, and is proudest of a portrait he painted of Abraham Lincoln. If these extra-time interests were not enough, he experiments with photography, collects sea shells and races his speed boat."

The idyllic setting of the Long Island Sound shoreline also provided an opportunity for a fan magazine, Modern Screen, to do a spread titled "Let's Join Sal Mineo at a Beach Party." Two pages of photographs showed Sal in a polka-dot bathing suit drinking Coca-Cola from a bottle and holding a lengthy barbecue skewer with a hot dog dangling at the end. With him vaulting a fence, batting around a beach ball, and having a cookout on the sand are his brother Mike, Jim Stewart (a friend), and a trio of models identified as Loretta Schatzkin, Phyliss Roseman, and Gaye Sheldon, also an actress and cited in a caption as Sal's date for the day.

Another fan-magazine story at this time related another beach outing in Santa Monica, California, in which Sal found himself the object of desire by "an aging but still sexy actress, noted for her frantic quest for the magic fountain of youth." The article stated, "When Sal found himself being chased from one end of the beach to the other by the aging sexpot, he finally told the actress off in no uncertain terms."

Many of the fan letters from teenage girls opened by Josephine's team of neighborhood helpers contained photographs and girls' addresses. Sal told a fan magazine that he copied them into a little black book. "In case I'm ever in Detroit, or Chicago, or Memphis," he said, "I'll have a date just like that."

His girls were also categorized by which sport they liked. One preferred horseback riding. Another was a bowler. A third was an enthusiast of waterskiing and boating. Sal boasted, "I've got a girl for every sport."

Not all of these admirers were girls his age. In addition to the aging sexpot who'd chased him all over Santa Monica, beach, there was an actress whom one magazine writer described as a certain flaming redhead whose name was synonymous with glamour to almost two generations of moviegoers. "She's a three-time loser in the marital sweepstakes and has a son virtually the same age as Sal," the article said. "She was a starlet when Rin Tin Tin was a pup. She's dated every big-time star since Rudolph Valentino. She is also famous for the out-sized dimensions of her bosom. As a reigning queen in cinemaland, she considered it her privilege to be the first to personally initiate newly arrived actors into the Hollywood version of the age-old game of musical beds. She latched onto Sal soon after he hit town."

As Sal told the story, after making the rounds of Hollywood nightlife they pulled up in front of the star's swank house in Bel-Air and parked in the driveway. Before anything happened, she let out a yelp. "I couldn't figure out what was wrong," Sal confided to a friend. "Then I noticed something bouncing around on the floor of the car. It was her foam rubber falsies."

Among the attentions being paid to Sal's romantic life was an item by gossip columnist Walter Winchell. He announced that Sal and actress-singer Anna Maria Alberghetti were about to become engaged on the West Coast and that Sal was bringing 72 relatives to Los Angeles for the wedding. At the time Sal and Anna Maria had not met.

However, he had met girls who'd lost in the Miss Universe contest. He was a consolation prize. "I took them all out," he boasted. "Miss Italy one night, then Miss Hawaii. It was a very interesting week."

Concerning Sal's attractiveness to older women as much as to girls his age, his drama teacher, Claudia Franck, said, "There is an unusual quality about this boy. It's a fierce earnestness which is noticeable because it is combined with—and almost covered by—a hesitant and appealing shyness."

Sal's family saw his appeal stemming from a natural sweetness and gentle nature.

No one who knew him spoke in terms of the delinquents he had portrayed in most of his films in the 1950s. They looked forward to seeing him in roles that were closer to the true Sal, as they put it. But his life as The Switchblade Kid was far from over.

His tough, troubled teenager burst onto movie screens in 1958 in the form of the kid he'd brought into American living rooms via television in June 1956.

With the nation's worries about juvenile delinquency showing no signs of abating, and perhaps being exacerbated by the rampaging popularity of rock and roll among the country's youth, Reginald Rose took an adaptation of his teleplay "Dino" to Allied Artists Pictures and had no problem selling it as a feature film.

The logical actor to play the title role was the one who not only had created Dino for television, but also had been the star of Allied Artist's *Crime in the Streets*. In this picture, however, there would be no need for the studio's publicity department to make it appear that Sal Mineo was the film's star. Sal would legitimately be billed ahead of the title.

Posters, lobby cards, and advertising would show him in a tight tee shirt and blue jeans and declare, "Sal Mineo explodes like a skyrocket in his most electrifying emotional role." The film would be touted as, "The body and soul story of youth with a chip on its shoulder."

Brian Keith was signed to reprise the role of Sheridan (no first name, just the initial L) as Dino's psychiatrist. Veteran Hollywood character actor Frank Faylen was cast as Dino's parole officer. Playing an abusive father was Joe De Santis. (Brutal or ineffectual fathers were a theme of juvenile-delinquency films.) The role of the suffering mother went to Penny Santon, a short and somewhat plump actress who resembled Sal's own mother. Juveniles in a settlement house to which Dino was ordered to report by his parole officer were portrayed by Pat DeSimone, Richard Bakalyan, Rafael Campos, Mollie McCart, and Cindy Harvey. A street gang calling itself the Silk Hats, whose members look up to Dino because he'd done time for a murder, included Sal's brother Michael as Dino's brother Tony. Although Michael was two years older than Sal, Michael appears younger. Tony informs Dino that the gang members want him to lead them in sticking up a gas station.

Sal's love interest would be a girl at the settlement house named Cheryl (Susan Kohner). Making her second film in two years, Susan was three years older than Sal but she also looked younger. She was the daughter of Hollywood talent agent Paul Kohner and Mexican film star Lupita Tovar. Her previous film was *To Hell and Back*, the movie autobiography of war hero Audie Murphy (playing himself). At age 14 she'd appeared with New York's Circle Theater players in *The Girl on the Via Flamina* and had been in *A Quiet Place*, a play starring Tyrone Power. She also had one theatrical experience in common with Sal. She'd been in a production of *The Rose Tattoo*, but not on Broadway.

Directed by Thomas Carr, *Dino* was shot in black and white by cinematographer Wilfrid M. Cline almost entirely on sound stages. Rose's script gave Sal some colorful lines.

Just released from the reformatory, an embittered Dino declares, "I'd like to go back there and cut their guts out."

To the psychiatrist concerning being confined to a reformatory: "Did you ever sleep 40 guys in a room? What goes on in there—everything you can think of."

Told by the psychiatrist that it's all right for a boy to cry: "Cry? You think I'm gonna cry? What arm do you take it in?"

During an emotionally wrenching soliloquy, as Dino lies on a leather couch in the office of the psychiatrist, Dino recalls abuse he has suffered from his father. "I don't remember no one ever kissing me," he sobs. "How come nobody ever kissed me?"

The kiss he receives from Susan Kohner persuades Dino that life isn't so bad after all. He meets the Silk Hats at the gas station but refuses to go through with the stickup. The film ends with Dino asking the psychiatrist if it would okay for his brother to come in to see him.

Dino marked a milestone in Sal's acting career: it called for his first screen kiss.

So important was this event to the teen magazine *Dig* that its May 1957 edition's cover proclaimed "Sal Mineo's First Movie Love Scene." Inside were an article titled "Big Smooch" and three pages of pictures immortalizing what the magazine called "a momentous occasion."

The article (by an unnamed writer) took *Dig*'s readers step by step through the scene:

> First, Sal and Susan are carefully readied for the camera, both by the wardrobe people fixing their clothes and makeup men applying fresh makeup for the scene. Susan's lips are given extra-special attention, for it isn't every day a girl gets kissed by a fellow like Sal.
>
> Director Tom Carr then steps in with some last-minute instructions on the clinch. He has to take into account the camera angle and make certain that both stars are shown, *with* the kiss, to best advantage. After everything is checked through again, they are ready to begin.
>
> Sal gazes deeply into Susan's eyes and places his hand gently on her cheek. Her hand reaches his, her eyes half-close, they whisper a few romantic words for each other . . . and their lips finally meet in a long kiss.
>
> Teenage girls reading this account were no doubt as envious of Susan Kohner as were the girls who watched the kiss on a movie screen.

Not every fan-magazine article about Sal adopted the angle of Sal Mineo, heartthrob. In what appeared to be a sincere effort to persuade youthful readers that belonging to a teen gang was not cool, *Filmland* ran a long article purportedly written by him (it was actually the result of an interview) that asked, "Must a teenager join a gang to be popular?"

"This is a problem I've certainly had to face," Sal said truthfully, "and I have to admit that kids have a good point in wanting to be like, dress like, and act like the 'gang.' I think it takes courage to be an individual, to stick up for what you believe is right. Yet, you can't be an individual if you feel that being one of the gang is the most important thing. I believe it's okay to follow the crowd—as long as you know where you, yourself, are heading. It's not so bad to dress like everyone else. For a while I wore tight pants and sharp jackets like the rest of the kids in the Bronx where I was raised. It was a rough neighborhood so it made it doubly difficult not to conform. Yet, when I began to get work as an actor and started going out on interviews I found that the people looked at me very peculiarly for the way I dressed."

He continued about his experiences in the Bronx, admitting, "I had my share of fights. That's how I broke my nose. I was fighting with a kid at school once and we went at it for so long we could hardly stand up. My brother Mike got involved in my battles, too, because he was always trying to help me out. He'd give me a hand and when he got me home he just gave me a lecture."

Sal's "lecture" to the magazine's young readers concluded, "Dress like others if you want to, talk the way they do if you must, but have the courage to be different enough to be able to look at yourself in the mirror and not feel like crawling into a hole. Put your sights on things that will bring you happiness even if you have to be apart from the crowd. Don't be a carbon copy."

Although his performance in *Dino* received praise from film reviewers, Sal worried that he was becoming a carbon copy of himself on screen as Hollywood's perennial juvenile delinquent. Consequently, when Walt Disney Studios offered him a role as an American Indian in a proposed production titled *Tonka,* he seized the opportunity to shed the Switchblade Kid image.

In a film advertised as "the untold story behind the West's strangest legend," it's not Sal who plays the title role. Tonka (also known in the film as Comanche) is a horse. Sal's character's name is White Bull.

A young brave of the Sioux tribe, he captures and tames a magnificent wild horse and names it Tonka, meaning "great one." When a cousin claims the horse by virtue of the cousin's higher standing in the tribe, White Bull sets Tonka loose. Freedom, however, is short-lived. Captured by a U.S. Cavalry troop and tamed to army standards, Tonka is renamed Comanche. Ridden into the Battle of the Little Big Horn, in which General George Armstrong Custer's 7th Cavalry was wiped out by Indians under Chief Sitting Bull, Comanche survives and is declared a hero, never to be ridden again except by his exercise boy. Through a sequence of fortuitous events, that boy is White Bull.

Costarring Phillip Carey and Jerome Courtland, and directed by Louis R. Foster from a screenplay by Foster and Lillie Hayward (based on a book by David Apel), the film reunited Sal with a member of the cast of *Dino,* Rafel Campos, another non-Native American playing one.

Despite having injured a knee while learning to ride, Sal proved to be a fine horseman. Riding bareback and racing the chestnut quarterhorse one day at 42 miles an hour, he outran the camera truck that was supposed to keep up with him. He also put the obviously well-trained horse through a series of trick moves in a corral.

The movie afforded Sal's fans ample opportunities to see his bared chest and to admire a muscular physique, the result of Sal's daily regimen of exercises with weights. However, there's no evidence of his hallmark mane of thick, curly black hair. He wears a skull-hugging black wig with two long braided pigtails. A color photograph of Sal as White Bull with bulging biceps and wearing a chest-revealing open buckskin vest as he sits astride Tonka was used as the cover of a Dell comic book telling the story of the horse that survived Little Big Horn. The drawings of Sal were lifelike.

With *Tonka* completed, Sal's next role would have him portraying another youth who was far removed in distance and time from the rock-and-roll world of increasingly unruly teenagers in America in the waning years of the 1950s. He would be a boy who discovered a magic lamp, which, when rubbed, brought forth a genie who granted wishes.

*   *   *

While Sal had been making movies in 1957, one of the greatest composers of pop music in pre–rock and roll America was engaged in writing the musical "Aladdin" for CBS-TV's *Du Pont Show of the Month,* to be broadcast on Friday, February 21, 1958. He was Cole Porter and he had created some of the grandest musicals in the history of Broadway.

To write the book for "Aladdin" Porter had turned to humorist S. J. Perleman

The location is Peking, China, in an unspecified time, but long ago. The musical opens in a marketplace as the audience is introduced to a magician. When the emperor and his daughter pass through the market, the princess notices a boy named Aladdin. She is smitten and so is he. The magician tries to persuade Aladdin to join him in a nefarious scheme. When Aladdin finds himself trapped in a cave, he discovers the magic lamp with its wonder-working genie. In the end, love conquers all.

To perform Cole Porter's "Aladdin" producer Richard Lewine assembled an amazing cast. The magician was Cyril Ritchard, a distinguished Australian actor, singer, dancer, and director. The emperor was Basil Rathbone (his indelible characterization of Sherlock Holmes in 14 films in the 1930s and 1940s long since left behind). The princess was Anna Maria Alberghetti. A beautiful 21-year-old actress and classical singer who was born in Pesaro, Italy, she had made her American singing debut at age 14 at Carnegie Hall. Since 1950 she had been in six motion pictures. The genie was played by a tall black actor with a mellifluous voice, Geoffrey Holder, who would go on to many other roles, including a villain in a James Bond movie. Others in the musical were Dennis King, Una Merkel, and Howard Morris.

Although the title of the production was "Aladdin," the role of the boy is secondary to that of the magician. Sal's performance was energetic, in keeping with the script, but Ritchard dominated. Of the musical's ten Cole Porter songs Sal performed one, "I Adore You," reprised with Alberghetti for a happy ending. The show's cast album was originally released in monaural sound, although stereo recordings had made their debut. But in the 1990s when Sony Corporation was planning to reissue the record on CD, it was discovered that the original recording session had also been captured on three-track stereo tapes. As a result, the Sony CD is in stereo.

Despite the reputations of Porter and Perelman and the extraordinary cast, the show was a flop both in terms of the size of the audience and in the opinion of critics. One wrote, "Sal Mineo was a fine Aladdin indeed, once he devoted his vocal cords to dialogue instead of singing, at which he is, frankly, hopeless though sincere."

Viewers preferred to tune in for *Adventures of Rin Tin Tin, Jim Bowie,* and *Colt 45* on ABC and *Studio 57* (a mystery), *Truth or Consequences,* and *The Life of Riley* on NBC.

Sal's consolation in undertaking what proved to be a failure was his salary for portraying Aladdin. He was paid an unprecedented $100,000.

The next Sal Mineo movie was also a musical of sorts, titled *A Private's Affair.* Directing it would be one of Hollywood's most distinguished and durable moviemakers, 60-year-old Raoul Walsh. It's a tribute to his abilities and forward outlook on life that he undertook a movie aimed at a rock-and-roll audience and with a cast consisting of some of the youth culture's most popular personalities. With Sal in the starring role, playing an army private named Luigi Maresi, the picture's cast included Christine Carrere, Barry Coe, Barbara Eden, Gary Crosby, and Terry Moore. It also reunited Sal with Jim Backus. Made by 20th Century-Fox in Cinemascope, the picture involved its likeable and energetic actors in putting on a show at an Army base. The plot may have owed its inspiration to the fact that the country's No. 1 rock-and-roll star, Elvis Presley, had been drafted into the Army.

Hardly a touchstone in movie history, *A Private's Affair* may retain some interest to film students as a prime example of a 1950s teen movie. It certainly kept the fires of Mineo Mania well stoked and it carried Sal another step away from the Switchblade Kid. But this lightweight film provided no challenge to the serious actor who created Plato, Romolo, Baby Giola, and Dino.

How well or poorly *A Private's Affair* fared among film critics and performed at the box office mattered little to Sal. He had something more personal to worry about. In this period of continuing success and increasing salaries he was informed that his infected right eye had become ulcerous. Unless he had surgery he could lose all sight in it.

The operation proved successful, requiring him to wear a black eye patch for a few weeks and tinted glasses in the sun and in conditions of bright lights (except in films) for the rest of his life. The surgery also resulted in that eye being very slightly askew.

A fan magazine joyfully notified Sal's fans that he had recovered and that the "pain and worry brought him fresh insights, a renewed faith, a more solid perspective on life and living." He was "a stronger, better, wiser man for it, with a richer, fuller, capacity for living, for feeling, for enjoying, and for participating." All true.

Sal was soon energized by preparing for a role that nearly everyone in Hollywood said he was ideally suited to play. So did the man whose life story the picture would tell.

In the world of music in 1959 there was only one possible answer to the question, "Who is the greatest drummer currently on the music scene?" A short, black-haired, 50-year-old Italian from Chicago, Gene Krupa had provided the beat for a dancing public in the Jazz Age that was born during Prohibition and grew into the syncopation of the swing era of the big bands. He was described as "the archetypical showman-drummer, the man who brought the drummer to the public's notice in a way that hitherto had not been accomplished."

Name a successful band, and Gene Krupa had been in it, from McKenzie and Condon's Chicagoans in 1927 to Red Nichols and the Five Pennies in the early 1930s to Benny Goodman from 1934 to 1938, as well as the bands of Tommy Dorsey and Harry James, and then with his own group into the fifties. Gum-chewing and wisecracking, he had beat out a song called "Sing, Sing, Sing" in a concert at Carnegie Hall in 1938 that had the audience wildly enraptured. A repeat performance on a Goodman recording made the song a hit.

A Columbia picture produced by Philip A. Waxman and directed by Don Weis, *The Gene Krupa Story* reunited Sal with Susan Kohner as his love interest. Trumpeter and singer and friend of Krupa, Eddie Sirota, would be played by another actor/singer with a huge youthful following, James Darren. Red Nichols would play himself, and Bobby Troup would be bandleader Tommy Dorsey. Jazz singer Anita O'Day and bandleader Buddy Lester would play themselves.

Krupa's drumming would be on the soundtrack, matched by Sal's drumming on screen.

The script was generally true to Krupa's life. Defying parents who wanted him to enter the priesthood, Gene chooses to play drums professionally. He sets out for New York with his best friend and the friend's sweetheart Ethel (played by Kohner). She and Gene fall for each other, providing the secondary plot of the film. Finding success in the world of jazz and swing music, Krupa also discovers the seamy underside of that world in the form of drugs. An arrest for possessing marijuana nearly ends his career when he finds himself blacklisted.

"I'm Gene Krupa," declares Sal as Krupa, "and all I need is to get back to work."

Screenwriter Orin Jennings provided an intelligent and witty script with some memorable lines. Among them, concerning teenager Krupa's drumming, "How can an angel like that explode and knock everybody's plaster loose?" When a Krupa girlfriend is asked to help him in the drug case by testifying that the marijuana had been planted on Krupa, she refuses, declaring, "I've got a town I'd better get out of." On being blacklisted by the New York music world, Krupa says, "This town is like it died and left me." Krupa's pal Eddie philosophizes about life with, "Anguish and absurdity, that's all there is."

Except for the part of Plato, no role was desired more, or sought more vigorously, by Sal than this one. He'd taken up the drums after *Rebel Without a Cause* and they'd become almost an obsession. He'd gotten to be good; so good that Gene Krupa gave his blessing to him in the role. Sal threw himself into the picture as he had with no other, including *Rebel*. His own life also had much in common with Krupa's. They were Italians, sons of immigrants, who had found their life's calling as boys and had steadfastly and passionately pursued it against all odds. They'd each achieved amazing success, some people said, meteorically.

Playing an adult for the first time, Sal brought to the screen a body that was more mature and developed, thanks to weight workouts. That physique is revealed in Sal's first movie scene in which he's been to bed with a woman. In later scenes, as Krupa achieves the success he'd longed for, Sal is nattily attired in perfectly tailored suits with tie and vest and shoes with spats. He sports a Frank Si-natra–like porkpie hat in some scenes and a dapper homburg in others. At age 20, he is more handsome in this film than in any before or after.

His physical representation of Krupa is astonishingly accurate. He captures the legendary drummer's mannerisms, quirks, and distinc-tive facial contortions while drumming. But most remarkable in Sal's portrait of Krupa is Sal's own drumming, matching the soundtrack that Krupa had laid down. Actors, actresses, and singers had been synchronizing mouth movements to recordings almost since the ad-vent of talkies (it's called lip-synching), but Sal was required to match his drumming with Krupa's recording beat for beat.

Krupa was so impressed by Sal as a drummer that when the film was completed, he gave Sal a set of Krupa's own drums.

Sal's performance caught the attention of another notable in Hol-lywood who had made a career playing movie gangsters. Half-Italian George Raft said that if a movie were made of his life, he wanted Sal to play him. The same wish was voiced by a real-life, but Jewish, criminal, Mickey Cohen, whose Los Angeles home had been turned into a fortress against gangland rivals, complete with flood lights, alarm systems, and an impressive arsenal.

Sal found the news that Cohen thought he could be a convincing gangster flattering because he and brother Mike enjoyed dressing up like mobsters. One of his favorite outfits was a snug velvet-collared coat, dark shirt, white tie, and a slouch hat pulled down over the eyes. That he and Mike might be taken by a passerby for hoods delighted them. But one night in New York as the brothers walked along a midtown street with their wise-guy swaggers, they found themselves facing cops bounding from police cars, guns drawn, and yelling, "Get-cher hands up!"

Only after they were frisked and their ID cards checked were they offered apologies and the explanation that a robbery had occurred at a nearby restaurant. To the coppers, Sal and Mike looked like a couple of guys who might have pulled off such a thing.

Sal once approached a studio executive and offered the opinion that he would be perfect in a gangster movie in which he would die at the end in a hail of bullets.

"You're a leading man," the shocked executive exclaimed. "Leading men don't get killed off. If you want to make pictures like that, get your own movie company."

Of the era of gangsters such as Al Capone and Lucky Luciano, Sal told an interviewer in 1959, "Those gangster days! That was the era. I wish I had been born then, because that was when everything was going. Mike and I should have been there. Prohibition! Everybody was swinging."

Sal expressed these thoughts to Dean Jennings in a *Saturday Evening Post* article dated October 31, 1959. Titled "The Boy Called Sal," it filled five lengthy pages and was accompanied by six photographs on the first two pages. Jennings chose to begin by quoting a brutally unflattering description of Sal by Terrence O'Flaherty, the television critic of the *San Francisco Chronicle*.

O'Flaherty's piece had noted that he had heard that "twenty-year-old actor Sal Mineo had been signed to star in a remake of *The Pagan,* a steaming South Seas idyl that had the ladies swooning over a Latin lover named Ramon Novarro back in 1929." O'Flaherty blasted the idea, calling Sal "the baby-faced hero of the popcorn set." He continued, "The casting points up an interesting switch in Hollywood's changing concepts of male beauty. It is also a comment on the age level of today's movie-going public. Gone is the classic Greek profile with body attached. In its place we have the moon-faced teenager with the Pablum personality."

Jennings's article then noted that after O'Flaherty's article had gone to press "the roof fell in" as Sal's fans rallied to their idol. "The Sal Mineo Fan clubs far and wide," Jennings noted, "cried out in fury, and O'Flaherty was figuratively lynched, shot or burned at the stake."

What the San Francisco TV critic had not appreciated, Jennings pointed out, was that the American teenager, with an estimated spending power of $9 *billion* a year was the new and dominating force in the world of entertainment. "With millions of adults staying home nights to gape at television screens," he wrote, "the movie theaters are filling up with youngsters in the thirteen-to-nineteen age bracket. They, in turn, have created a whole new class of movie stars who, like themselves, have more or less just learned the art of shaving or daubing on lipstick."

Rather than being a moonfaced actor, Jennings advised O'Flaherty, "Probably the most versatile member of the group [of new actors] with the most promising future is Sal Mineo, a lad with a delicate, almost girlish face, wild black hair he deliberately musses up for effect, eyelashes half an inch long, full, sensuous lips and enormous brown eyes."

But the "prettiness is deceptive," Jennings warned, pointing out that Sal had been trained in "the street-gang warfare" of the Bronx. "Now, at the age of twenty, when some of his former pals are either putting the bite on dad for the family car or working up to the penitentiary, Mineo has a formidable record [of movies] that rolled up huge grosses."

Regarding the Krupa film, in which Columbia Pictures had invested more than a million dollars, producer Philip Waxman said, "We're not losing any sleep. Sal will draw them in."

Waxman was not guessing.

"The teenage movie-goer is ubiquitous," Jennings noted in the article, "far more impulsive and vocal than most adults, and easily influenced."

Regarding Sal Mineo, no better proof of that was needed than a recent joke in a monologue by Bob Hope on his TV show. "No school tomorrow, kids," he said. "It's Sal Mineo's birthday. All those in the Bronx can stay home."

It wasn't Sal's birthday, but the next day the absentee rate in Bronx schools shot way up.

A photo accompanying the article showed Sal arm in arm with Josephine outside the house he had bought for the family in Mamaronek. "From here," said the caption, "Mrs. Mineo energetically directs Sal's fan-club campaign." There were nearly half a million fans alone in the midwestern branch headed by Edward Gould from his home in Detroit.

One of Sal's fans, though not a member of a club, was David Cassidy, the son of actor Jack Cassidy and stepson of Shirley Jones. A friend of Sal's, Jack brought Sal home one evening for dinner. It was an event that four decades later still had David recalling it with amazement. "All I could do was talk with him about the Krupa movie. He told me that Gene Krupa gave him a set of his drums. I said, 'Ah, a set of drums!' *Nobody* had a set of drums. The next day, there in a huge box was the drum set with a bow on it and a note from Sal to me, saying, 'David, here's the drum set that Gene gave me. Enjoy them.' "

So interested were Sal's admirers in everything about him that the fan magazines found themselves hard-pressed to come up with ideas for stories. Perhaps the most ingenious fresh angle was that of *Screen Stories* in its pages devoted to the first film in which Sal had played the drums (*Rock Pretty Baby*). The magazine decided to engage the editor of *Horoscope Magazine,* Edward A. Wagner, to cast an astrological chart for an unnamed person who'd been born on January 10, 1939, in New York City. Accompanying a synopsis of *Rock Pretty Baby,* results of Wagner's work were headlined, "Sal Mineo: His Stars Tell a Success Story."

The astrologer found in Sal's chart "an ambitious and energetic individual . . . intent upon achieving success and riches." While describing his subject as possessing a degree of sympathy and imagination where other people are concerned, particularly in lower walks of life, with whom he may feel a bond of understanding, he warned against "foolish or extravagant" expenditures, particularly in pursuit of social gains, heart's desires, or attention from others based upon ostentatious outlay. "When disappointments or frustrations come into his life, he will be inclined to periods of depression and self-doubt. However, he will show a strong capacity for snapping out of setbacks and going into action with the purpose of building anew."

The forecast concluded with a prediction: "The period around his 28th and 29th years will be crucial and events then may mark an important turning point in his life."

Legitimate questions concerning the validity of horoscopes aside, all of this would prove true.

seven

Dov

In *The Gene Krupa Story,* screenwriter Orin Jennings had unwit-
tingly given two lines to Krupa that turned out to be Sal Mineo's
approach to a life that a phenomenal success afforded. In the film,
Krupa asks his friend Eddie, "What good is making good if you
can't have anything that goes with it—the parties, the kicks." In the
same scene, he says, "That's what making money is for, to have a
good time before it caves in on you."

Having reached 20, Sal took those sentiments to heart. He had
plenty of money and he was determined to enjoy it. He had nice
cars, an apartment in New York, and a roomy California house in
Laurel Canyon, rented from actor Scott Brady.

"If you're a movie star," he said, "you should live like one, not
a plumber."

Sal appeared never to have heard what Spencer Tracy once remarked about the field in which Sal was making his money. "Acting
is not an important job in the scheme of things," Tracy said.
"Plumbing is."

Among the audience whose tickets to movies and purchases of
records had made Sal Mineo a very rich 20-year-old at the end of
the 1950s, the worship of celebrities of their age showed no sign
of diminishing. Indeed, their fervent embrace of Sal's generation of
actors on the movie screen and on television had saved Spencer

Tracy's Hollywood. A motion-picture industry that had trembled with fear of television now found itself making enormous profits by making TV shows on its sound stages and back lots, and frequently on the streets of Los Angeles.

Warner, Columbia, and 20th Century-Fox and independent production companies such as Desilu (Lucille Ball and Desi Arnaz having taken over the RKO studios), Four Star Productions, and Ziv Television were producing almost everything on the tube except news and sports. Some of the shows had created instant stars, including Edd "Kookie" Byrnes; Robert Conrad, in an imitation of 77 Sunset Strip set in Honolulu (Hawaiian Eye, also known jokingly in the business as 77 Surfboard Strip); James Garner in Maverick; Roger Moore in The Alaskans; Gardner McKay (Adventures in Paradise); Chuck Connors and Johnny Crawford in The Rifleman; and tight-jawed, squinty, taciturn cowhand Rowdy Yates on Rawhide, played by Clint Eastwood.

On September 29, 1959, Sal watched the actor who had played the parole officer in Dino, Frank Faylen, debut in a TV show aimed directly at the audience of adolescents who now dictated popular entertainment. Faylen played the father of the youth in the title role of The Many Loves of Dobie Gillis. The part would make one-time child actor Dwayne Hickman a star, along with the actor who played his zany sidekick Maynard G. Krebs (Bob Denver). Introduced on the show in 1959 were Warren Beatty as handsome Milton Armitage and Tuesday Weld as Thalia Menninger.

Five days later, on October 4, 1959, Sal tuned in to catch Nick Adams as he leaped to TV fame as Johnny Yuma on a show called The Rebel, which had nothing to do with Rebel Without a Cause. On October 11 he flipped on the TV set in his rented Laurel Canyon house to catch the debut of Robert Stack in a new show that promised to vicariously satisfy his longing to have lived during the era of Prohibition. While Italian-Americans across the country expressed outrage at the show's inference that all gangsters were Italians, and perhaps vice versa, Sal thoroughly enjoyed The Untouchables.

By every measure in this revitalized Hollywood Sal Mineo was entitled to think of himself as a movie star, and to appreciate a remark about being at the top expressed by a glamour queen of old

Hollywood. "After a taste of stardom," Hedy Lamarr had said, "everything else is poverty."

For Sal stardom meant having clothes tailored by designer Ron Postal of Beverly Hills and going on to a workout at the Beverly Wilshire Health Club. The session usually lasted an hour or two, lifting weights, shadowboxing, and other exercises to sharpen an already impressive build.

Noting Sal's "preoccupation with health and strength," the profile of him in *The Saturday Evening Post* speculated that he was "sensitive about his height and keeps an anxious eye on his upward and outward progress." The story added, "Sal naturally burns up a lot of calories in his pursuit of muscle, and in order to maintain energy he gulps down pep pills at the rate of ten a day when he's working on a picture or under pressure from other jobs. He carries a rosary and won't work without a Christopher medal around his neck."

Articles about him had become fairly routine for Sal, but such a prestigious magazine as *The Saturday Evening Post* devoting attention to him signified that Sal Mineo had become more than an idol for teenagers. This was a publication that had been founded by Benjamin Franklin and that was famous for its covers by Norman Rockwell. In the same issue as his profile was an excerpt of a book by James Roosevelt, *My Father F.D.R.* The magazine also carried the first of a seven-part serial by short-story writer Paul Gallico. It would be delivered to scores of thousands of homes and sold on newsstands coast to coast.

To have such a magazine describe him as "an engaging, intelligent, and intense young man who labors with consuming frenzy" could not be dismissed as just another movie-studio publicity department puff piece. The only thing better than a profile in *The Saturday Evening Post* would be to have his picture on the cover of *Life*.

But there was a downside to celebrity. One evening as Sal drove his car into the parking lot of the Beverly Wilshire Health Club he was spotted by five girls. (That his sports car bore a New York license plate, SM 95, undoubtedly alerted them that the person they were probably hoping to catch a glimpse of had arrived.) How these teenagers managed to gain entrance to the health club was not recorded, but they not only got inside, while Sal was working out they also located his street clothes and stole them, including his wallet (subsequently returned by mail, minus the money).

When word of this daring heist made it into newspapers across the country, Sal received an offer from a manufacturer of young men's slacks. If he would endorse them in advertising, he was advised, he would receive a pair of pants each week for a year. Similar offers came in from a shirt maker, a sweater company, and a manufacturer of wallets.

He heard from a cosmetics firm about an endorsement of hair cream. (That the firm waited so long to contact an actor famed for his unruly hair was a mystery.) A car maker in Detroit said it would supply its new model each year in return for his complimentary comments. A manufacturer of knives made a pitch to be allowed to market switchblades and zip guns bearing Sal Mineo's name. A leather-jacket maker asked him to endorse a black one. And a promoter proposed selling plastic-encased locks of his hair.

Being so famous affected his choices in restaurants. If he decided to go out to dinner he was limited to places accustomed not only to serving celebrities, but also to shielding them from being accosted by fans and autograph-seekers. In Sal's case that vigilance extended to anyone who might decide to see how tough Sal Mineo really was.

Being seen in Hollywood's swankiest spots and the "in places" was encouraged by people handling the publicizing of *The Gene Krupa Story*. There was no shortage of such spots. Inroads by television notwithstanding, Hollywood was still the Hollywood of the Brown Derby, Chasen's, the Coconut Grove, the plush dining rooms of Beverly Hills hotels, and all the other glamorous nightclubs that had been closed to the kid from the Bronx who'd arrived in town to do some looping on *Six Bridges to Cross*—and even to the star that ascended into the glittery firmament of Tinsel Town following the release of *Rebel Without a Cause*. While Sal Mineo was a year shy of the legal age for drinking in such places, he was now a "name" for whom all doors opened, red-velvet ropes in the control of headwaiters were let down, and the best of tables were available, even without a reservation.

When Sal found himself in a swanky restaurant in Beverly Hills he was in a place of which screenwriter Herman J. Mankiewicz had quipped, "It only goes to show what God could do if He had the money."

Sal also understood that he was in a business that judged success not only by how well your last picture did, but by what you were working on at the moment. If he wanted to stay on top, he couldn't rest on laurels such as good box office and good reviews for *The Gene Krupa Story*, and certainly not on having been nominated for an Oscar for his role as Plato, which had been five years ago.

"If you've made a hit movie," counseled Marlon Brando, "then you get the full 32-teeth display, but if you've sort of faded, they say, 'Are you still making movies?' The point of all this is, people are interested in people who are successful."

Two new movies being talked about at this time fired Sal's imagination and ambition.

Director David Lean was preparing to make the story of an Englishman who'd become a hero of World War I for his exploits in leading an Arab army against the Turks. His name was T. E. Lawrence, and Lean's epic film was to be titled *Lawrence of Arabia*. The script had a part for an Arab boy whom Lawrence took as a lover.

The other film was to be Otto Preminger's screen adaptation of a bestselling novel about Jews who had survived Nazi gas chambers and concentration camps and made their way to Palestine with the intent of assisting Jews in that Arab land in creating a Jewish state. Written by Leon Uris and published in September 1958, *Exodus* had skyrocketed to the top of best-seller lists. In advance of the book's publication, Preminger had acquired the property from MGM, which had an option on the movie rights to Uris's work. The deal had been struck by Dore Schary, who had long since left Metro. Learning that the studio was at best lukewarm about making the book into a movie, Preminger had launched a campaign to have MGM sell him the property. He'd made the announcement that he'd succeeded on May 25, 1958, four months before the book's publication.

Preminger announced that he would begin casting on August 15, 1959, in New York.

One of the characters in Uris's story was a youth who'd survived the Warsaw Ghetto and the death camp at Auschwitz.

His name was Dov Landau and Sal Mineo set his sights and heart on playing him.

Analyzing where he was in terms of his career, Sal feared he was typecast as the perennial youth. He found that prospect so depressing that he occasionally thought of giving up acting. He confided, "I wasn't happy. I was being given parts in pictures that may have been commercial, but I wasn't happy with it. I thought, 'If I have to make one more of those little epics, I'll feel like I'm prostituting myself.' I was miserable."

He saw Dov Landau as a golden opportunity.

"Everyone has his own ideas on who should play the leads," Preminger told the press. "I even have some of my *own*."

Bald, imperious, and speaking with an accent everyone assumed was German, Otto Preminger was born in Austria in 1905. His father was a lawyer who had been attorney general of the Austro-Hungarian empire. Otto studied law but preferred acting and directing. He'd come to America to stage a courtroom drama (*Libel*) in 1935, followed by a move to Hollywood.

His most recent film as a director before taking on *Exodus* had been *Anatomy of a Murder*. It raised eyebrows because the theme of the courtroom drama was rape and James Stewart talked about women's panties.

Having established a reputation for creating moneymaking films, Preminger at the same time engendered displeasure and outright contempt from actors who found him to be an ill-tempered martinet. Lana Turner said of him, "I thank God that neither I nor any member of my family will ever be so hard up that we have to work for Otto Preminger."

Sal felt no such aversion as he sent his résumé to Preminger's office, with a note stating not only his desire to play Dov but also his belief that he would be ideal in the role. Then it was a matter of waiting and hoping to hear from the director with an invitation to read for the role.

Meanwhile, Preminger announced that in making *Exodus* he

planned to employ no sound stages and back lots. As he had done in *Anatomy of a Murder,* which had been shot on location in a rural area, he would film *Exodus* at places where the action in Uris's book occurred: the Mediterranean island of Cyprus, and Israel. To ensure the blessings of government officials in both countries, he visited with the British Governor of Cyprus, Sir Hugh Foot, and the Archbishop of Cyprus, Makarios. In Tel Aviv he called on Prime Minister David Ben Gurion.

Declaring that the film would be in color in order to show Israel as "the real star" of the picture, he set out to scout locations. He was particularly interested in being allowed access to a famous old fortress in Acre. Built in the 17th century and currently used by the Israeli government as a mental hospital, the fortress was the site from which Israeli freedom-fighters ("terrorists," to the British and Arabs), including the character Sal hoped to portray, staged a dramatic escape by dynamiting a wall. Preminger intended to destroy the rebuilt wall in the same way as the escapees.

More explosive than his intentions regarding stone and mortar was Preminger's announcement on January 19, 1960, that he had chosen as screenwriter for *Exodus* one of the "Hollywood Ten" who had defied a congressional committee that investigated "Communist infiltration" of the movie industry in the late 1940s, Dalton Trumbo. Convicted in 1947 for refusing to answer the committee's questions, Trumbo served a prison term but then found himself on a blacklist of writers. He'd gotten around this by writing scripts using a fake name.

Said Preminger, "In our free democratic way of life, we do not keep on punishing a man once he has paid for violating the law. And inquiring into a man's politics and religion and discriminating against him because of them is not the American way."

His hiring of Trumbo effectively undermined blacklisting.

Having cleared the way for filming at the required locations and hired a writer, the director now turned to the task of filling 11 major roles in the film. They included the novel's main character, Ari Ben Canaan; Kitty Fremont, an American nurse; British General Bruce Sutherland; Major Fred Caldwell, an officer opposed to resettlement of Jewish European exiles in Palestine; Barak, Ari's father; Doctor

Lieberman, in charge of a refugee-camp hospital; Akiva, leader of the Jewish underground organization, Irgun; Karen Hansen, a teenager in the camp; and Dov.

As is the case with many bestselling novels sold to the movies, readers of the book had their own ideas concerning which actors and actresses should bring characters off a printed page and into life on the screen. A good deal of the publicity ballyhoo preceding the making and release of *Gone With the Wind* had centered on a search for a Scarlett O'Hara. To pick the young Karen Hansen, Preminger repeated the stunt. He announced "a worldwide search" for an actress to play her.

Casting the role of Ari was not left to chance. Preminger had announced on August 31, 1959, that as he'd read Uris's novel he'd pictured only one actor in the part—Paul Newman.

"I never considered anyone else," he said. "Before the book was published, I sent a copy to Paul, and he was crazy about it. He told me he would love to play Ari. And that was that."

Noting the casting of Newman, Sal was thrilled by the idea that if he got the part of Dov he would be working again with the actor from whom he had learned so much during the making of *Somebody Up There Likes Me.*

Two weeks after naming Newman as Ari Ben Canaan, Preminger announced that Kitty Fremont would be played by Eva Marie Saint. She had burst onto screens and into stardom with *On the Waterfront,* holding her own opposite Marlon Brando in Elia Kazan's screen realization of Budd Schulberg's gritty story of labor racketeering on the New York docks. Like Sal, she'd done television and Broadway before breaking into movies. Since *Waterfront* she had assured herself a place in Hollywood stardom with successes in *That Certain Feeling, A Hatful of Rain, Raintree County* and, costarring with Cary Grant, Alfred Hitchcock's *North by Northwest.*

Both Newman and Saint would have scenes with Dov, Sal noted as he read and reread the book and waited anxiously for a call from Preminger's office.

Meanwhile, other major roles were being filled. Distinguished Shakesperean actor Ralph Richardson would be General Sutherland. Peter Lawford, who'd come to Hollywood from England during World War II, was to play Major Caldwell. The Welsh-born character actor Hugh Griffith, who'd been cast as a horse-loving sheik in *Ben Hur,* won the role of a Cypriot Greek named Mandria, a shipping company owner. The part of Barak Ben Canaan went to one of the great actors of the American stage and films, Lee J. Cobb. The coveted role of Akiva was given to a veteran of the New York Yiddish theater; David Opatoshu had been seen most recently on the movie screen in *The Brothers Karamazov.*

Waiting for a reply from Preminger and beginning to fear he would not receive one, or that he'd be told he'd been turned down as Dov, Sal celebrated his 21st birthday surrounded by his family in Mamaronek. Not since he had learned that Nicholas Ray and Stewart Stern were preparing a script about teenagers with a kid in it named Plato had he felt so right for a role in a movie. Yet he had been an actor long enough to understand vagaries of casting. He knew the cruel realities of casting according to type. Anyone looking at his résumé had to be impressed. He'd been on Broadway twice. His TV credits filled a page and a half, including a nomination for an Emmy for "Dino." He had made a dozen movies and had earned an Oscar nomination at the age of 16. In all of those films he'd played American youths, all but one of whom was an Italian and most of whom had been switchblade kids with Bronx accents.

Dov Landau was a youth, of course—11 years old when first met on the pages of Leon Uris's novel—but a Polish Jew who learned tricks of survival in the Warsaw Ghetto that would pay off for him in the death camp of Auschwitz at age 14. Dov Landau was blonde with blue eyes, making him in the novelist's description "the least Jewish-looking" of those in the ghetto.

Sal Mineo was, in his favorite phrase for himself, "a wop from the Bronx" who had curly black hair and, in the words of the *Saturday Evening Post* article, "velvety brown eyes." What director in his right mind could ever look at him and picture him in the role of Dov Landau? Hollywood was known as a dream factory and a place where an Esther Blodgett could one day find herself starring in the movies, but Hollywood was also the town filled with people in charge of an industry whom director Frank Capra had said could best be described in one word: "Nervous."

As time passed with no word from Preminger, Sal's hope of playing Dov Landau seemed more and more a pipe dream.

Then, one day in February, Josephine walked into Sal's bedroom in Mamaroneck to tell him that Mr. Preminger's office was on the phone. The caller inquired of Sal whether he was free to come into the city tomorrow to see Mr. Preminger.

With charming understatement, Sal recalled, "I rushed down."

Preminger gave him a script and told him to take it home, study it, and return the next day to read for the role of Dov Landau.

That night Preminger screened the only Sal Mineo picture in which he'd played an adult. With *The Gene Krupa Story* fresh in his mind the following day, he heard Sal read, left the room without a word, and returned a moment later to tell Sal, "I'll see you in Israel."

Sal was so pleased and excited that he left Preminger without asking about money.

On February 25, 1960, a Preminger press release announced, "In one of the most off-beat castings in recent years, Sal Mineo was today assigned to play Dov Landau, 17-year-old survivor of the Warsaw Ghetto and Auschwitz, in the film version of *Exodus*. Mineo, long a teenaged favorite due to his films, records, and TV appearances will be reverting to the kind of acting that made him the youngest performer ever nominated for a best-supporting actor award for his role in *Rebel Without a Cause*."

While Preminger's press release obviously recognized that Sal was best known to the public because of *Rebel,* it had been Sal's performance in *The Gene Krupa Story* and his reading for the role of Dov that convinced Preminger that Plato had not been a fluke and that Sal was a fine actor. At the same time the director exhibited the shrewdness of George Stevens in discerning that Sal Mineo's name had marquee value that would attract a youthful audience to *Exodus* as it had to *Giant*. Preminger must be nonetheless credited for seeing that Leon Uris's blond and blue-eyed Polish Jew could not be brought to life on screen better than by a 21-year-old, black-haired, brown-eyed, Roman Catholic American with a Bronx accent.

That a name which would fit nicely into newspaper ads and on billboards could be counted on to bring many thousands of people to see *Exodus*—people who otherwise might not go to a movie about Jews fighting for a homeland—was a plus that would prove good for the film. And the film would be good for Israel.

Sal would be billed sixth, after Newman, Saint, Richardson, Lawford, and Cobb. Behind his name were those of some of the finest actors in the world. They included David Opatoshu, Hugh Griffith, Felix Aylmer, and Gregory Ratoff, a producer-director who sometimes acted in films. (His most memorable role had been Max Fabian, an irritable Broadway producer with an upset stomach in *All About Eve*.) Also billed after Sal was young and handsome John Derek, who took Hollywood by storm as the kid who went bad in Nick Ray's first delinquency film, *Knock on Any Door*. In the Cecil B. DeMille 1956 remake of DeMille's *The Ten Commandments* he was Joshua to Charlton Heston's Moses. In *Exodus* he would play an Arab sympathetic to the Jews.

Preminger's search for an unknown teenage actress to play Karen Hansen came to an end on March 14 with the announcement that the role had been won by 14-year-old Jill Haworth. The press release asserted, "Petite (5 foot 2), golden haired, and blue eyed, Jill at first couldn't believe that she had won the role. It will be her first important part. Born in Sussex, England, she is an only child. Neither of her parents were in show business, but Jill has attended the Corona School in London (which specializes in professional children) since she was 11. She started as a dancer."

Jill's name and picture had been submitted to the searchers for Karen by her school.

Perhaps mindful that in the film Karen falls in love with Dov, the press release continued, "An avid movie-goer, Jill's greatest thrill came not at winning the part of Karen but at the news that Sal Mineo would be playing Dov opposite her. She is an ardent Mineo fan, and his photographs decorated her wall at school."

Between the date of Preminger's announcement that Sal had been cast as Dov and the start of filming, Sal had less than a month to prepare for his first trip out of the United States and the longest period he'd ever strayed from the safe haven of his family. He would be on location in Israel 14 weeks. Before packing his bags, he took a crash course from a voice coach who specialized in teaching foreign accents to American actors; in this instance, Warsaw-Polish. He also read everything he could find on the subject of the Nazi persecution of Jews and experiences of those who had survived the death camps.

Right on schedule, filming of *Exodus* began at the port of Haifa. In Technicolor and Super Panavision 70 Todd AO with six-track stereo sound, the scene captured by director of photography Sam Leavitt and camera operator Ernest Day was Dov Landau wandering through the streets of the ancient port that had felt the tread of the Roman soldiers of the Caesars and other armies of conquest in thousands of years of Jewish history. To create Haifa as it appeared in the spring of 1947, set dresser Dario Simoni had converted a sidewalk café across the city's Paris Square from a police station into an Arab enterprise selling Egyptian cigarettes (banned in Israel since the Arab-Israel war of 1948 that followed the proclamation of a Jewish state called Israel). The setting also required placement of barbed-wire barricades, tanks, and British soldiers, not seen since the last days of British rule.

As the camera rolled, the script called for Dov to be almost run down by an Army truck. To be certain that this "most off-beat casting" would not be injured, Preminger rehearsed the scene several times with himself standing in for Sal. Costume coordinator Hope Bryce had outfitted Sal in a loosely hanging double-breasted brown leather jacket, open-collared blue shirt, well-worn pants and boots, and a flat-topped brown leather cap with a short brim. None of the Jewish spectators who were being kept behind barriers in Paris Square that day complained that the young actor playing Dov Landau did not look Jewish.

While Sal's first scene before the camera was the first to be shot, it was not the start of the film. The epic tale begins on Cyprus where a ship called *Star of David* has disembarked a flood of Jewish refugees from Germany. They are packed into trucks for transportation to a detention camp established by the British but run by Jews. It's as the convoy makes its way toward the camp that the film introduces Dov Landau. Leaping from a truck, he dashes for freedom and is pursued by soldiers. When he is cornered, a soldier slugs him with a rifle, sending him plummeting from a wall and rendering him wounded and unconscious. Picked up roughly by soldiers, he is carried off to the camp's hospital. Shirtless, bandaged, sullen, and defiant, he rails against the Jews who run the camp for the British. The only person he lets tend his wounds is a pretty blond girl named Karen (Jill Haworth), a refugee from Holland.

Into the camp hospital comes widowed American nurse Kitty Fremont (Eva Marie Saint), who has a few days on her hands before leaving Cyprus for England. To "while away the time," she offers her nursing skills to the overworked camp doctor. While this is going on, a plot is afoot to spirit the *Star of David* refugees onto another ship that has been obtained by Ari Ben Canaan (Paul Newman) for the purpose of taking the refugees to Palestine. The ship is the *Olympia*. In reality, she was the *Olga,* rented by the moviemakers as a set and as a means of transporting film equipment and crew members to Israel. The *Olympia* is ultimately renamed *Exodus* as Ari and the refugees stage an onboard hunger strike to protest the refusal of the British to allow the ship to leave port. Rather than face worldwide condemnation for keeping Jews from reaching Israel, the British government permits *Exodus* to depart for Haifa.

Sal's next scene is on board the ship as Dov Landau informs Karen that he intends to join the anti-British underground. "I'm going to kill Englishmen," he vows to Karen. He will join the Irgun because "they know how to do it."

When the *Exodus* reaches Haifa, Dov seeks out the group (avoiding being run down by a truck in Paris Square on the way). Greeted with suspicion, Dov is subjected to questioning about his experiences in the Warsaw Ghetto and at Auschwitz. The interrogator is the group's leader, Akiva. Played by David Opatoshu, the balding, goateed inquisitor is soft-spoken. He sips a glass of tea while Dov attests to having blown up lots of Nazis with dynamite in Warsaw.

When asked to describe his arrival at Auschwitz, he pictures Jews being divided and ordered to enter the camp through three gates: one for those who had been marked for death, one for those deemed fit for hard labor, and the third for young girls to be used for the sexual gratification of the guards. Dov tells Akiva of being sent through the work gate.

"Now may I tell you something, Dov Landau?" asks Akiva. "At no time did the Jews use dynamite in the Warsaw Ghetto. They had no dynamite."

Dov had learned how to use dynamite in Auschwitz, Akiva continues, by using it to make mass graves to receive the dead bodies of "your people, hundreds and hundreds of thousands of them." He had saved his own life, Akiva says, by working in that camp as a *Zonderkommando*, whose job was to shave the heads of other Jews, to remove dead bodies from the gas chambers, to collect gold fillings from their teeth.

During this ghastly, almost whispered soliloquy by David Opatoshu, Preminger's camera is in a tight close-up of Dov's anguished face. Velvety brown eyes of the heartthrob of so many fan magazine stories were now wide open and brimming with tears. The Cupid's-bow, pouty lips that could cause the hearts of millions of teenage girls to flutter quiver as Dov answers "Yes" to each of Akiva's gentle but damning statements about what Dov had done at Auschwitz.

With a wrenching sob deep in his throat, Dov pleads, "What could I do?"

Taking into consideration that Dov was less than 13 years old when he arrived at the death camp, Akiva continues, "Even so, we must have the truth."

Was there anything else?

Head down on a table and buried in his arms in shame, Dov replies, "Yes."

"Tell us."

Dov grasps Akiva's arm and begs, "Please don't make me tell you. Kill me. I don't care. I won't tell you."

"Tell us."

Hunched over, back to the camera, wracked with shame and sobbing, Dov blurts out, "They used me. They used me like you use a . . . a . . . woman."

A moment later, eyes bright with determination and with a glowing expression of pride, Dov is sworn to give his body, brain, soul, and being without reservation and qualification to the freedom fighters of the Irgun.

Running more than three hours, Otto Preminger's screen realization of Leon Uris's nearly 600-page novel, said *Life* magazine in a cover story in its December 12, 1960, issue, "goes beyond the book" to present "a tale told in proud passion of how well and skillfully Jews had to fight" to forge a Jewish homeland called Israel.

The story was related through the characters of Dov, the Polish Jew who had survived the Nazis to become a dynamiter to drive out the British; Ari Ben Canaan, the Sabra (a Jew born in Palestine); and brothers Barak and Akiva, who chose different paths toward a goal of an Israeli state (Barak preferring negotiations, Akiva taking the route of violent resistance).

The film is also about two women: Kitty, who falls in love with Ari; and Karen, who offers herself to Dov as they crouch in the grass at his guard post, only to hear Dov fiercely refuse.

First they will be married, he tells her. Then she will be Mrs. Dov Landau, a respected woman. People will tip their hats to her when she walks by. For now, she must return to the camp where she lives while he fights the Arabs.

The next day, Karen is found dead, her throat cut by an Arab.

The Gjon Mili photo chosen by *Life* for the cover of its *Exodus* issue was of Sal and Jill Haworth about to kiss. The eight-page spread featured nine photos, three of which were of Sal. He was pictured twice with Jill in scenes from the film.

While *Exodus* was being shot, rumors flew from Israel to Hollywood that Sal Mineo and Jill Haworth had fallen head over heels in love. If so, the affair was a validation of a maxim of the motion-picture business that had been enunciated by director Alfred Hitchcock: "All love scenes started on the set are continued in the dressing room after the day's shooting is done. *Without exception.*"

The lore and legend of show business was replete with stories, true and fanciful, of leading men who fell in love with leading ladies. Some married them. Some even stayed married to them.

The caption under a smaller version of the *Life* cover photo of Sal and Jill in a scene from the movie might have been interpreted as indicative of an offscreen romance. The slug line of the page-two picture said, "In love in *Exodus.*"

That 21-year-old Sal Mineo, who was far away from home and unable to pluck a name from an address book crammed with the phone numbers of willing fans, might have felt the pangs of amour for pretty Jill Haworth made perfectly good sense, even if she was only 15.

The third picture of Sal in the *Life* spread is posed. It shows him as Dov standing before a barbed wire–enclosed British police station.

His grimly determined face is shadowed. The hands grip the strap of a knapsack containing dynamite. He definitely is not Plato.

The most dramatic sequence catches the action as the freedom fighters battle their way out of the British prison at Acre, where Dov's dynamite has blasted apart a wall in order to free 250 prisoners. After the scene was completed, a head-count of the mental institution, which had been used to simulate the prison, revealed that 253 people had dashed through the hole in the wall. A trio of inmates had seized the opportunity to make a run for it, but were soon rounded up.

Life's sister publication, *Time* magazine, hailed *Exodus* as "a terrific show . . . a serious, expert, fighting and inspiring thriller." A review in the *New York Times* called it "dazzling." Film critics everywhere lauded the picture, and most singled out Sal's portrayal of Dov Landau for extravagant and deserved praise.

It was a performance like none other. In *Rebel* and subsequent roles he'd been required to bring little more to parts than himself. To bring Dov Landau to life on the wide silver screen had meant finding and plumbing the depths of soul of a character that had nothing in common with Sal Mineo but closeness in age. Plato had introduced moviegoers to a pretty boy. Dov Landau had relegated Plato and all of Sal's angst-and-hormone-driven teens, and even his polished portrayal of Gene Krupa, to parts on the résumé of a kid player who'd had a great deal of luck. Dov Landau was the achievement of a serious actor.

The quality of that accomplishment was recognized with his second nomination for an Academy Award for actor in a supporting role.

"I wanted to win that Oscar for *Exodus*. I wanted it real bad," Sal admitted. "The first time, when I got a nomination for *Rebel*, I was very excited. I was 16 and thrilled, but I knew I did not have a chance."

Encouraged by rave reviews for *Exodus,* Sal felt optimistic about being called to the stage to an accept an Oscar on the 1961 Academy Awards show (by then "the Oscars" had become an extravagant television broadcast).

"I wanted it very much," he said. "I felt that at this point in my career winning an Oscar would firmly establish respect for my acting ability."

Amazingly, *Exodus* was not nominated for best film. The nominees were *The Alamo, The Apartment, Elmer Gantry, Sons and Lovers,* and *The Sundowners.* Nor was Otto Preminger's name on the roster of directors. Nominated were Jack Cardiff (*Sons and Lovers*), Jules Dassin (*Never on Sunday*), Billy Wilder (*The Apartment*), Fred Zinneman (*The Sundowners*), and Alfred Hitchcock (*Psycho*). The award went to Wilder, as did the best-film Oscar for his picture.

Among the contenders in Sal's category were Chill Wills for *The Alamo,* Jack Kruschen for Wilder's film, and Peter Ustinov for his role as a Roman slave dealer specializing in gladiators in *Spartacus.* A curiosity regarding Ustinov was that he was also in *The Sundowners.* His performance in *Spartacus* was that film's only acting nomination.

The fifth best supporting nominee was Peter Falk, for his fourth movie role. The film, *Murder, Incorporated,* was based on a book by a crime-busting district attorney named Burton Turkus who broke up a Brooklyn Mafia murder-for-hire gang. Falk played gangster Abe "Kid Twist" Reles. The hoodlum had agreed to become Turkus's star witness against the mob. For the gangland treachery, he was thrown from a sixth-floor window of the Half Moon Hotel in Coney Island, apparently by the cops who were guarding him. Reles's death provided one of the great quotes in the annals of American crime: "The canary could sing, but he couldn't fly."

Falk's Oscar nomination was his first.

In a *Cigar Aficionado* magazine interview in the 1990s, Falk— who went on to star as a rumpled, stogie-chomping Los Angeles homicide detective who specialized in collaring the killers among the rich and famous on *Columbo*—recalled talking about his Oscar nomination with Sal on a rainy afternoon in a bar in New York's Greenwich Village. When Sal advised Falk that he ought to campaign for the Oscar (a generous suggestion considering that Sal was up for the same Oscar), Falk was astonished.

Sal told him that actors campaigning for an Academy Award had been going on for years. "You take out ads," Sal explained.

The practice was confirmed for Falk by no less an expert on Hollywood than the head of the William Morris talent agency, which handled Falk. According to Falk, Abe Lastfogel said, "You should campaign for an Academy Award."

Falk replied, "That's what Sal Mineo said."

"Well, do it!" exclaimed Lastfogel.

Just such a campaign was launched by Chill Wills. The twangy-voiced character actor in countless Westerns, who was up for the supporting actor Oscar for *The Alamo*, blanketed Hollywood trade papers with ads promoting his performance. The campaign seemed to outdo previous attempts at influencing Academy members who might not have seen all the films up for awards.

The Wills blizzard of self-promotion had one unexpected consequence. One day as Oscar time neared, an ad was taken out by Groucho Marx. It declared, "I'm voting for Sal Mineo."

A Jew, Groucho had been so moved by Sal's performances as Dov that he'd contacted Sal to commend him for it. They became friends.

Not everyone in Hollywood was in a laudatory mood regarding Sal's portrayal of a Jew. He'd come to town to help promote the movie, and one day found himself under attack by a gang of thugs wearing Nazi armbands.

As Sal told the story, "I was staying in a hotel apartment just off Sunset Boulevard. It had a garage down below. When I went to get into my car, there were about six of these football-player types wearing swastika armbands. They were waiting for me. I saw them jump out of a pickup truck in broad daylight. They came over and started attacking my car. But there was just enough room from where they parked their truck and the driveway, so that I could jump in my car and drive right through them. I knocked three of them down. I called the police but they said there wasn't anything they could about it."

As the Academy Awards approached, newspaper polls of movie fans indicated an even split in preferences between Sal and Ustinov.

For the second time in five years Sal donned a tuxedo to attend the Academy Awards with his name listed in the program.

Again he left the theater empty-handed.

Although he had won the Golden Globe Award, given by the Hollywood Foreign Press Association, as best supporting actor for *Exodus*, nothing signified a movie actor's success more than an Oscar.

Leaving the Academy Awards without a golden statuette for his performance in *Exodus,* he walked alone aimlessly, dejected and depressed.

When he did not arrive at his apartment when his brother Mike expected to see him, Mike drove around frantically searching for him. Recalling the incident in the garage with the thugs in Nazi armbands, he grew increasingly alarmed. When he discovered Sal wandering in Beverly Hills, he was safe but he had roamed for hours and walked miles from the theater in Hollywood where the awards had been presented.

He'd gone to the ceremonies confident that Dov Landau had changed everything. He'd believed that the intense freedom-fighter with a backpack stuffed with dynamite to blow away the enemies of the Jews would liberate Sal Mineo from the image of heartthrob of teenage girls.

Gone forever would be the adorable boy with the tumble-down locks and the velvety eyes in movies for the popcorn crowd.

Blasted to oblivion would be the dreamy kid promoting his latest 45 platter by jabbering with Dick Clark on *American Bandstand.*

Thanks to Dov, so long to The Switchblade Kid!

Instead, the Oscar had gone to a chubby Englishman whose performance as a buffoonish seller of gladiators in *Spartacus* had been no different than his Outback Australian in *Sundowners.* Ustinov had played the parts admirably. But how in the scheme of things could Ustinov's rolypoly character in the story of a freedom fighter against Rome before the time of Christ convey anything more important in 1961 than Dov Landau's struggle to forge a homeland for Jews? How could Academy voters choose a clown over a symbol of millions of Jews whom the world had let go to the gas chambers and then be shoveled like manure into the flames of crematoria?

On January 20 of that year, in Washington, D.C., standing in the blinding, cold light after a blizzard, the young and handsome new President of the United States, John F. Kennedy, had proclaimed that the torch had been passed to a new generation of Americans poised to cross a New Frontier.

But had anything changed?

Were the thugs with swastika armbands who'd attacked him in a garage any different than the Nazis who had wrenched sexual pleasure from a 14-year-old Jewish boy? Did *Exodus* amount to nothing more in Kennedy's America and to Hollywood's moguls than another night at the movies and very good box office that was in large measure attributable to kids interested in seeing Sal Mineo in another picture in which he took off his shirt?

Sal had expected that in a business that had been to a large extent invented by Jews, a film about the struggle to create a Jewish homeland called Israel would have been heaped with laurels. Yet the only nominations had been his and Ernest Gold's for his music, which was the only award garnered by *Exodus* that night. During his meanderings, Sal wondered if he'd lost because even in Hollywood there was a streak of anti-semitism. Had he been denied because he had appeared in a pro-Jewish film and played a sympathetic Jew who'd shot Arabs? Some months later he went so far as to express that question aloud. No one would ever know.

Assertions, meant to comfort, by his family and friends that he had been honored in being nominated, and stories of great actors, actresses, writers, and directors who'd been making movies for decades and never been nominated once, let alone twice, failed to bolster his spirits.

Others discerned in Sal's pouting mood the callowness of a youth who ought to be happy with what he had. No gold statuettes adorned a shelf in his living room, but that room was in a very nice house with ample closet space stuffed with designer clothes. In its driveway and garage were expensive automobiles. Less than a decade of making movies had showered him with cash to buy his parents Mary Pickford's former waterfront home in Mamaroneck. Films had given him the funds to pay for college for his brothers and sister if that's what they wanted, and if they did not, enough money to support them comfortably. He was 22, handsome, and wealthy, and the dream date of girls and women, young and not so young, not just in America but all over the world, wherever his movies were shown.

Rather than pine about not getting an Academy Award for portraying Dov Landau, he was advised by sympathetic friends to cheer himself up by putting into practice the philosophy of life he'd stated to James Darren's Eddie in *The Gene Krupa Story*. "What good is making good if you can't have everything that goes with it—the parties, the kicks."

Having gotten a second Academy Award nomination, and being a young, good-looking, and a very rich single guy, Sal found himself not only on Hollywood's A list for parties, but also able to ask people on the A list to his own affairs and count on them coming to his big house in Beverly Hills. The kid from 217th Street in the Bronx who'd arrived in Hollywood in 1954 could now afford to hire a maid and butler and anyone else he might need to serve food and drinks to the elite of moviedom.

Of these halcyon Hollywood days he recalled, "I gave fabulous parties to which I invited fabulous people. When you have the facilities and the money, you can meet the kind of people you want to be with, and the communion of these people—great artists, great writers—generates so much excitement. That's not saying they'll come only because you have money, but in order to entertain, you have to be in a position to do so."

Along with guests invited to his parties and dinners who might at some point prove to be helpful in the development of his career, as well as those from whom nothing was expected but good companionship, Sal's guests lists included old friends. Yul Brynner came whenever he was in town. Natalie Wood attended with Robert Wagner. If work on *The Rebel* allowed, Nick Adams showed up. Peter Falk frequently attended with his and Sal's friend John Cassavetes. Others who had been in Sal Mineo movies came. There was Peter Lawford, whose fame as a movie star had been eclipsed by the fact that he was President Kennedy's brother-in-law and a charter member of the Rat Pack, consisting of Frank Sinatra, Lawford, Dean Martin, Joey Bishop, and Sammy Davis, Jr.

Sal's leading lady in *Dino* and *The Gene Krupa Story*, Susan Kohner, was a guest from time to time. Among other gorgeous young women who found themselves invited were Portland Mason, daughter of James Mason; and Yasmin Khan, daughter of Rita Hayworth and Aly Khan.

One beautiful feature of Sal's parties was Jill Haworth. She had moved in with him soon after the completion of *Exodus*.

A frequent guest (and at almost every A-list party in Hollywood) was Roddy McDowall. A child star who had left England when Nazi planes were bombing London at the start of World War II, Mc-Dowall had become a star as a boy in John Ford's film about a Welsh coal-mining family, *How Green Was My Valley*, in 1941. He confirmed his child-star status in *My Friend Flicka* and *Lassie Come Home*. An accomplished photographer, he knew practically all the stars in Hollywood and enjoyed a reputation as a trustworthy confidant. The keeper of others' secrets all his life, he also managed to keep the movie public from learning that he was a member of the circle of Hollywood's homosexuals, which included Rock Hudson.

Having met Sal during the making of *Giant*, and because he was firmly at the top of the A list, Hudson also accepted invitations to Sal's parties. While Hudson courteously extended invitations to Sal to attend similar A-list parties at Hudson's home, Sal did not find himself asked to Hudson's other affairs at which the guest list was restricted to handsome young men.

In addition to enjoying the rewards of his work by "living it up," Sal hoped that being the genial host at lavish parties for the A list would result in obtaining roles. When he'd completed *Exodus* he found himself with no picture commitments, except to narrate an anti-drug film to be shown in schools. It was titled *Insight or Insanity?* With that finished and nothing in the way of film work to occupy him, he accepted an invitation to appear in a stage comedy being presented by Casa Mañana Theater in Fort Worth, Texas. Titled *Operation Madball*, the play had been the basis for a 1957 movie of that name starring Jack Lemmon and former TV comedian Ernie Kovacks. The plot involved a group of Army misfits planning to throw a party. The Fort Worth production ran three days (April 26–29).

Back in town, Sal went to other people's parties and to restaurants and nightclubs with his choice of beautiful women. To the people who saw him in these places he was always the same fun-loving, handsome, polite, soft-spoken, gentle Sal Mineo who happened to be, in the lingo of their peculiar town, "between pictures."

While Jill Haworth was living with him at his rented house on Santa Monica beach, she had a loving family in England with concerns about their 16-year-old sharing a house with a young man in what in 1961 was still regarded as living in sin. Haworth was also an actress with a career to build. When she was offered a role in a film to be shot in France, *Ton Ombre est la Mienne* (*Your Shadow Is Mine*), she departed for Europe. Except for a Weimaraner dog he'd bought and named Dov, Sal found himself alone.

One day he decided to go for a walk on the beach. It was a classic California afternoon of blue sky and tan-enhancing sunshine that was a cliché scene from so many cliché movies about the Golden State of California in which a young man with troubles to sort out pulls off his shirt. He walks slowly along the fringe of foamy, spent surf sliding in to erase the footprints he's left in the sand. If this were a Sal Mineo picture, the scenario would have called for the youth with the muscular physique, wind-blown curly black hair, and pensive expression on a flawed but still handsome face to look ahead and discover a beautiful girl strolling toward him.

Sal looked up and saw a beautiful boy. He recognized Sal and greeted him as so many of Sal's fans had done more times than he could remember. In such situations Sal had overcome his natural shyness with strangers and been polite and patient while wishing the fan would go away. But without fans, where would he be? His fate had been sealed by Sylvester's girlfriend in *Major Benson* when she sighed and said, "Isn't he a dream?" The girls who'd idolized him and wished that they could meet him and maybe marry him were counted in hundreds of thousands. Photos of him sent out by Josephine Mineo's helpers had been slipped into purses, pockets, school books, and lockers and kept on vanity-table mirrors in bedrooms and in heart-shaped lockets. Now those girls were in their twenties and probably married to guys who were nothing like the fantasies they'd entertained of Sal Mineo in the darkness of a movie theater or with their heads on pillows when they went to bed wishing Sal were beside them.

That boys could have the same feelings toward him had not come as a surprise. He learned about homosexuals on the streets of New York. He'd been approached by men in the subway. He worked beside homosexuals on Broadway and in Hollywood. He'd heard the Tab Hunter–Anthony Perkins joke, gossip concerning Rock Hudson, and about James Dean getting his cock sucked by five of the top men in the movies. And he'd heard the rumors that Jimmy and he had been to bed.

Suddenly, he'd met a boy on a beach and found himself wanting the boy to stay and to walk the beach with him. To spend the rest of the afternoon with him. To have dinner with him. To ask him to come to his next party. Coaching Sal in how Plato should feel about Jim Stark in *Rebel Without a Cause*, James Dean had said, "You know how I am with Natalie. Well, why don't you pretend I'm her and you're me, Pretend you want to touch my hair, but you're shy. I'm not shy like you. I love you. I'll touch your hair." He found himself wanting to touch this boy's hair.

The boy talked about having seen him in all his movies and spoke of how close he'd felt to Plato in *Rebel* and of his understanding Plato's feelings toward Jim because he had felt that way about the young actor playing Plato. Sal wanted to say to this boy on the beach the line that Plato had said to Jim as they'd stood by the door of the garage where Jim kept his Mercury. "Hey, do you want to come home with me? I mean, there's nobody home at my house, and, heck, I'm not tired, are you?"

When the boy accepted the invitation, Sal was pleased. Excited. Scared.

A dozen years later as Sal and I talked in an all-night restaurant in New York, joking from time to time about me writing his biography, he looked back to that day on the beach and spoke to me of it with astonishment. If I were to write the biography of Sal Mineo, I thought as I listened to how he'd been introduced to homosexual love, I would compare the discovery of his true sexual nature to 13-year-old Sal Mineo looking at the lights of Broadway theaters and realizing he'd been born to be an actor. He had gone from playing Crown Prince of Siam to Dov Landau without ever being a boy named Salvatore. Instead, he'd been the heartthrob on covers of fan magazines, guarantor of good box-office receipts, singer with records that hit the top of the charts, and The Switchblade Kid. He'd filled every role to the best of his ability, done what was required by studio bosses and directors, and garnered all the glitzy trappings due a movie star. In achieving all this he'd remained the sweet-natured son of Josephine and Salvatore and devoted brother of Victor, Mike, and Sarina. He once had an idol, but Jimmy Dean died.

Then, not long after having lost the Oscar he believed he deserved for Dov, there was a chance encounter with a boy on a beach.

There are moments after which nothing can be the same. Graduating from school. The first job. Marriage. Birth of a child. Death of a loved one. The breaking up of an old friendship. A young man or boy coming to grips with his true sexual nature. Milestones of life, watershed moments, turning points, they are spun by playwrights into dramas, tickled by comedians for laughs, and spotted by historians who analyze them from the certainty of the long perspective. A biographer searches his subject's life hoping to be able to write, "From this time things had to be different."

In recognizing and accepting his true nature, Sal faced the reality that if he were to go on making movies, the people who went to see them must never find out.

eight

Epic Efforts

On January 17, 1962, one week after Sal had celebrated his twenty-third birthday with his family in New York, I was still living in Boston and working as a news producer for WHDH-TV. Leafing through *The New York Times,* I read on page 67:

SAL MINEO FINED $50

Singer's License Is Revoked

for Speeding in Bronx

> Sal Mineo, the actor and singer, was convicted yester-
> day of speeding in the Bronx last June 1. As a result,
> his New York State operator's license was revoked; it
> was the third time within eighteen months that he had
> been found guilty of speeding.

Sal had appeared at Bronx traffic court wearing a black eye patch because the old inflammation had flared up. Magistrate Maurice Downing imposed the fine after learning that Sal had gotten a ticket on the Henry Hudson Parkway the previous November 10 only five minutes after he'd received a speeding ticket on the Manhattan portion of the highway. And in October 1960 he'd been convicted in Bronx traffic court of speeding. Because he had three offenses in a period of 18 months, Judge Downing revoked his driver's license.

What troubled Sal about the news article more than the embarrassment of appearing to be "a hot rodder" was that the headline identified him as a singer rather than an actor who happened to be appearing at that time on Broadway.

The play, by Ernest Kinoy, was titled *Something About a Soldier.* It had opened January 4 at the Ambassador Theater. It starred Sal, Kevin McCarthy, and Ralph Meeker. For the part of a recruit, Sal wore his hair in a crew cut. He turned in a good performance, but the show ran for only a dozen performances. Not long after it closed, Sal found himself being fitted for another uniform.

He'd been signed by 20th Century-Fox for a role in Daryl F. Zanuck's production of an epic feature about the D-Day invasion of France during World War II. The film would be called *The Longest Day,* which was the title of the bestselling true account by Cornelius Ryan of the Allied assaults on the Normandy Beaches on June 6, 1944. The picture had an international cast.

In the credits for the American actors Sal was listed eleventh, following John Wayne, Robert Mitchum, Henry Fonda, Robert Ryan, Rod Steiger, Robert Wagner, Richard Beymer, Mel Ferrer, Jeffrey Hunter, and Paul Anka. Sal was to play Private Martini, a member of the 82nd Airborne Division, whose troops were parachuted behind German lines hours ahead of the landings on the beaches by the main elements of the Allied forces.

The film was shot in black-and-white Cinemascope on the very beaches of the landings and in the French countryside of "hedgerows," which were not hedges in the sense of those found around American lawns. These were huge, thick embankments studded with dense brush and even trees. Because the paratroops would drop at night into this strange environment and in the midst of enemy forces, the Americans carried small metal clickers as a means of identifying one another. Unfortunately, Private Martini believes he's heard a clicker behind a hedgerow when the sound is actually the cocking action of a rifle bolt in the hands of a German.

It was a small part—minuscule, actually—in a huge, sprawling movie shot over a period of ten months at 31 locations with 50 international stars and thousands of extras. Yet it is a movie with three truly memorable scenes involving individuals in the vast panorama of war.

One is of comedian Red Buttons turning in an amazing dramatic performance as Private John Steele. When his parachute snags on the steeple of the church of Ste. Mere-Eglise early on D-Day, he dangles helplessly, playing dead. This was a real ordeal for Buttons, who suffered from a fear of heights.

The second indelible scene involves Richard Beymer. Fresh from playing Tony in the film of *West Side Story*, he is a lost, bemused, and weary G.I. who gets through the entire invasion day without firing a shot.

The third is Sal's, as Martini's boyish face beams with relief and joy at hearing what he believes is a buddy's clicker. It's Sal's second movie-death scene, but there is no James Dean to weep and show Sal what it would be like for someone close, someone he idolized, to grieve.

Although *The Longest Day* provided Sal an opportunity to play a different kind of role and to be part of another film spectacle soon after *Exodus*, he had wanted to be in a second screen epic of 1962, David Lean's *Lawrence of Arabia*. It was after being turned down for the role of Lawrence's young Arab lover that Sal expressed his belief that he'd suffered professionally because the Lean film was made in Jordan, an Arab country, and he'd played a Jew who shot four Arabs.

Sal's next film in 1962 also took him on location overseas. An action-adventure movie in color and Panavision, titled *Escape from Zahrain,* its chief attraction for Sal—other than the money he earned—was being reunited with the actor he fondly called "the old man." The film starred Yul Brynner. It was their first collaboration since the *Omnibus* production of the Hemingway story "The Capital of the World" in which Sal was a Spanish boy dreaming of starring in the bullring.

Now he was a 23-year-old man and a bona fide movie star with two Academy Award nominations. Brynner was delighted to be working with him and had warm memories of Sal as the prince in *The King and I.* Of that experience he told a reporter, "Sal treated me like a father. To me he was like family, like one of my own kids."

The cast of *Escape from Zahrain* included Jack Warden, Madeline Rhue, Jay Novello, and James Mason. Directed by Ronald Neame, the film's plodding plot involved five prisoners who escape from a jail in the Middle East and are pursued across the desert. The picture got little attention from reviewers and at the box office.

Back in Hollywood in the autumn of 1962, Sal found himself in an Army combat uniform and again on a battlefield in France following D-Day, but this time it was re-created for TV. He appeared in an episode of a new weekly ABC television series called *Combat*. Sal would have much preferred to have been a guest star on a show that followed *Combat* in the ABC Tuesday night schedule at 9:30, *The Untouchables*.

That television was offering more steady work than movies was evidence that an era had ended. Its demise was noted in a sensational book filled with lurid tales of the seamy side of the film capital, *Hollywood Babylon*. Author Kenneth Anger wrote, "By the Sixties, Old Hollywood had died. The battlements of those feudal fiefdoms, the studios, fell one by one to the enemy."

An undisputed lord of the Hollywood feudal system almost from its beginning was director John Ford. A director since 1917, he'd made some of Hollywood's greatest pictures. In 1963 he was about to make an epic feature for Warner Bros. that would be the last hurrah of his trademark Westerns.

Titled *Cheyenne Autumn*, it was a sentimental treatment of American Indians and deemed by film students to be Ford's apology for having killed so many of them in his numerous sagas of the frontier.

Ford told Peter Bogdanovich, a young writer on the subject of movies who visited the Monument Valley, Utah, location of the film, "I've killed more Indians than Custer."

Ford explained that his purpose in *Cheyenne Autumn* was "to show their point of view for a change." He insisted in production notes that the Cheyennes were "not to be heavies, nor are they to be ignorant, misguided savages without plan or purpose to their warmaking."

He wanted the two main Indian roles to be played by Native

Americans. This put him in conflict with Warner Bros. The studio
wanted the parts filled by two of its actors, Ricardo Montalban and
Sal Mineo. The studio's motivation in insisting on Sal was both self-
serving (Sal's name still had marquee value) and generous toward
Sal (the studio saw the film as a way to help Sal out of a professional
slump).

Ford argued that Sal Mineo looked nothing like an Indian and
spoke with a Bronx accent. The studio reminded Ford that Sal had
played an Indian very well and with good box office for Disney in
Tonka.

When the studio would not back down, Ford had no choice but
to cast Sal in the role of a headstrong and defiant brave named Red
Shirt.

Sal is billed after Richard Widmark, Carroll Baker, and Karl Mal-
den, and ahead of Montalban, Dolores Del Rio, Gilbert Roland, and
Arthur Kennedy. Special billing was given to James Stewart as Wyatt
Earp and Edward G. Robinson as "the Secretary of Interior," both
cameo roles.

The screenplay by James R. Webb was inspired by a story by Mari
Sandoz about the historic trek of the Cheyenne in 1878, when a
resolute band of 286 men, women, and children walked through
flood, drought, intense heat, and freezing cold from an enforced
settlement in Oklahoma to their natural habitat in the shadow of
Wyoming's Teton Mountains.

In Technicolor and Super Panavision 70, most of the film was
shot in John Ford's favorite Western setting, Monument Valley.

To prepare for his role (and acutely aware of Ford's misgivings
about his Bronx accent), Sal sought the aid of Native Americans to
help him achieve an authentic sound. However, Ford resolved what
he considered a problem with Sal's speech by cutting all of Red
Shirt's lines. Sal utters not a word in English in the picture.

Sal felt offended, but his natural impulse to take a line from Romolo in *Somebody Up There Likes Me* and tell Ford to take the role
and "Eat it" was overridden by a need for money.

He also found himself insulted by Ford on a daily basis either by
being ignored or by being called "Saul."

Ford insisted that all of Red Shirt's riding be done by Sal, but
without the help of an expert horseman, even though Sal had not

been on a horse since *Tonka* six years ago. In one scene Sal was to run to his horse and leap onto its back. When the camera rolled, Sal ran but missed his footing and failed to jump astride the horse. He asked Ford for a second take. Ford replied that he could have a second take if he wished, but the camera would not be rolling. Sal's only take was in the final cut despite the effect of making Red Shirt the clumsiest Indian ever to mount a horse.

Unlike his role in *Tonka,* in *Cheyenne Autumn* Sal keeps his shirt on through most of the film. His hair is again a black wig with long braids.

During the filming Sal stepped on a nail, injuring his foot. When Ford saw him hobbling, he griped that Sal was "a problem to work with." The damaging remark made its way back to Hollywood.

Film historians and Ford's biographers have well documented Ford's irascibility and his reputation as a very difficult director who enjoyed picking one actor in a cast and giving him a hard time. In Sal's case, however, Ford went from rude and abusive to downright cruel.

The script called for Red Shirt to die at the hands of his tribesmen because he has taken another man's wife. On the day the scene was to be shot Ford declared with obvious joy, "Okay, let's kill Saul."

Montalban shot Sal. Sal fell. Ford said, "That's swell."

Sal recalled the scene and the date on which it was filmed. It was Friday, November 22, 1963, around one in the afternoon. "Just about that time in Dallas, Texas," he said, "Lee Harvey Oswald was shooting President Kennedy."

One day, into the Monument Valley location drove Peter Bog-danovich. Because the writer was close to Sal in age, he introduced himself. The two hit it off. During their conversation, Sal handed Peter a dog-eared paperback novel that he had been reading. Peter looked at the title and supposed *The Last Picture Show* was about the movies. Written by a Texan named Larry McMurtry, it was a novel about a youth in a small Texas town in the 1950s. Sal said it was a pretty good story and that if he could raise money to make it, he would also star in it. He let Bogdanovich take the book with him.

Four years later, Bogdanovich made the movie with Timothy Bottoms in the part Sal had wanted to play. Bogdanovich believed Sal was too old for it. In a 1998 book of quotations about the film business, *Hollywood and Whine,* author Boze Hadleigh includes this undated quote attributed to Sal about Bogdanovich: "As a director he's repetitive and unimaginative. As a man he has numerous insecurities, which I legally don't dare elaborate on. As a friend—he ain't."

With his role in the current film completed, Sal left the insults and abuses of John Ford, the blue skies, burning sun, freezing nights, and breathtaking, rugged scenery of wind-sculpted stones and monoliths of Monument Valley and happily returned to a Los Angeles of smog, freeways, and beaches. He came back jobless and with no roles in the offing.

Cheyenne Autumn opened in 1964. Generally favorable reviews faulted Ford for packing too many subplots into it and for moving away from the plight of the Indians in the middle of the picture for a long scene in a saloon with James Stewart as Wyatt Earp and Arthur Kennedy as Doc Holliday. New York film critic Kate Cameron admitted the scene was fun, "but has no place in the story of the Cheyenne walk."

People who ran the National Cowboy Hall of Fame and Western Heritage Center in Oklahoma City thought the movie was such "an accurate portrayal of the American West" that the museum named it "the outstanding Western of the year."

Sal's performance did not fare well in some reviews. One critic found his portrayal of a brave "inept." Another opined, "Sal Mineo has been practicing his Method Preparation for the role by studying statues of Cigar Store Indians."

Reviewers and theater audiences looking at Sal's next movie would find in it much to talk about, but no one could accuse him of turning in a wooden performance.

nine

Who Killed Teddy Bear?

In the Hollywood of 1964, as in every year since the Horsley brothers leased the Blondeau Tavern and a barn at Sunset and Gower in 1911 and made a motion picture called *The Law of the Range,* the question for them and moviemakers who followed them to "Hollywoodland" was, "What do we make next and what new face can we find to put into it?"

Embedded in the sidewalks of Hollywood Boulevard were pink terrazzo star-shaped plaques with names in bronze of people with one thing in common; once upon a time they were movie stars. Like Sal, some had been described as heartthrobs. Like Sal, some were guaranteed box-office draws. Some had been fine actors. Some were in great pictures. Many had gotten rich. But now, were it not for their names on The Walk of Fame, many—perhaps most—of them would have been forgotten by people who'd paid to watch them on a movie screen.

You stayed a star just as long as studio bosses believed you could put people's asses in theater seats. If the day came that the bosses feared you couldn't because they thought people were tired of seeing you, well there were plenty of new faces out there who could.

By growing older Sal had gone from baby-face heartthrob to a man in his twenties whose face was no one's idea of a leading man's. He was perfect for Red Shirt and Private Martini, but carry a picture by himself? As a gangster, perhaps, but gangster pictures were passé. The only mobsters anyone cared about lately were on *The Untouchables* and its last show had aired on September 10, 1963.

Sal had outgrown juvenile-delinquent parts, but nobody was interested in j.d. pictures anyway. The era of kids with duck's-ass haircuts and black leather jackets was past. The fifties were over. James Dean was dead.

Sal found himself in the same professional pickle as previous kid actors in transitioning to adult roles. The number who'd done it successfully could be counted on one hand. Judy Garland, Mickey Rooney, Roddy McDowall, Natalie Wood, and Elizabeth Taylor managed. But the greatest kid star of all, Shirley Temple, had tried to go from a darling little girl to teenager and grown-up and hadn't really clicked. She finally gave up pictures altogether. The sad truth about audiences since the dawn of the business was that they were a fickle lot with very short memories and an unquenchable thirst for something different, from their taste in movies to enthusiasm for the actors and actresses they saw on the silver screen. Last year's hot ticket could quickly cool.

"There was this whole new craze, 'Let's get new faces,' " Sal said about the period after he'd made *Cheyenne Autumn*. "All of a sudden all the good roles I wanted went to the new faces. You work so hard to make a name for yourself and suddenly it doesn't count."

He said to Hollywood columnist Marilyn Beck, "It's a situation I've never been able to fathom. One minute it seemed I had more movie offers than I could handle, the next—no one wanted me."

Talent manager Phil Gittleman noted, "Sal had talent. Everybody knew that. They just didn't know how to cast him. He wasn't somebody from the fifties trying to make a comeback."

For Sal it was a matter of staying in the movies, not only because he'd gotten used to the lifestyle it provided, but for the thrill of being a movie star. He'd fulfilled the fantasy of the little Salvatore Mineo who'd calculated the size of a theater marquee to see if his name would fit. He'd justified his mother's faith. In ten years he'd gone from 217th Street to palm-shaded lanes of Beverly Hills.

He loved where he was. Mention the name Sal Mineo and it was met with recognition. Ask who he was, you were answered, "A movie star."

Somebody's got to love him ...or he'll explode!

"Baby" Giola, 16 and seething with all the pent-up fury of today's adolescents... hungry for "kicks" and ready to go, Go, GO all the way!

SAL MINEO
...the sensation of "Rebel Without a Cause" plays the furious role that makes him a star!

ALLIED ARTISTS present

CRIME IN THE STREETS

TV's brilliant young star JOHN CASSAVETES bursts on the screen like a bombshell!

JAMES   JOHN   SAL
WHITMORE · CASSAVETES · MINEO

MARK RYDELL · with DENISE ALEXANDER
A VINCENT M. FENNELLY PRODUCTION · Directed by DONALD SIEGEL
Story and Screenplay by REGINALD ROSE
Music by FRANZ WAXMAN

403
(560 Lines)

3   4 cols. x 10"

-wspaper ad for *Crime in the Streets.* To capitalize on Sal's success in *Rebel Without a Cause,* -ied Artists promoted this film as though Sal was its star.

Sal's much publicized first movie kiss, with Susan Kohner./ AUTHOR'S COLLECTION/ALLIED ARTISTS.

A lobby card for *Dino*, the movie that saddled Sal with the epithet "the switchblade kid." S. brother in the film was played by his actual brother, Michael./ AUTHOR'S COLLECTION/ALLIED ARTISTS.

START MOVIN'
(IN MY DIRECTION)

Words and Music by DAVID HILL and BOBBY STEVENSON

As Introduced on the Kraft Television Theatre and Recorded on Epic Records by

SAL MINEO

SHELDON MUSIC, INC.
48 WEST 48th STREET
New York 36, N.Y.

SAL MINEO 5-9227

LASTING LOVE

YOU SHOULDN'T DO THAT

LASTING LOVE

sheet music for "Start Movin'," a song
Sal introduced in a 1957 *Kraft Television*
ter production; the recording under the
: label sold 1,200,000 copies and
iched his brief career as a pop singer.
ior's collection. (TOP)

record jacket for "Lasting Love," which stands among Sal's several Top 40 hits.
Author's collection. (BOTTOM)

Fan photo card of Sal as Aladdin.
AUTHOR'S COLLECTION.

In 1958 Sal played the title role in the *Du Pont Show of the Month* "Aladdin," which was writt
by composer Cole Porter and which also starred Cyril Ritchard and Anna Maria Alberghetti.
AUTHOR'S COLLECTION.

The cover for *Comanche,* the authorized comic book based on the film *Tonka*.

WALT DISNEY'S

COMANCHE

starring
L MINEO as
White Bull

...as White Bull, the young brave who tames the horse he calls Tonka in the 1959 Walt ...ney film of that name.

THE BOY CALLED
SAL

By DEAN JENNINGS

Twenty-year-old actor Sal Mineo, who once fought in the streets of the Bronx, now has many thousands of adoring fans who enable him to make $300,000 a year out of movies and records.

Sal with Susan Oliver in a scene from his forthcoming movie, *The Gene Krupa Story*.

A lengthy feature article in the *Saturday Evening Post*, published to coincide with the release of *The Gene Krupa Story*, reflects Sal's star status in 1959. As Krupa, Sal played his first adult role

...ith director Otto Preminger at the seaside city of Haifa for the shooting of the 1960 epic film *...s.* / AUTHOR'S COLLECTION.

...al as Dov Landau in *Exodus*. His performance secured him his second Oscar nomination. / APWIDE WORLD.

Sal and Jill Haworth on the December 12, 1960, cover of *Life* magazine, which featured a pictorial article on the making of *Exodus*. The on-screen romance of Sal and Jill was rumored t-
be flourishing off screen as well.   AUTHOR'S COLLECTION/*LIFE*/GJON MILI.

* * *

But who was he, *really*? Who was the Sal Mineo inside the muscular torso and behind the velvety brown eyes in the pictures in the fan magazines? To the public he was a list of adjectives, all superlative. To the Mineos of Mamaronek he was still a sweet, shy kid who grew up in the Bronx; only richer, but generous to a fault. Double Academy Award nominee. A handsome guy out on the town in Hollywood with a different glamour girl clinging to his arm every night. The envy of young men and the erotic dream of countless females.

How much of all that was real and what part of it was Hollywood hype? One writer who made a living reporting observations of the stars of moviedom decided Sal was entirely an act. "He was always playing Sal Mineo. He had that star aura. He had a Little Caesar complex. He was always trying to be outrageous, larger than life, making up for his physical stature."

This was certainly a defensible observation. Sal lived the way he thought a movie star should. He liked nice houses and lived in them. He admired expensive cars and bought them. He enjoyed lavish parties and threw them. He loved fine clothes and sported them. He dated the most beautiful women in Hollywood and New York.

Occasionally, someone whispered that the women in Sal Mineo's life were arranged by a studio to cover the fact that Sal was homosexual. There'd been talk about him having had a love affair with James Dean. But gossip like that surrounded almost every good-looking new guy who took Hollywood by storm. It was almost a rule that an actor was not really a star until he walked into a room and overheard someone whisper, "There's that faggot."

Just because Sal had played a "fairy" in *Rebel Without a Cause* didn't prove he was one.

Yet the director of the film that catapulted Sal to fame had recognized more in Sal than potential for stardom. When Nicholas Ray spotted a boy in the crowd of teenagers at the casting call for *Rebel Without a Cause* who looked like Ray's son, "only prettier," he had also sensed the sexual nature of Sal Mineo. "There was no limp wrist or swish," Ray recalled 20 years after Sal auditioned for Plato, but Sal's submerged sexuality had surfaced when he played scenes with James Dean.

"I know he loved Jimmy," said Ray. Encouraging the love that

Sal apparently did not understand had been good for the film and
Rebel had made Sal a movie star.

Six years later, when Sal finally recognized what Nick Ray had
perceived buried within him—the kind of love he'd felt but hadn't
understood with Jimmy Dean—Sal embraced it with the same passion he'd shown when he discovered he enjoyed taking dancing classes. When he was learning how to waterski, he had begged Yul
Brynner to drive the boat faster. Everything he liked in life was
pursued with zest, sometimes recklessly, as he had done with a
sportscar on the Henry Hudson Parkway.

To find pleasure and fulfillment in homosexual love yet not accept
and indulge it would be untrue to himself.

It would be contrary to the philosophy for living to the fullest
that had marked all other aspects of Sal Mineo the movie star.

If it was true to a man's nature to make love with young men, as
did Rock Hudson, Tony Perkins, and plenty of other actors who
suffered no damage to their careers, and if Jimmy Dean had felt no
qualms about having sex with men, why shouldn't Sal Mineo?

Since arriving in Hollywood, he'd also observed that it was a
place where secrets could be kept. If it was okay for a male movie
star to go to bed with men he was free to be himself, as long as the
public didn't find out about it.

What truly mattered to the moguls of the movie business was
successful films. All that was expected of a star was that audiences
wanted to see his next picture.

Sal's problem in 1964 was not that he'd discovered he liked
having sex with guys, but that the movers and shakers in a Hollywood in love with new faces were doubting that Sal Mineo on a
theater marquee could still generate that kind of enthusiasm.

The day his telephone didn't ring, or no messengers arrived from
producers and directors with scripts for him to consider, he was
finished.

The call that came was from Joseph Cates. At first, Sal thought
it was from Gilbert Cates, a producer and director of games shows
for NBC-TV. Joseph, however, was Gilbert's older brother. He was
also in television, but he was making a career shift into theatrical
film production.

When Cates briefly described the story, it was like nothing Sal had ever experienced in a mainline movie. Cates was planning a savage portrait of a perverse subculture of a decade that social commentators were calling the Swinging Sixties. Sal would get star billing as a character named Lawrence Sherman, a busboy in a New York discotheque. After reading the script, Sal informed Cates he was not only available, but also excited about the project.

He did not tell Cates—and perhaps did not have to—that at that moment he would have accepted any part.

Written by Leon Tokatyan and Arnold Drake, Cates's low-budget, black-and-white picture was to be shot on New York City streets, including Times Square, with interiors in a studio just across the East River from Manhattan in Long Island City.

The cast consisted of dancer Juliet Prowse, Broadway star Elaine Stritch, Margot Bennett, Frank Campanella, Bruce Glover, Daniel J. Travanti (future star of TV's *Hill Street Blues*, listed as Daniel Travanty), and a surprising choice by Cates as a police detective, comedian Jan Murray, in his first film. (Murray's daughter Diane Moore was cast as his screen daughter.)

Discussing his movie debut in the film magazine *Scarlet Street*, Murray said, "None of us, outside of Sal Mineo, were really motion picture artists. We weren't names in motion pictures. So we all had a chance to do what we felt was a good picture, an interesting picture. Sal was the only bona fide motion-picture personality in it. He was an awfully nice guy. A nice young man."

Sal's busboy character was not.

The film was titled *Who Killed Teddy Bear?*

The reason for that title is revealed to the audience in the opening scene. Clutching a teddy bear, a small girl sits by an open door. Frightened by what she sees in the room, she runs away screaming and falls down a long stairway. A close-up finds her looking dead with eyes open and staring at the ceiling. She still holds the bear.

A cut reveals the bare, muscular belly of a young man lying on a bed. When he gets up, he is wearing snug white briefs (it's a film first; heretofore when a man's underwear was shown in a movie it had to be baggy boxers). Moving to a mirror, he admires his reflection. Returning to the bed he picks up a phone, dials a number, lies back, and lovingly strokes himself as he says to the person who's answered, "I know you don't know me, but I know you . . . very well. I know what you look like right now. I can see your skin."

The woman on the receiving end is Norah Dain (Juliet Prowse). Living in a sublet apartment, she is an actress and dancer currently employed as a hostess at a definitely downscale Manhattan discotheque.

Manager of the nightspot is Marian Freeman (Elaine Stritch).

Norah's chief responsibility is to keep the customers dancing. This proves difficult to do when one of the men is more interested in coaxing Norah into a bed somewhere. Referring to her body, he says, "I just want to borrow it . . . maybe rent it if I have to."

Observing this, busboy Lawrence (Sal) informs Marian, who in turn orders the club's bouncer, Carlo, to give the offensive customer the bum's rush. Carlo is played by Daniel Travanti, who for reasons not explained is a mute. In the course of ejecting the customer, Carlo is wounded with a knife. The police are called. When Norah offhandedly tells Detective Dave Madden (Jan Murray) about the strange phone call she'd received that morning, Madden takes a professional interest.

He escorts Norah home. Soon after he leaves, Norah gets another call.

The same voice as in the morning says, "Hello, my love. I want to talk to you. I'm a man and I will make you feel like a real woman. I know you so well. I know every inch of you. . . . Oh, Norah, my love."

Horrified that the caller knows her name, Norah turns again to Madden, who is a cop who specializes in cases involving serial sex offenders. He gives Norah a short course in the nature of "the telephone psychotic." Some are fetishists, some are sadists, some are masochists, others are simple voyeurs. And there are combinations. He warns Norah that while her caller is content to talk with her at the moment, he might try to venture beyond the verbal to the physical.

To this point in the film the audience has not been shown the face of the man making the phone calls and has been led to consider it might be Madden. It's a ploy that might have been believable had the audience not seen rippled belly muscles, narrow hips, and hard buttocks that could not belong to the middle-aged detective. That the stalker is Lawrence is confirmed about halfway through the picture when Lawrence is shown peering into Norah's apartment with binoculars and venturing as close to being shown masturbating as legitimate movies allowed in 1965. Lawrence turns to the camera and lights a cigarette, revealing his face.

While Norah is contending with these anonymous calls, she turns to Marian for comfort, only to discover that Marian is a lesbian who would like nothing more than to tumble into a bed with Norah.

About midway, the film reveals that the young girl looking into a room was Lawrence's sister. What she saw was Lawrence and a woman having sex. When the sister survived the fall down the stairs and was left mentally impaired, Lawrence felt so guilty that he spent his life caring for her and expressing his sexual appetite by becoming a peeping-tom predator with a phone, and a patron of Times Square pornographic book stores and sex shows. In scenes with his sister Lawrence is either stripped to the waist or wearing a form-fitting tee shirt and a pair of white chino pants so tight that his penis is visible in startling relief.

The detective is right about Norah's caller trying to get closer to her. Lawrence moves from telephone calls to stalking Norah. He turns up at the health club where she exercises with a swim in the pool. The following sequence shows Lawrence working out in the gym.

Sal had often appeared in films without a shirt, including *Exodus*, but as Lawrence pumps iron and flexes his muscles in *Who Killed Teddy Bear?* the audience sees impressive evidence of the result of Sal Mineo's years of weight-lifting and body building. Biceps and pectorals bulge, the torso is V-shaped, abdominal muscles are taut, and his skin is as tight as one of his snare drums.

After working out, Lawrence decides to go for a swim. He changes from workout shorts to a bikini swimsuit. In a photo essay ("Sal Mineo's Workout") using photos made in the gym during the filming, the 1980s gay-oriented magazine *In Touch* noted that as Lawrence headed for the pool he "offered one incredible, jaw-dropping moment when he stands by the edge of the water in tiny black Speedos—clearly displaying an enormous semi-hard cock through the skin-tight fabric." (The scene was cut from a 16-mm version for home viewing in an era before videocassettes made adult-rated movies common as rentals.)

When Lawrence finds Norah in the pool and gazes at her while indulging in a sexual fantasy, Norah remarks with amazing under-statement that Lawrence has a "nice body." Deciding that a swim-ming pool is not the place to realize his fantasy, Lawrence returns with Norah to the disco. They dance wildly. (The place is closed because Marian has been murdered while wearing Norah's fur coat, being mistaken for Norah by rape-minded Lawrence.)

Recalling her role in *Teddy Bear* more than 35 years later, Elaine Stritch rolled her eyes and grinned as she said, "I was a lesbian owner of a disco who fell in love with Juliet Prowse and got stran-gled on 93rd Street and East End Avenue with a silk stocking by Sal Mineo. Now who's *not* going to play that part?"

After Lawrence has attacked Norah in the disco, he is caught by Detective Madden. In a foot chase through Times Square, he is shot to death.

Sal's agent, Tom Korman, matched Norah's understatement about Sal's physique when he said of Sal's first foray into an inde-pendent film, "It was a provocative movie."

Thirty-five years after the release of *Who Killed Teddy Bear?* and its quick disappearance from circulation, film historian George Haitch's "an appreciation" of the movie in *Scarlet Street* said, "Shrewd direction, crisp dialogue, and exceptionally strong perform-ances from an enthusiastic cast more than compensate for typically low-budget production values, but it is the bold presentation of some provocative and downright lurid subject matter that gives this film its edge, and a sordid atmosphere of uncompromising tawdri-ness that makes it memorable. . . . It was, no doubt, this radical con-cept that eventually relegated the film to a kind of cinematic limbo, in that the subject matter was deemed too overwhelming for mass consumption, while its oblique and tempered presentation ultimately disappointed the hardcore aficionado primed for a few vicarious thrills. Nevertheless, this ingenious application of provocative and unusual story material, intelligently crafted within the constraints of an extremely low budget, surely qualifies the film for cult consid-eration. And the movie's inherent momentum, twisted logic, and the star turn by Sal Mineo in one of his best, but least remembered, performances make for riveting viewing."

Not many people went to see the picture. Sal's family was shocked by it. His performance was exceptional, but it was not the kind of film to persuade the movers and shakers of Hollywood that Sal Mineo was still a property worth supporting and promoting as a star.

With stoic resignation, a bemused Sal said, "I found myself on the weirdo list."

Never in better condition physically, he returned to a Hollywood in which many of its leading personalities sympathized personally, politically, and professionally with a social upheaval in America in the second half of the sixties, which some hailed as a revolution by the youth of the country. The rallying cry was "Sex, drugs, and rock and roll."

A warning shot from a new generation had been fired across the bow of the old in 1963 in a song by Bob Dylan. "The times," it said, "they are a-changin' "

The counterculture's epicenter in Los Angeles was a stretch of Sunset Boulevard known as the Strip. It included youth-dominated clubs where sex pervaded the atmosphere, drugs were plentiful, and the music was rock performed by the Byrds and the Doors. Among these clubs were the Galaxy, London Fog, the Unicorn, Sneaky Pete's, and Elmer Valentine and Matio Maglieri's Whisky-A-Go-Go.

"It was a 24-hour party," said an article in *The Los Angeles Times*, "but it was all very innocent. It wasn't until later that the scene turned ugly."

Everything would change in 1967 when the older businesses along the Strip complained to the city about the late-night crowds leaving the sidewalks a mess of trash and puddles of urine. The result was a police crackdown aimed at the underage patrons of the clubs. The police action met resistance. It was immortalized as the "Riot on Sunset Strip" in a documentary film of that name.

Until then the Strip was the symbol cited in a story in *Life* magazine that gave an older America derided by counterculture kids as "the establishment" a glimpse of the "new generation" dancing the night away at a spot that had supplanted an old-style Hollywood club (Crescendo). The new place was the Trip.

In the new lexicon of the new generation, "trip" had two mean-
ings. It meant to enjoy, as in, "I was really tripping on the music."
But "to trip" also meant taking drugs.

Whether Sal used drugs to escape his woes or simply because they
were the "in thing" is not known. He probably did it for both reasons. He certainly had good reasons to seek at least momentary
respite from cares about his place in an industry that suddenly
seemed to not know what to do with him, or perhaps didn't want
him anymore. And it was not in the character of the man who as a
boy smoked a cigar to be accepted by a gang to court rejection by
the Sunset Strip's version of the kids on East 217th Street by turning
down a joint or a hit of acid.

On these forays into the clubs of the Strip he could not forget
that he was still regarded by the people he met in them, and in the
world at large, as a movie star. They might ask for an autograph,
but they knew nothing—nor did they care to know—of whether his
latest picture made money at the box office. All that mattered was
that he was in the movies and that he obviously was a guy of their
generation. He liked to have as good a time as they did and he didn't
mind at all that they weren't stars, or even in show business. There
was nothing stuck up about Sal Mineo.

Nor did he dress any differently than them. Chances were, when
he walked into a club on the Strip he'd be in blue jeans, cowboy
boots, and a leather motorcycle jacket. That he wore tinted aviator-
type glasses was not an affectation, he explained. He had eye trouble.

When he spoke, he sounded like a New Yorker. But his attitude
was right in line with the image of Californians extolled by the songs
of the Beach Boys. It was easy to picture him hanging ten on a surf
board on the beach at Malibu. All in all, except for his line of work
and the big Harley-Davidson bike or sportscar that he parked in
front, the people in the clubs saw Sal as your average young guy
checking out what the clubs had to offer on that night in the way
of the object of life extolled by a Beach Boys' hit, "Fun, Fun, Fun."

Sal Mineo was a movie star, but also a man of the new generation
looking for rock, dope, and sex. What the kids in Sunset Strip clubs
did not know was that sooner or later on many nights when Sal
was out on the town, he headed for another kind of club. A restau-

rant and bar on Santa Monica Boulevard at Crescent Heights, the Gallery Room was a place where no one looked at him with disdain as he came in and whispered to a companion, "There's that faggot."

On any night, or during the daytime if Sal wished, there was a vast array of such places in which he could relax and talk with a good-looking guy, buy him a drink or two, and if they clicked, invite him home for an hour or the night.

The search for companionship with attractive young men was not limited to the clubs and bars where the like-minded were found. He had roving eyes for a cute guy anywhere. One who sparked his interest was 14-year-old Michael Mason. Sal found him selling clothes at Lenny's Boot Parlour in Beverly Hills. Sal had wandered in as a customer.

In an article in *Crawdaddy* magazine in 1979, Mason recalled, "He saw me looking at him and he came running over, practically, and said, 'Can you help me, please?' He was kind, and I was excited because he was a star."

To Mason's amazement, Sal called him at the store the next day and almost every day after until Mason accepted an invitation to dinner at a restaurant on Sunset.

After the meal, when Sal asked Mason to Sal's home, Mason expected to enjoy an evening of conversation with a movie star. "So we smoked a couple of joints," Mason recalled, and then Sal showed Mason around the house.

When they got to the bedroom, Sal asked, "Do you like my new bed?"

It was king-size.

Sal said, "Why don't you try it?"

Mason sat on the bed.

Sal sat beside him and said, "Swing with me. Swing with me."

It was a new term to Mason.

"All I saw were those big dark eyes," he recalled. "We fell onto the bed, boom boom."

When Sal called Mason again, Mason told him, "It was my first time. I didn't enjoy it all. I don't want to see you again."

A month or so passed, but Mason kept thinking about what had happened.

"I'd been hanging around with the Monkees, really grooving on one kid's body," Mason continued in the *Crawdaddy* interview. "It [having had sex with Sal] started to make sense to me. So one night I knocked on his door. He opened it and said, 'Michael, it's you. It's really you.' "

He and Sal had sex a few more times and then Michael moved in with him for a while. He regarded the friendship with Sal the best of his life. But he found Sal at that time to be sexually repressed. He said, "It took him years to feel comfortable on the gay beach with me in Santa Monica. By the time we'd get down to the sand, the sun would be down. For years he didn't even strip down to his bathing trunks. He'd sit there in his pants and tee shirt for a couple of minutes, then say, 'Let's walk.' "

That the Sal Mineo who'd felt no restraint in appearing on a movie screen in a see-through Speedo in a state of arousal was reluctant to undress on a gay beach indicates that while Sal had accepted his sexual nature and had no problem patronizing the Gallery Room and other such bars and clubs, he was reluctant and probably afraid to break the Hollywood code requiring its homosexuals to keep their love lives to themselves. At a time when his future in pictures was in the balance, to declare his sexuality publicly would only invite someone with the necessary power to decide that his career had reached the moment when the screen flashed two words that appeared in every movie ever made in Hollywood: THE END.

During this anxious time, Sal discovered that his finances were teetering on bankruptcy. When tax returns for several years were questioned by the federal government, a review of records revealed that his accounts were a shambles. Money that he believed was there, wasn't. He found himself virtually broke. He'd heard tales of movie stars going bust but had never dreamed that it could happen to him. "I made millions," he said. "Not *one* million. A *few* million."

It was true that after the huge bite taken from his earnings by taxes he had spent freely on expensive cars and houses, on his family and friends, collecting art, and throwing splashy parties, but surely he had not blown it all! Yet there could be no disputing the cold, hard numbers. Somehow, he found himself in financial disaster. Money supposed to be in a trust fund wasn't there. Huge tax deductions that had been taken were disallowed. He was ordered to pay back taxes in the amount of a quarter of a million dollars.

The house in Mamaronek would have to go. The speedboat. The cars. He would have to make some changes, including the painful one of telling his family that from now on he would be running his affairs himself. The "family business" that had been Sal Mineo came to an end. The management firm that had been hired was dismissed. He found a new business manager and for the first time in his career he got himself a Hollywood agent.

The man who took him on was one of the ablest and most respected in the business. Tom Korman, a savvy veteran of Hollywood wars, had seen it all before. As *The New York Times* had observed, Sal was a young man riding the Hollywood crest. "When he had the money, he spent it freely," Korman noted. "Go out and buy clothes. Buy a car. He loved it."

Now, with breathtaking suddenness, the bottom had dropped out at a time when Sal Mineo wasn't a hot property anymore. With no film offers to rescue him, he had to retrench.

Tom Korman understood what had happened. "The business changes, times change," he said as he looked back to the time when parts were not coming his client's way. "Sal grew up. He wasn't a boy anymore."

For a decade Sal believed he was riding an up elevator. Instead, it was a roller coaster and now it was hurtling downward.

Years earlier, one of his friends in the Bronx had jokingly told him that if his movie career didn't work out, he could come back to the Bronx and find another line of work. It was a friendly sentiment, but it showed that the kid who'd expressed it did not understand Sal Mineo. Accepting defeat was not in his character. In a fistfight with a boy on a school playground at the age of nine he'd continued slugging it out even when he thought he wasn't able to stay on his feet for another minute. When he'd decided that Jesus should step onto a stage carrying a staff, Jesus entered with a staff. No amount of harassment and bullying by street gangs could get him to change his mind about being the Crown Prince of Siam. Nick Ray's misgivings about him as Plato could not stop him from going after a part he knew belonged to him. He'd made up his mind that only he could play Dov Landau and he'd justified Otto Preminger's "offbeat casting" by being the only one of the brilliant actors in *Exodus* to earn an Oscar nomination.

So what if he was on the down side of a roller-coaster ride? The wonderful thing about roller coasters was that they climbed up again and always glided to a smooth and happy ending.

Although some people in Hollywood were prepared to administer last rites to Sal's movie career, he was not prepared to lie down and die quite yet. He believed something would happen to turn things around. *Somebody* would want him.

The somebody was the director of *Giant*. George Stevens offered Sal a small role in a film based on one of the bestselling books of all time, *The Greatest Story Ever Told,* Fulton Oursler's account of the life of Christ. Seventeen years after the nuns of St. Mary's school cast Sal as Jesus, George Stevens offered him Uriah, a crippled young man whom Jesus commands to get up and walk. Sal does so convincingly and movingly.

Soon after, Uriah is present when Jesus summons his friend Lazarus from the tomb.

While it is always dangerous for a biographer to seize upon a metaphor, a bankrupt actor being asked to play a character who is healed by Christ and then witnesses another young man restored to life after being pronounced deceased was nothing less than a miracle.

For nine days' work and about eight minutes on the screen he would be paid $92,000.

ten

Down but Not Out in Beverly Hills

Back in Hollywood with 92 grand in the bank, Sal resumed the lifestyle that he thought was expected of a movie star, that he believed he deserved, and that he enjoyed. He rented a house in the Hollywood Hills and a beach place in Malibu, replaced the Harley, bought a bright red Corvette, leased a Bentley, and threw parties.

When a friend suggested he ought to be more careful with money, Sal replied, "A movie star shouldn't be stingy."

Almost immediately after he came back from filming *Greatest Story*, he was again a regular in the clubs along Sunset Strip and at the bars of the Gallery Room and other haunts that had become a major part of the secret life of Sal Mineo. One of the Sunset Strip clubs he frequented upon his return featured a hypnotist named Pat Collins. He enjoyed her act and even participated in it by going on stage and letting her hypnotize him. People in the audience who recognized him were not sure if he was actually hypnotized, or whether he was going along with Collins' act. In fact, he was hypnotized and enjoyed the experience.

On one of these occasions a hip young personality who had a telephone talk show on radio came to the club to tape an interview with Collins. His name was Elliot Mintz. As he entered the club and looked around, he spotted at the bar a good-looking young man, bearded (Sal had grown a beard and mustache to play Uriah), with black leather pants, black leather jacket, and sunglasses. A cigarette dangled rakishly from a corner of his mouth.

Beneath the beard Mintz recognized Sal Mineo. He was the first movie star Mintz had ever seen in the flesh. Suddenly more interested in Sal than Collins, he asked Sal for an interview. Sal agreed to grant it after the show. After about an hour of answering questions and with Mintz still interested in continuing, Sal suggested they do so in more comfortable surroundings. He invited Mintz to his house in the hills.

Mintz remembered, "We got into his red Corvette convertible. I had never seen a prettier car in my life. He loved revving it up. We took off to his house. When he opened the door, there in the middle of the living room was a full-blown Harley Davidson. Sal explained that he didn't like to leave it outside because he looked on it as a work of art. That night we spent talking. I slept upstairs on a couch. He went downstairs."

A friendship was forged and Mintz was invited to stay at Sal's Malibu house. It had six bedrooms, each with a fireplace. Mintz thought it was paradise. Looking out at the Pacific, Sal said, "Welcome to the end of America."

"He had the 92 thousand," Mintz recalled. "He had a Bentley. He had a maid, a butler. He knew how to spend money better than anybody I knew. Parties every other week with everybody. Sybil Burton, Jane Fonda, Natalie Wood, whoever was the Hollywood vogue. They weren't orgies, they weren't sickic trippics. There were just bands, great music, and people dancing on the beach."

One of the beach dancers at one of the parties was the ballet star Rudolph Nureyev. He gave Sal a lesson in ballet moves on the sand.

"We'd sit up all night laughing and playing music," Mintz remembered of the parties.

Although Jill Haworth attended them, she did not live with Sal. They were friends, but she knew her romance with him was over. Sal explained, "I love Jill. I always will, but I'm not for marriage and kids. I've been on my own since I was about 15, and I can't adjust to the responsibility of one person. I've tried it a number of times—I mean, living with someone—and it just hasn't worked out. Jill and I have incredible feelings for each other, but to get married is another thing. The idea of settling down goes against my makeup.

What I need is totally different. I need companionship, I need love and all the things that go with it, but I don't need married life. I like my freedom too much."

When he no longer needed to conceal his sexual nature, he said, "I've found a lifestyle that is much more satisfying in total to me than complete commitment to one person. I really do dig the freedom—I always have."

In a 1970 interview in *Cavalier* magazine in which he said he did not "start living" until he was in his mid-twenties, he explained, "I stopped trying to make people think I really spent my time taking chicks to Wil Wright's ice cream parlor, like the fan magazines said. I started dressing like I wanted. Acting like I wanted."

He needed to be free to enjoy the life of a handsome young movie star who had discovered that he preferred fleeting and unfettering companionship with young men. But as the money from *The Greatest Story Ever Told* rapidly dwindled, he also needed to get back to work.

He hoped to win the role of a young man who, with his partner, murdered a farm family in the film version of Truman Capote's bestselling "nonfiction novel" *In Cold Blood*. He was rejected for the part of Perry Smith because the producer wanted "a new face." He also sought the role of Ratso Rizzo in *Midnight Cowboy* and was turned down.

With no one knocking on his door with movie offers, he looked to television.

He'd recently appeared on TV as a guest on *The Patty Duke Show*. But the part required no acting at all. He played himself in an episode in which he returned to his former school (Brooklyn Heights High in the script). The comedy series was written by Sidney Sheldon, who would leave sitcom TV to become a bestselling novelist. The Duke show was directed by Don Weis, who'd directed Sal in *The Gene Krupa Story*.

When starstruck Patty asked Sal if he liked being a movie star, he replied, "If I told you I didn't enjoy it all, I'd be a liar. Sure, it's wonderful. The only problem is that it's very difficult to have any privacy."

In the late 1960s Sal felt he needed to guard his privacy more than ever. He was regarded as a star by an admiring public, but what would they think if they knew the truth about his sex life? Star status notwithstanding, producers, directors, and casting directors apparently felt he wasn't important enough to carry a feature film. When MGM offered him a part in a Western feature for TV, *The Dangerous Days of Kiowa Jones,* it wasn't the starring role. That went to Robert Horton, who'd started on TV in 1955 in a soap opera (*King's Row,* based on a movie that had vaulted Ronald Reagan to stardom). Between 1957 and 1962 Horton had a leading role on *Wagon Train* and had just starred for one season in the Western *A Man Called Shenandoah.* Horton's Kiowa Jones was a cowhand who crossed paths with a U.S. Marshal escorting two convicted killers to Fort Smith to be hanged. When the marshal is dying of "fever," he deputizes Jones.

On the trail to the fort he must contend with bounty hunters, Indians, a pair of vengeful brothers and their father, and the prisoners: "The Gypsy," played by Nehemiah Persoff, and Bobby Jack Wilkes. With long sideburns, and remaining clad throughout the film, Sal plays Bobby Jack a hired gunman with more then 20 notches on his pistol and a macho swagger even with hands and feet shackled. He harasses Jones with a half-maniacal laugh and a string of taunts.

Bobby Jack is Sal's most physical role. He is knocked or dragged from a horse three times, kicked, cut with a knife, slapped, slugged, beaten up in a fight in a driving rainstorm, and nearly strung up with a rope.

He accepted the role strictly for the money, as he did in 1967's *Stranger on the Run,* also known as *Lonesome Gun,* in which he played George Blaylock. That same year he was Angelo in *The Challengers.* In 1968 he was guest star on the third episode of the hit detective show *Hawaii Five-O.* Broadcast on October 10, the episode was "Tiger by the Tail." His role was aspiring nightclub singer Bobby George, who staged his own kidnaping for the publicity.

The salaries for these performances were so quickly spent that Sal's business manager, Phil Gittleman, put him on an allowance of $25 a week and paid his rent of $250 per month. When Sal made no money, Gittleman urged him to collect unemployment benefits. He even took Sal to the office. On Santa Monica Boulevard, it was known among out-of-work actors as the Polish Embassy. "I set it up with a friend who worked there to get it over in an hour, not the usual half a day," Gittleman recalled about that day. "Sal was too proud. He took a look around and then he had to leave. He had to live high. Sal didn't know that if you bought your Levis outside Beverly Hills, you paid less than $4."

Elliot Mintz noted that Sal never invested his money. He spent it on rent, dinner parties, and gifts for friends. "If he went out to dinner with eight people, six of whom were strangers, and the bill came to $180, Sal paid for it," Mintz recalled. "He even signed bills he couldn't pay."

If he was broke, transportation was provided by a friend who managed a car-rental firm; she let him drive one rent-free. If his wardrobe needed sprucing up, Michael Mason got designer clothes for him. When he was flush, he rented a house. "He lived all over Beverly Hills, in ten or 15 places," recalled Mintz. If the money was plentiful the house was palatial. If cash wasn't abundant, the houses were modest and the furnishings were cheap rentals from a friend whom Sal called Crazy Nate. Mintz remembered, "He'd lease Sal a bed for $9, a quarter for the top sheet and a quarter for the bottom. Nate would lease him anything—a television for $10 a month, a table for a buck and a half, plants for 85 cents. He'd charge a nickel a month for each piece of silverware. We had it down so we could get all this stuff into a truck in an hour. Toward the end Nate wouldn't rent him stuff, so he'd get crates from the supermarket, or wooden boxes, and he'd cover them with marble contact paper and use them for end tables. He'd use candles, and he'd say, 'If we keep the room dark, who's going to notice the difference?' "

At times Sal wondered if the plummeting roller coaster he was riding would ever start back to the top. But he was on it and there was no way of getting off, short of giving up the only work he'd ever done or wanted to do.

"Cry?" Dino had said to his psychiatrist. "You think I'm gonna cry? What arm do you take it in?" When Gene Krupa was black-listed, he declared defiantly, "I'm Gene Krupa, and all I need is to get back to work."

In 1968 Sal decided that if Hollywood no longer wanted him, perhaps someone elsewhere might. He chose to find out by going to Europe. His welcome was warm and encouraging. He met people who expressed interest in several of his ideas for projects. But none of them materialized and he found himself left holding the bag with $2,500 in bills.

"I ran off to Europe," he said, with typical stoicism, "and discovered you can't run away from yourself."

Nicholas Ray opined that Sal had come too far too fast. "I think to have success so young was a problem," he said many years after *Rebel Without a Cause*. "A star needs to have the steel of a Joan Crawford, a restlessness, a selfishness in a creative sense. Actors also have to betray. They are all things to all people. Sal had the will but he didn't have the steel. I doubt if Sal knew he was being ripped off."

Ray's assessment of Sal Mineo as lacking steel was wrong.

In an episode of *Janet Dean, Registered Nurse,* as a kid named Jose Garcia, he'd exclaimed, "Jose Garcia is strong as a bull." So was Sal Mineo. He was down on his luck in Beverly Hills, but he was not out. Not by a long shot. If movies didn't want him he would return to his roots in the theater, but not as an actor. He would follow the counsel given to one of the old lions of the movie business by his own father. When Samuel Goldwyn said he wanted to be an actor, his father advised, "Don't become an actor. Actors starve. Become the person who *hires* actors."

In the theater that responsibility belonged to a producer, but the ultimate decision was in the hands of the director.

If he were to become a director of a drama, the question was, "Which one?"

While browsing through the shelves of plays in a Martindale's bookstore he believed he'd found the answer in a work by a Canadian.

eleven

_____

Fortune and Men's Eyes

When Toronto-born John Herbert was a teenager, he ran afoul of the law and found himself locked up with other youths in a reformatory. The experience resulted in a bitter play on its degradation and brutality. The central figure is Smitty. Naive and essentially noncriminal, he has been sentenced to six months for a minor offense. He has three cell mates. Queenie is a raging homosexual who exploits every situation to his own ends. Mona is a boy who copes by separating his mind from his surroundings. Rocky is a bullying opportunist. The theme of prison brutality is employed to depict how a good person (Smitty) is transformed into a cynical, unfeeling prisoner even more callous than the others. The motivation for his transformation was a homosexual rape, played offstage.

Herbert found a title for the play in a sonnet by William Shakespeare:

> When in disgrace with fortune and men's eyes
> I all alone beweep my outcast fate,
> And trouble deaf heaven with my bootless cries.

Produced in New York in February 1967 by David Rothenberg and Mitchell Nestor, who directed, *Fortune and Men's Eyes* was first presented in association with The Little Room at the Actors

Playhouse. The role of Smitty had been created by Terry Kiser (who would later achieve fame as the dead host in the movie comedy *Weekend at Bernie's.*)

The play was published in book form in 1967 by Grove Press. Glancing through its pages in Martindale's bookstore two years later was an actor who had portrayed a teenager who'd been confined to a reformatory in *Dino* and asked his psychiatrist, "Did you ever sleep forty guys in a room? What goes on in there—everything you can think of."

Sal said that he became interested in Herbert's play because he was "looking for a good play to do with young actors. I thought that the first time out as a director I'd have more rapport with young actors."

In order to direct the play he would have to obtain performance rights from the playwright. The price, he was told, would be $1,000. Had it been $10,000, the fee could not have seemed more out of reach. Sal's only hope of raising it was to try his luck at gambling. The cash he had on hand was just enough to take him to Las Vegas on a one-way ticket with a few dollars left to hit the roulette tables in the hope of building a pot to allow him to go for higher stakes at a game he knew well, chemin de fer. He arrived in Las Vegas dressed to the nines and looking every inch the movie star with thousands to blow in the casinos and feeling like Sean Connery as James Bond going up against Auric Goldfinger. With skill and luck at the wheel and the chemin de fer table Sal won enough to cover Herbert's fee and a return ticket to L.A.

With performance rights obtained, he decided that before he undertook the project he needed to know more about life in prison than what he learned from reading Herbert's play, seeing Jimmy Cagney movies, and playing Dino. In a phone call to the warden's office at San Quentin prison to ask if he might visit California's toughest lockup, he explained his purpose and was amazed to find the prison's officials eager to extend a welcome to a movie star.

Of the visit Sal recalled, "I was in with convicted murderers and guys who'd been there 35 years. The cell doors were open and the guards were outside, but they couldn't hear what we were talking about. I was up in isolation, where a man spends 23 hours a day in a tiny cell and gets to walk outside the cell an hour a day. The inmates always prefaced what they said to me with, 'Look, this is between us—*I* have to stay here after you go.' "

While he was talking to the prison warden, a report came in of two stabbings in the yard.

"He got on the phone," Sal remembered, "and referred to these two men by their numbers, and I learned that you don't turn your back at any time in these prisons. I felt the play needed that kind of tension."

Sal claimed that the experience left him with nightmares, and a determination to use the play to vent his angry feelings about the glimpse he'd had of prison life. But bad dreams did not deter him from continuing the learning process by visiting prisons in New York. Of a lockup for young criminals called Greenlands in Westchester County, he said, "The isolation cells are about seven feet by five. They have toilets without a flush and a sink without knobs for hot and cold water. The kids have to ask the guards for water. The bed is cement, maybe a foot and a half off the floor. There's no mattress, no pillow, no blanket. They spend 24 hours a day in that cell. When they come out, guards use hoses to quiet them because the kids are raging animals."

On a later visit to New York City's Riker's Island jail he was told by a guard, "Right now a kid could be getting raped or getting the shit beat out of him and we wouldn't know it."

Studying Herbert's play, Sal decided it was not forceful enough in making the case that he wished to present against prison conditions. He revised it accordingly. Because Herbert could not enter the United States as a result of his criminal conviction in Canada, Sal sent him a script of the play as he'd altered it.

"While he didn't agree with everything I was doing," Sal noted, "he didn't forbid my doing it my way."

In Herbert's playscript Rocky exerts his dominance of his cellmates by attacking the new boy, Smitty. Because the action takes place offstage the audience does not know if Rocky raped Smitty, beat him up, or did both.

Sal's version of the play made clear it was rape by putting it center-stage.

Produced by Moe Weise and Phillip Gittleman, *Fortune* was booked to open first at the Coronet Theater in Los Angeles. Uneasy about staging it with unknowns, they wanted Sal to portray Rocky. Sal felt that he was wrong for the role. He pointed out that he was 30 years old and Rocky was 20. Smart business won the argument, temporarily.

Rocky was a "hippie type who could be dangerous if he exploded," Sal explained, adding, "I like Rocky. He's the kind of character I dig. For all his hang-ups and his weaknesses, he's kind of a really pathetic kid. Not the brightest kid you'd want to meet, and yet I find it very moving that he is affected by another kid. He's something that he could never be. He could never be Smitty."

Sal saw Rocky intimidating Smitty verbally, not physically. "After the rape scene," Sal pointed out, "Smitty says it was the verbal threat that made him submit—the threat that without Rocky to act as his protector Smitty would be gang-raped by 15 or 16 guys."

The actor Sal chose to portray Smitty had been starring in San Francisco in a rock musical called *Your Own Thing*. Eighteen years old, Don Johnson (born Donnie Wayne Johnson in Flat Creek, Missouri) had dropped out of the University of Kansas to join the American Conservatory Theater in San Francisco.

Five feet six inches tall with blue-green eyes and fair hair, the handsome youth had always thought of himself as a future star. After 200 performances in *Your Own Thing,* he was seen by Sal and invited to come to Los Angeles to audition for Smitty. He was the 255th actor to try for the role.

Recalling the occasion in a 1973 interview, Johnson admitted he had heard that Sal Mineo had a reputation for preferring sex with men. "I played it really super-butch," he said of meeting Sal. "I told him, 'Look now, if you think I'm letting anybody fuck me for this role, you're out of your bean. Forget it. I'll just forget my career and the whole damn thing, because I am not getting involved in that shit.' And that just put him on the floor, laughing. He said, 'You don't have to do any of that.' "

Johnson returned to San Francisco and the next day got a telegram from Sal that he had the part, but he had to lose ten pounds.

In addition to being offered a good role, Johnson found the idea of appearing nude on the stage appealing. In an article in *Scarlet Street* a few years later, Johnson said: "Basically, I guess I'm an exhibitionist. I'm very proud of my body. I'm pleased with the way

I look and the way I carry myself. I feel that it's all there to be used—the looks and everything else. Some people have great minds, and they were given them for a reason. I have never been accused of having a great mind, but I do have my looks."

While preparing for his directorial debut, Sal lived with his dog Dov and Johnson in a theatrical hotel, the Montecido. The arrangement caused a lot of talk. Of rumors that Johnson and Sal were lovers, Johnson said, "Of course there were some wild stories that went down because of us, which was fine, because they helped sell a lot of tickets. And there have been some outrageous stories about us! God, God, God!"

The suite in the hotel had been obtained on the basis of Sal's movie-star status, but when he moved in he had no money for the rent. When no payments proved forthcoming, the anxious owner broached the subject with Sal. To fend him off Sal said he was thinking of buying the place. The stall worked for a couple of months, but when the owner pressured Sal to make the deal or pay his $10,000 bill, Sal moved out in the middle of the night.

Elliott Mintz assisted and later boasted that everything he learned about "finances" had been picked up by watching Sal operate without cash. "He was not a hustler or thief," Mintz said. "He just believed things were owed to him."

Joe Bonelli, who spent more time with *Fortune and Men's Eyes* than anyone connected with the show but Sal and the producers, remembered Sal always being broke.

How Joe found himself part of the production in both New York and Los Angeles is an illuminating portrait of Sal at that time. A native of Mississippi, Joe had come to Hollywood in the 1960s expecting to be a movie star. Like so many actors with that dream, he'd found it easier to land a job waiting on tables in the restaurants and clubs on the swinging Sunset Strip.

One of the celebrity hangouts was an Italian restaurant. Among the regulars were Peter Fonda, Dennis Hopper, rock musician Jimi Hendrix, and Sal Mineo. With a knack for "chatting up" stars, Joe realized that Sal liked him. Personal circumstances caused Joe to leave L.A. and return to Mississippi for a few months. When he came back to Los Angeles in December 1968, he read in a show-business trade paper that Sal was holding auditions for understudies in *Fortune and Men's Eyes*. Joe wanted to see Sal again. He went to the auditions and took along a friend to impress the friend by showing him that "a celebrity knows me."

"It was an open reading, and I'm sitting there waiting," Joe recalled, "when Sal walked in and saw me. He said, 'Where the hell have you been?' "

Sal liked Joe's reading and offered him a job. But the next day Joe got a phone call informing him there'd been a change and the job offer was withdrawn. It was a temporary setback. A month or so into the run of the play he was taken on to understudy the role of Mona. When the show was taken to New York, he was hired for a backstage job and eventually became stage manager, a job he held for a year and a half.

Having met Sal on the Sunset Strip and observed him living up to the popular image of a movie star, Joe was astonished to hear from Sal that one day he had discovered that because of mismanagement of his business affairs all his money was gone. Joe later witnessed the dismal state of Sal's finances. During the Los Angeles run of *Fortune* Sal was slapped with court papers filed by a creditor. "Sal took the summons with a big grin," Joe recalled, "then he told me to give the process server tickets for the show. Sal said, 'The guy's just doing his job.' As for the person to whom he owed the money, Sal let out a laugh and said, 'Let him join the line.' "

Joe remembered Sal successfully avoiding other showdowns with people he owed.

"Yet, he always looked as prosperous as a star was expected to be," Joe recalled.

Just how devastated Sal had been after losing the Oscar for his performance in *Exodus* was driven home to Joe when Joe expressed surprise that Sal had not gotten the award and asked him who had gotten it.

Sal replied, "Peter fucking Ustinov."

"Well, there's only one thing to say about that," Joe said. "If you had to lose the Oscar, at least you lost it to a first-class real actor."

Sal stiffened and snapped, "It was *my* fucking Oscar."

Joe and audiences of *Fortune and Men's Eyes* also saw how deeply emotional Sal could be regarding James Dean. A page in the program dedicated the play to him. When Sal did a guest shot on Joey Bishop's late-night TV talk show, Bishop surprised Sal by running a clip from *Rebel Without a Cause*. It was a scene in which Plato gazed lovingly at Jim Stark. When the clip ended, Sal came back on the TV screen in a tight closeup that revealed the same worshipful look in his eyes. After the taping of the Bishop show, Sal returned to the Coronet Theater and told Joe what had happened. He said, "The world saw my soul for ten seconds."

Except for a pan by *Hollywood Reporter*, reviews of *Fortune and Men's Eyes* by the Los Angeles critics were favorable. The warmest praise came from the gay press. The magazine *in* declared it "one of the most exciting evenings in the theater this season." Part of the reason, said the reviewer "surely is that Sal Mineo has been starred in it. Another part is this production marks the debut of Sal Mineo as a director. It is auspicious."

A national gay magazine, *Avanti,* made its debut on newsstands with a lengthy interview with Sal and a glowing review of the play that paid attention to the other actors. Reviewer Dustin Halliday wrote, "Of exceptional note was Michael Greer's truly magnificent portrayal of Queenie. Don Johnson as Smitty and Rogert Garrett as Mona by no means fell short of the excellent caliber of performance set by Mineo's deft direction. The production from start to finish is a successful display of teamwork resulting in excellent ensemble staging."

Sal noticed "a big change in the audience." For the first couple of weeks it was entirely male. "All of sudden it changed," he observed. "We're getting a lot of students, getting a lot of women coming in. What I dig about it is that both sexes find it moving. The play doesn't gear itself to one specific society. I think anyone can find something within the play that they can identify with, maybe some of them too closely."

The play was not everyone's cup of tea. When distinguished actors Edward G. Robinson and Sam Jaffe and their wives came to see it, they left after the first act.

With *Fortune and Men's Eyes* a hit in L.A. it was scheduled to open in New York City at Stage 73 in October 1969, produced by Kenneth Waissman and Maxine Fox. At 321 East 73rd Street in the heart of the Upper East Side, known as the Silk Stocking district because of its concentration of rich residents, the theater was as far off-Broadway as it could be.

Sal's interpretation of *Fortune and Men's Eyes* was not the first play to broach the topic of homosexuality on a New York stage. On April 12, 1968, Theater Four on West 54th Street presented *The Boys in the Band*. It was described by theater critic Clive Barnes as "by far the frankest treatment of homosexuality I have ever seen on the stage." Barnes pointed out that the play was not about homosexuals at a birthday party but about homosexuality as a way of life. A film version of the play went into production in July 1969.

The generally critically praised and box-office success of *The Boys in the Band* had been followed on October 5, 1969, by John Osborne's play *A Patriot for Me*. About a homosexual and a spy, it received mixed reviews. "One of the problems," said Osborne, "is that no leading actor wanted to play a 'queer.' It was turned down by several people. Their wives didn't want them to play that sort of part. Even the queer actors didn't want to take the risk." (The lead role was taken by German-born actor Maximilian Schell.) Another play about homosexuality appearing at the off-Broadway Bouwerie Lane Theater as Sal readied *Fortune and Men's Eyes* in the autumn of 1969 was *And Puppy Dog Tails*.

All this theatrical attention to homosexuality had followed an event in Greenwich Village that had splashed homosexuality onto the front pages of the city's newspapers and at the top of television and radio newscasts in a way that left heterosexuals astonished. Homosexuals were proclaiming "Gay Power" and the beginning of a "Gay Revolution."

The rebellion commenced shortly after midnight on June 27 at a homosexual bar at No. 53 Christopher Street, called the Stonewall Inn. When nine plainclothes detectives raided it on a complaint that drinks were being served to minors and dancing was going on without a permit, patrons and bystanders on the street pelted the cops with coins, beer bottles, and bricks.

A *New York Daily News* headline proclaimed:

HOMO NEST RAIDED
QUEEN BEES ARE STINGING MAD

The front page of *The Village Voice* noted GAY POWER COMES TO SHERIDAN SQUARE. On October 31, 1969, *Time* magazine took notice of these events with a seven-page feature, "The Homosexual: Newly Visible, Newly Understood."

In this atmosphere of turmoil and perplexity, confusion and anxiety among heterosexuals and many homosexuals, Sal Mineo made his New York debut as a theatrical director.

The program stated that the play at Stage 73 was "Sal Mineo's *Fortune and Men's Eyes*." Although he was not in the play, a drawing of a young man's face in black and white on the front of the playbill was clearly his portrait. The program's biographical sketch of the director, written by Sal's friend Elliott Mintz, began provocatively with, "Mr. Mineo is an erotic politician."

Top billing in "Who's Who in the Cast" was given to Michael Greer as Queenie. At age 26, the native of Galesburg, Illinois, had played a draft dodger in a wacky film called *The Gay Deceivers* that had failed at the box office. A singer and comedy writer with an act of his own, he had been seen by Sal in performance at San Francisco's The Purple Onion. He was hired for the L.A. production and brought east for the New York version.

Mark Shannon had toured in summer stock with Martha Raye in *Hello Sucker* and had been back in New York only two weeks when he auditioned for Sal. He got the part of Smitty.

Rocky was played by Bartholomew Miro, Jr. His professional stage career began as a tribesman in the hit rock musical *Hair*. Sal had seen him in it and asked him to audition. He found that the actor had gone overnight from a "flower child" to an aggressive street kid. Rocky was played later in the show's run by a graduate of Harvard who'd been on Broadway in *A Patriot for Me* and in a minor role in the movie *John and Mary*. He was billed in *Fortune and Men's Eyes* as Tom Lee Jones. Movie and TV audiences would get to know him as *Tommy* Lee Jones.

Making his New York debut after performances in college productions at the University of Texas, Jeremy Stockwell (formerly Sockwell) was cast as Mona.

A guard was played by Joe Dorsey, a veteran of Shakespearean productions in England and the United States. His wife, Halyna Harcourt, was an actress and their four-year-old son was a veteran of TV commercials.

When this cast assembled for the first rehearsal, Sal greeted them with, "Welcome to our prison. None of us will be the same after this play. You can argue pros and cons about capital punishment. I'm more interested in the treatment of prisoners. Physical brutality will always exist. I'm concerned with the mental brutality of reprogramming one's life and censuring one's attitudes or beliefs as a way to persevere."

The latter statement was perhaps Sal's subconscious assessment of the treatment he felt he'd received in the Hollywood that sought new faces and claimed to have struggled to find a new place for the Sal Mineo who was no longer the heartthrob of teenagers.

Sal's play was set in the present in "a boys' prison." This was a change; the original script placed the action in a men's prison. The action unfolded in three acts, on a mid-October evening, three weeks later, and Christmas Eve.

Sal had made one more adjustment in the play for the New York opening. The onstage rape in the L.A. production had been a brief scene. For New York he stretched it to three minutes of what Joe Bonelli called "a gladiator battle in the shower."

As the date for the opening approached and word got around that the play contained an onstage rape, Sal discussed the scene in a feature in the Long Island newspaper *Newsday*. He speculated that "some people might in their minds conceive of the rape to be romantic, sensual, or even humorous," rather than one of "irrefutable horror and brutality."

The violent scene was as strictly choreographed as a dance number in a musical.

After the opening-night performance, the fledging director, producers, cast, and backstage crew headed downtown to the traditional 44th Street venue for such bashes, Sardi's restaurant, to await the reviews in the newspapers, especially that of the critic for the *New York Times*. That Clive Barnes had written an enthusiastic notice for *The Boys in the Band* left them hopeful of a good review from the man whose opinion could make a show a hit or doom it to oblivion.

Barnes's review asked, "How far can you go? Or, if you think it more pertinent, how far are we going? In the theater, that is. And in the business of breaking old taboos, and all that nonsense." Answering this rhetorical question, Barnes continued, "Sir or Madam, I suggest that if this is the play you would like, you need a psychiatrist a lot more than you need a theater ticket."

As to the director, "I am not sure what kind of reputation Mr. Mineo has—he is a minor Hollywood player, I believe—but I am perfectly certain what reputation Mr. Mineo deserves."

Barnes continued, "I consider the changes Mr. Mineo has made in this play have been made in the interest of sexual titillation— chiefly of the sadomasochistic variety—rather than in the interest of drama. . . . It will be interesting to see whether this show, following the enlightened economic practices of *Oh! Calcutta* [a show with nudity], starts to charge extra for its front rows, possibly on the grounds that you can hear better from there. I shall also be following with fascination the show's advertising—as, I trust, will the Police Department."

The effect of Barnes's review was to turn the Sardi's party into a wake.

Jill Haworth attended. She could sympathize with everyone in the cast because Barnes had recently panned her performance as Sally Bowles in *Cabaret*. She had seen *Fortune* in L.A. and although she had been shocked by its nature, she went to the New York opening to show her continuing love for Sal.

Sal had expected his directorial debut in a controversial play to evoke both positive and negative reviews. But he was stunned that Barnes had ignored the performances and singled him out for vituperation. He asked, "What about the actors? They're good kids, they should be seen. They need the recognition."

He interpreted the fact that Barnes "devoted three columns to the show" and named only him as meaning that Barnes saw him as a threat to traditional theater. Sal said, "He was reviewing Sal Mineo, not the play."

Joe Bonelli agreed. "Clive Barnes did not review *Fortune and Men's Eyes*," he said. "He decided he was going to take the Hollywood Whiz Kid and put him in his place."

Sal bitterly expressed a wish that he could appear on the *Tonight Show* with Barnes in a discussion of the play in which he would denounce *Barnes* as the person who was "destructive to the theater."

In an interview published by *Cavalier* magazine a few months later, Sal still felt stung. "I think it must be a personal point of view and a personal reaction [by Barnes] based on his own insecurities," he said. "He talks about the changes in the play being in the interest of sadomasochism—well, the *point* of the play is that this kid, Smitty, turns into an animal and can only feel pleasure through pain. So far as my reputation goes—after I've been 18 years in the business, show business, and he doesn't know the *name?* And as for the reputation I've gotten from the play, I don't care. It's on that stage, and if you want to identify me with it, okay."

Despite Barnes's blast, *Fortune and Men's Eyes* continued its run. Gay men who hailed "the Stonewall rebellion" considered it a duty and act of loyalty to flock to the box office of the small theater on 73rd Street. But front-row ticket prices remained at $10 and the advertising for the play was simply a reproduction of the cover of the playbill. How many of those who trekked to Stage 73 to see Sal Mineo naked is not known. No doubt, many did. But when the word spread that Sal was not in the play, there was no decline in attendance. Sal found a repeat of what had happened in L.A. The almost entirely male and mostly gay audience soon became a mix of genders of all ages and sexual orientations.

The New York production continued well into 1970. Before the producers decided to close it, another young actor who had been a star on television and found himself struggling to make the transition to adult roles was preparing to take over the role of Smitty. One can only imagine what the public would have made of Jay North, the boy who had played Dennis the Menace, being the victim of a center-stage rape.

The audiences that had filled the seats of the Coronet in L.A. and Stage 73 in New York did not solve Sal Mineo's financial woes. His deal with the producers was that in lieu of salary he'd get a share of the profits. Noting that three months into the show he'd not seen a dime, he told an interviewer, "I've experienced many peaks as an actor. I'm sure there are still more peaks, but I had to come to terms with myself. Do I want a nice home with a nice car, do I want a steady job and pick up a script and learn lines and do that number? Or maybe do what I've always wanted to do—even if there is no bread in it. The point is that you do your thing and you go where your heart takes you and that's where you should go."

In an acting career that so far had spanned 18 of his 30 years, that had been Sal Mineo's unflinching approach to acting and to life.

twelve

"I Find It Very Baffling"

Having directed *Fortune and Men's Eyes* in Los Angeles and New York, Sal Mineo longed to put his version of John Herbert's play on movie screens.

However, the right to do so belonged to someone else.

When *Fortune and Men's Eyes* first appeared in 1967, film director Joseph Schwerin took an option on the movie rights. A man who was passionately involved in the cause of prison reform, he saw the play as a cinematic vehicle to promote those views. "I was not interested in exploiting homosexuality," he explained. "It's not why I became interested in the play."

A man with that outlook was not interested in having his film directed by the man who had taken an offstage homosexual rape and splashed it in full view of an audience as a three-minute gladiatorial struggle in a shower room. Schwerin saw the prison itself as the villain. Also aligned against Sal in the matter of making a film from the play was its author, John Herbert. He had done an about-face regarding Sal's revisions and had made his disapproval public.

But it was not Schwerin's version that reached the screens. The studio, MGM, and the producers, Lester Persky and Lewis Allen, arranged to have Schwerin replaced by Harvey Hart, who had directed *Bus Riley's Back in Town* in 1965.

"What emerged," wrote Vito Russo in his 1987 book on homosexuality in the movies, *The Celluloid Closet,* "seemed like a story about a country club for sadomasochistic homosexuals, backed by a Galt McDermot score of country and western hijinks more appropriate to a *Bonnie and Clyde.*"

"With no pretensions to greatness as a playscript," wrote Parker Tyler in *Screening the Sexes, Homosexuality in the Movies,* published in 1973, "*Fortune and Men's Eyes* had the misfortune in film to be overdocumented with prison atmosphere and sentimentality saddled with Rocky's implausible suicide when committed to solitary for his sins. Film cameras seldom have the sense to let well enough alone."

As in *Rebel Without a Cause* in 1955, in 1970 the "queer" had to die at the end.

The Los Angeles to which Sal returned (always with an eye peeled for a process server or a creditor demanding settlement of an outstanding debt) was in the full bloom of the "Gay Revolution." In addition to the Gallery Room, he had at his disposal gay bars and restaurants, which included the Corner Pocket at 8800 West Sunset, Le Tom Cat on Santa Monica in West Hollywood, B.J.'s on La-Cienega, and Entre Nous on North LaCienega. "Bob Damron's '70 Address Book" in the gay magazine *in* categorized them according to geography and type of clientele. M meant a mixed crowd and/or tourists. P was a private club. RT was "raunchy types" who were often commercial, meaning hustlers (male prostitutes). YC designated younger and/or college kids. SM stood for both sadomasochistic and "some motorcycle" (enthusiasts in black leather gear from head to foot).

There was even a map of Griffith Park indicating the usual attractions of the zoo, tennis and golf, and picnic grounds. "Our paths" showed where gays could meet. A key feature of the route was the Planetarium, where Plato asked Jim if the world would end in the nighttime.

"From the snowy ski slopes of Mt. Baldy to the sunny surf of Santa Monica," boasted the magazine, "from the automated delights of Disneyland to the desert farm lands of San Fernando Valley, from the drag bars of Main Street to the sailor bars of Long Beach—it's all L.A.—from the tuxedoed glamour of the Music Center to the hip hang-outs of the Sunset Strip."

Preceding Sal's return to L.A. were stories that the nature of the play he had chosen for his debut as a director was actually Sal's declaration of a sexuality that embraced sadomasochism. Michael Mason recalled, "The rumors about S&M started while he was still with Jill Haworth. He wasn't particularly into it, but he loved to put people on. If somebody was talking about something strange, something sexual, he'd get a sly smile on his face, lick his lips, and pretend he was getting all hot and bothered."

The S&M impression was reinforced by Sal's penchant for motorcycle leathers. This impression was in turn bolstered by the fact that Sal had spent several weeks riding with the Hell's Angels, ostensibly because he was planning to do a motorcycle movie.

This indeed had been his intention. "I'd heard about the motorcycle gang long before it was publicized," he recalled in an interview several years later, "and I wanted to do a script on them. I contacted them and they tested me. They let me ride with them. When I had a screen treatment, a studio heard about it and contacted me. We started negotiations. Two weeks later, I found [the studio] had already assigned a producer and a director to the project and they wanted to talk to me as an actor. I said to them, 'Fuck you!' The movie they made was *Wild Angels*."

The project Sal had in mind after *Fortune* was a collaboration with Elliott Mintz entitled *The Moving Fist*. He told friends he would have a final draft of the script within days and that there would be six weeks of pre-production, with shooting to commence before the end of January 1970.

"It will be the first film I'll be directing," he said excitedly. "When you get into films, you have much more control of what you want the audience to focus on. You can direct your point of view to people who may never have noticed before and make them aware and conscious of these facts, simply because you are subliminally attacking their heads. That's what I want to do with this film."

The project did not materialize. He could not find backing because he was not going to be acting in it. He complained to friends that everyone looked at him and saw an actor. "I wanted to come back to Hollywood on my terms," he said, "not to open in other plays and act in them. The problem is I go to somebody and tell him I need $25,000 to do a play. He says, 'Oh, what part are you going to play?' I say, 'No, man. I'm not going to act in it. I'm going to direct it.' He says, 'If you act in it we can publicize you and we'll make our money back, but if you just direct it, how are we going to do that?' "

A desperate need for money put him in *80 Steps to Jonah*. It starred Wayne Newton and fared poorly in reviews and attendance. Next, Sal signed for a movie in Cinerama. An adventure story set in 1883, it was titled *Krakatoa, East of Java*. The climax of the story was the eruption of the Krakatoa volcano, which was, in fact, located *west* of Java. Sal was Leoncavallo, the son of Giovanni Borghese (Rosanno Brazzi). They are balloonists who have sunk to putting on a show for carnivals and become passengers on a merchant ship bound for Krakatoa. The true purpose of the voyage is to find a treasure. Just as the trove of pearls is being divided, the volcano erupts.

The movie's premiere was held in Honolulu. It was Sal's first look at it. Halfway through the screening he stood up in disgust and blurted, "This is the worst piece of shit I've ever seen." As shocked Cinerama officials and the audience gasped and gaped in shock, he walked out.

When the film made its debut in Hollywood, Sal took advantage of the event to get some publicity for *Fortune and Men's Eyes*. He showed up at the Cinerama Dome on Sunset Boulevard with a police escort and a paddy wagon. In it were the boys from *Fortune*. They were clothed but handcuffed together. As guests arrived for the gala premiere, they were interviewed live on Steve Allen's TV show by his wife, Jayne Meadows. She found herself talking not only to Sal but the three young men shackled to him. Sal ignored the movie and talked about his play. Cops then escorted them back to the Coronet Theater with sirens blaring.

"Nobody went to *Krakatoa*," Sal said. "To most people it sounded like a voodoo flick."

The film's only virtue as far as he was concerned was the salary. While again living like a movie star, he pursued projects and dodged debt collectors. His finances were also fortified by two guest roles on a television series, *The Name of the Game*. He was in "A Hard Case of the Blues" on September 8, 1969, and on "So Long Baby, and Amen" one year and one day later.

Money was not a factor when he agreed to participate in a television documentary/tribute to James Dean. In *The First American Teenager,* Sal said Dean was the first to give teenagers an identification. "Before Jimmy Dean you were either a baby or a man. In between was just sort of one of those terrible stages that you had to get out of rather quickly. And he didn't."

For the show's audience of mostly former teenagers, seeing Dean in his red jacket and '49 Mercury was a trip down memory lane to a time when they'd felt as confused as Jim Stark, his girl Judy, and his adoring friend Plato. Now they had kids of their own.

Those who'd been thrilled by James Dean and tried to emulate him could look back with nostalgia as adults and say, "God bless Jimmy Dean's soul. May he rest in peace."

For a page in the playbill of *Fortune and Men's Eyes* Sal had written, "Jimmy: In memory of your friendship and inspiration, I dedicate this production to you."

Sal told a friend, "Jimmy wanted a spiritual relationship with people he cared about. He drew from this and he needed it from his friends. It was this special need that singled him out and made him different from everyone else. He needed a friend and love. He found them with me."

This connection with Dean had not ended in the crash at the intersection of routes 466 and 41. Sal believed he and Dean were in psychic contact. According to Elliott Mintz, in the summer of 1963 at Sal's beach house Sal asked for "a sign" from Dean. Mintz said the temperature in the house went way up. The second time Sal asked for a sign, Mintz said, a radio turned on.

Whether these were signs from Dean or not, Sal believed he was in communication with the youth he considered to be his first love, even though at the time, he said to Elliott, "I didn't know what it was or how to cope with it."

Haunted by James Dean and the legend that had grown around him since his death 15 years earlier, Sal had a flesh-and-blood friend in Elliot Mintz. Wanting to help Sal out of financial difficulties and hoping to spark a comeback for him, Elliott persuaded radio station KABC, which broadcast Elliott's program, to give Sal a talk show. When Sal allowed a caller to use several four-letter words, he was fired.

Undaunted, Sal continued pursuing financing for his projects. While they proved fruitless, Peter Bogdanovich was validating Sal's perceptiveness in spotting properties with a potential for good films by making *The Last Picture Show*. Another property for which Sal had once owned the film rights was a novel by Leo Herlihy. But he had been forced by a need for cash to sell his rights to *Midnight Cowboy*. The role of Ratso Rizzo, which Sal hoped to play went to Dustin Hoffman.

When Sal heard that a movie would be made of a Mario Puzo novel about a New York Mafia family, he bought a copy of the massive book. When he'd finished *The Godfather*, he was convinced that he'd found a way to attain his goal of playing a gangster. He saw himself as both Michael, the young war-hero son of Don Corleone, and his older brother Fredo. Who better than a true New York–born son of Sicilian immigrants, who in the minds of Italians and all other Americans was a movie star worth putting their asses into the seats of movie theaters to see?

He sought a part with all the passion and confidence with which he'd gone after the roles of Plato and Dov Landau. But he was informed that producer/director Francis Ford Coppola was looking for new faces. He griped, "What difference does it make if the audience knows me? They certainly know Marlon Brando, and he's playing the Godfather. I'm a good actor and I'm hearing that 'new face' bullshit. I would have been perfect for *The Godfather*, but no, they said, 'Mineo's been around and everybody knows him.' "

Sal was told later that the actual reason for being rejected was the objection by a member of the cast (not named) to "acting opposite a faggot."

Ironically, the film for which Sal was acceptable in 1970 was one in which his face would not be seen. Knowing that Sal was desperate for money, his friend Roddy McDowall arranged for him to get a role in the latest of McDowall's hit *Planet of the Apes* series, *Escape From the Planet of the Apes*. Also in the picture was the other non-Indian actor in an Indian role in *Cheynne Autumn*, Ricardo Montalban. Though Sal's "familiar" face was undiscernable beneath a rubber mask as a chimpanzee named Dr. Milo, he had the satisfaction of knowing the audiences for the film would hear his voice. Unlike Red Shirt, Milo had lines. They were confined to a short scene early in the film in which he dies, strangled by a gorilla. They included:

"We have traveled from the earth's future to the earth's past."

"Our human captors will not be edified to learn that one day their earth will be cracked like an egg and burned to a cinder because of an ape war of aggression."

"Apes at this moment cannot talk. We should follow their example."

"Use your head and start thinking."

Sal said he had accepted the role of a chimp as a "gag gig." He really took it because he needed money. It was his last theatrical feature. He later made a TV movie, *Only One Day Left Before Tomorrow*. He was half of a team of repossessors who set out to retrieve a jet aircraft from the irresponsible son of a Latin American dictator. He was amused to be playing the kind of man he was dodging in his own life.

Money was available from time to time from other television producers who not only did not care that Sal Mineo's face was familiar, but counted on it to attract viewers. Such producers found it to their advantage to cast Sal as Nick in *The Family Rico*. At long last, he found himself in a movie about gangsters. Adapted from novelist Georges Simenon's tale about torn loyalties of a Mafia family, it was an above-average TV movie with an impressive cast that included Ben Gazarra, James Farentino, Dane Clark, Leif Erickson, and Jo Van Fleet (who had played James Dean's bordello-owner mother in *East of Eden*). Other TV producers signed up Sal for roles in the undistinguished films *Left-Handed, Man Running*, and *Such Dust As Dreams Are Made On*.

While Sal's face had not been seen in his friend Roddy's film, McDowall made sure that Sal's beauty at this time was immortalized in a photograph in one of McDowall's three books of portraits of actors and actresses. The photos were accompanied by brief essays written by actors and actresses who'd worked with them. Sal's essay was written by Dennis Hopper, who recalled Sal being tutored on the set of *Rebel* with Natalie Wood while Hopper yearned for a romance with Wood. McDowall's black-and-white shot captured only Sal's head and neck as he gazed askance into the distance. Four decades after it was shot, the photo was still being sold as a post-card. The impression is that when the picture was taken Sal was naked.

No longer worried about a negative effect on his career if it be-came known around Hollywood that he enjoyed having sex with men, or that his decision to direct *Fortune and Men's Eyes* was widely accepted as a dramatic "coming out of the closet," Sal felt free to be open about his sexual appetite. He found himself wel-comed into the Hollywood homosexual circle by most of its mem-bers, though not all. Those who were still closeted feared being seen with him. Others were turned off by the S&M rumors. One actor who exhibited no such reticence was Rock Hudson.

Sal coyly stated, "We dated." It was an affair that caught the attention of a gossip columnist for *The New York Post*. The item mentioned that the towering Hudson and the diminutive Mineo were frequently seen together, which in the veiled language of news-paper in 1970 was as close as the columnist could come to saying they were lovers.

Asked point-blank by an interviewer if he was homosexual, Sal said, "No."

He went on to say, "There are all kinds of people, all kinds of homosexuals, all kinds of heterosexuals. When I was working on Broadway, ages 11 to 16, there wasn't one day in my life on those subways and around 42nd Street going toward the theater when I was not approached by a homosexual, whether he be a cop, a priest, or a guy on the street. Because I knew nothing of homosexuality, all I saw was what I was confronted with. Therefore, as a kid, I said all homosexuals should be shot because they're evil. But working in this business and working with known homosexuals— playwrights, directors, actors—all of a sudden an education starts. It took that kind of exposure for me to understand."

By his definition, because he was capable of having sex with women and had done so, he wasn't homosexual; he was bisexual. "I don't like being told I can love only a woman," he said, "or only a guy."

In the parlance of a movement calling itself "Gay Liberation" Sal was "out," shorthand for "out of the closet." Because he was on Hollywood's "weirdo list" and unable to get parts in the big movies, he did not have to concern himself with whether the moviegoing public learned that he was a guy who had sex with guys. If he were seen "dating" Rock Hudson or dancing with a guy in a gay bar, so what? Should someone from a magazine, whether it was for gays or straights, ask about his sex life, he felt free to answer truthfully.

What puzzled him, he said to one interviewer, was that he was labeled gay, but others who were known to have sex only with men were said to be bisexual. He assumed this was to protect careers. "Half the gays in Hollywood pretend to be bi," he speculated, "as a matter of survival."

Since the deal-makers of the movie business considered him a has-been at age 30, that was no longer his problem. If he couldn't make a living as a movie star, he'd find another way, and whether the fact that he "screwed guys" was the subject of an article someone wrote about him would have nothing to do with it.

Consequently, in December 1972, when asked for an interview by a young journalist from Santa Barbara by the name of Boze Hadleigh, he not only agreed but also flew up to Santa Barbara to grant it. The result of his conversation would be published in Hadeleigh's 1986 collection of his interviews with celebrity homosexuals, *Conversation with My Elders*. But at the time of Sal's trip to Santa Barbara, Hadleigh was simply interested in meeting and talking to famous men he knew to be gay. He met Sal at the airport in a red Dodge Dart. They went to lunch. Sal asked him to put off "all those questions" till later.

This left Hadleigh frustrated. He enjoyed "Sal's easy company but fretted that he'd keep postponing our session until it was time to leave." So far, he didn't know much about Sal Mineo, other than the type of man he'd heard that Sal liked: "blond and supercilious."

Sal wanted to see the movie version of the musical in which Jill Haworth had played the role that Liza Minelli had in the film. As Sal and Hadleigh watched *Cabaret,* Sal nudged Hadleigh in the ribs and said Liza's handsome costar, Michael York, "What a hunk! That's my type."

After the movie, they went to a small outdoor café for the interview.

"Wearing sunglasses, a white shirt opening on his bronze chest, tight jeans, white socks, and penny loafers," Hadleigh wrote, "Sal Mineo looked like the eternal youth."

The conversation touched on every subject that anyone who found himself talking to Sal Mineo would have wanted to know about: his films, James Dean, his later costars, *Fortune and Men's Eyes*, and his love life.

Of his start in pictures he said, "They tried to change everything except my fuckin' gender. But they finally figured out that maybe what I had worked. And it did, for the kind of things I did at first, and kept on doing."

For shirtless scenes he had to shave his chest? "Hair is," he said "*vulgah.*"

The effect on Sal of *Fortune and Men's Eyes*? "I probably lost half my future chances. But that'll change—it's already changing. I think it's only going to change in a big way . . . if gay actors and stars and directors come out. That'll show the guys in charge that we're here, and we're gonna stick around and not keep playing bury the queer in the fairy tale."

As to his preference in sexual partners, Sal told another interviewer, "I like real men who are happy being what they are. I like English guys, because they've got good manners, and they're not so starstruck."

At the time he expressed this preference he was deeply involved with just such a young man. His name could not have sounded more English: Courtney Burr III. Sal had cast him in the San Francisco company of *Fortune and Men's Eyes*.

They were a fascinating pairing of opposites. Outgoing and talkative, Burr was five feet seven, with brown eyes, beachboy-blond hair, and a model's body that seemed to have been designed by Michelangelo. Sal was the dark-eyed and black-haired "wop from the Bronx" who was often introspective to the point of brooding. According to Michael Mason, Sal was attracted to Burr's openness. "Courtney was freer," he said. "He was into wilder sex, spontaneous sex."

With nothing happening in Sal's career to keep him in Hollywood, and because Courtney was English, Sal decided to try his luck in Great Britain. The project he had in mind was about drug trafficking, *The Wrong People*. He planned to film most of it in Morocco.

Shortly after arriving in London he was offered the role of gangland boss Al Capone, but the show was a musical. Although he'd always wanted to play a gangster, he informed the show's producers he could not see himself as a singing and dancing Scarface. He preferred to channel his enthusiasm into making *The Wrong People*.

The man who had won money at roulette and chemin de fer to buy the rights to *Fortune and Men's Eyes* said, "This project is a definite gamble. I've made a lot of money. I make money. I lose money. Money has lost its charm over the years. I've resigned myself to the gamble, and now I have to just roll the dice. I can't imagine this project not working. It's going to work. It's going to happen. I won't think negatively under any circumstances."

Unfortunately, someone in authority in Morocco did. Finding that the script dealt with drug traffickers and prostitutes, an official of the Muslim country refused permission for the film to be made there. Nor was Sal able to generate interest in the project in the nation where he had been welcomed as Dov Landau. The government of Israel was not excited about being associated with a movie that might further inflame anti-Israeli sentiments among Israel's Arab neighbors.

Again left holding the bag and feeling dejected, Sal packed his few belongings and left England. He said of the dismal state of his personal and professional fortunes, "I find it very baffling."

Not long after he was home again, people who assumed that Sal Mineo was all washed up in show business could pick up the April 5, 1973, issue of the *Hollywood Reporter* and find a headline that said they were wrong: "Mineo Will Produce New Play."

A story datelined New York reported, "Sal Mineo and Robin Moles will produce a new play by Frederick Combs, *The Children's Mass*, set for rehearsal April 9 for a May 16 opening at the Theatre De Lys." The production would be directed by Richard Altman. Playing the four leads would be Courtney Burr, Calvin Cutler, Kipp Osborne, and Donald Warfield.

Combs had been in the cast of *The Boys in the Band* and like

that drama, *The Children's Mass* had a homosexual theme. Courtney wore a blond page-boy wig and evening gown.

The show bombed with critics and audiences and quickly closed.

But Sal's inability to make *The Wrong People* and the failure of
The Children's Mass in 1973 were insignificant compared to being
informed that his father was dying.

Sal rushed to his bedside.

During the melancholy journey, he remembered one day when he
was a troublesome kid whose parents worried what would become
of him. He was watching his coffin-making father at work. Big Sal
had looked at him with a smile. Placing a hand on the casket, he
said, "You'll be wearing one of these someday, so get the most out
of living, and enjoy it while you can."

After five days at his father's bedside, "Little Sal," also known as
"Junior," eulogized him at the funeral mass held at the family's
church.

Salvatore Mineo, Sr., age 59, was buried in the Gate of Heaven
cemetery in nearby Hawthorne, New York.

"What I learned from him in those five days was how important
the moments are every day and how quickly time goes," Sal said.
"Being in the same room with him and looking at him, I realized
that one day I would be in the same position as he, facing death.
Before it happens I mean to do the things I want to do. I will not
end up saying, 'I wish I had.' "

When Salvatore Mineo, Sr., died, he and his family had accommodated themselves to the effects of the downturn in Sal's career
and they looked forward optimistically to a rebound. But coming to
terms with his sexual life was an ongoing struggle. Acceptance was
especially hard for Josephine. Confused and wondering if the manner in which she had raised Sal were the cause, she summoned the
nerve to ask, "How come you turned out gay?"

Sal answered the only way he could. "Ma," he said, tenderly putting an arm around her, "how come my brothers *didn't*?"

thirteen

———

One-Night Stand in Manhattan

One summer afternoon four years after I'd barged backstage at *Fortune and Men's Eyes* hoping to meet its director I answered the phone in an alcove in my apartment designated for the purpose of writing and there he was on the line asking, "Are you busy tonight?"

"Yeah, I have to work."

"Ah, fuck! I'm in town just till tomorrow and I thought we could have dinner, hang out for a while, maybe talk about my biography that you keep saying you're going to write, and then hit a few clubs, but since you're working—"

"I'll call in sick."

"Great!"

"Where do we meet and when?"

"Six o'clock at the Oak Bar?"

"You're staying at the Plaza? You must be feeling flush."

"We're *meeting* at the Plaza."

Waiting at the bar, he was wearing yellow-tinted aviator-style glasses, a white turtleneck, linen sports jacket, chocolate slacks, brown socks, and cordovan loafers. His left hand held a cigarette. The right circled a tumbler of Scotch. Since the hotel had an excellent restaurant, the Edwardian Room, we had steak dinners there. I paid. We returned to the Oak Bar for brandies and cigars, drank, smoked and talked about my work-in-progress, a novel that went unpublished, and of Sal having signed for a part in an episode of a new detective show, *Griff,* starring Lorne Greene. "Marked for Murder" was slotted to run on NBC on October 27. What he might do after that, Sal said, was up in the air, but he had ideas for a couple of projects which he would direct.

When I signaled the bartender for the tab, he said, "Whatdaya say we cruise some bars?"

In a 1967 guidebook "to the pleasure places of the most celebrated city in the world," *The New York Spy,* Leo Skir had noted, "Much is said, much is written, little is actually known about New York's gay world. Many suspect it is not gay at all, but rather kind of sad and lonely."

Two years later, as Sal Mineo arrived in New York to put a homosexual rape on stage, the belief that no one could be happy and homosexual was a theme of playwright Mart Crowley's *The Boys in the Band.* In the course of a long birthday party for a pock-marked, 30-year-old "queer" named Harold, the guests become progressively drunker and embittered toward one another and about themselves and their lifestyle. "Show me a happy homosexual," Harold declared, "and I'll show you a gay corpse."

By the time Sal presented *The Children's Mass,* homosexuals were saying they were not only happy, they were *gay.* And proud to be so. The Stonewall Inn had become to them as much a symbol of a declaration of freedom as Philadelphia's Independence Hall with its Liberty Bell. Indeed, "Stonewall" had become as much a synonym for the start of a revolution as "Lexington Green" and "Concord Bridge." The coins and bottles heaved at cops on Christopher Street were no less to gays than "the shot heard 'round the world," which launched the American Revolution. Yet for millions of heterosexual Americans who found themselves called "straights," the fact that 1) there existed such a place as a "gay bar" and 2) the men who patronized it would fight police to be allowed to dance with one another, was a rude awakening. Having heard of both phenomena, they were not surprised that the bar and the riot were in New York.

"The classic gay bars were by nature dark meeting places for clandestine sexual encounters," observed Wayne Sage, a contributing editor to *Human Behavior* magazine in a 1976 article in the gay magazine *In Touch*. "Those who went there were alone, hid their cars, gave false names, and otherwise hid from one another as well as the outside world."

After Stonewall, the gay bars and those who frequented them emerged into the light, not just in New York but in cities across the country.

Soon, the gay liberation movement coupled with the new popular music of the Sixties and Seventies in the phenomenon called "disco." In Los Angeles it was Studio One.

Owners of discos estimated their clientele to be at least 70 percent gay.

"Twenty years ago the gay superbars could not have existed," wrote Wayne Sage, "not only because society would not have allowed them, but because gays would not have patronized them."

In discos such as Studio One and in openly operating gay bars, the once-secretive life of the homosexual had become by the mid-1970s a late-night dance of the hours. If the New York Police Department had set out to arrest men for dancing with the men in the city in 1973, the cops would have had more on their hands than the handful of gays who'd greeted them with coins and bottles at the Stonewall. They might even have found themselves face-to-face on the dance floor with Sal Mineo.

No longer regarded as a movie star, he felt free of constraints. While he took roles in TV shows for the money, he considered himself a man of the theater. Since the days of Shakespeare, "the stage" had been an institution where the public expected to find homosexuals. Sal had met them and worked with them long before he realized he was one of them. Now that he knew, he didn't care how the public felt about him personally. He cared only about what they thought of his work in the theater.

Being in New York also provided a refuge from people he owed. While eating dinner one night in Downey's steak house on Eighth Avenue, not far from the Martin Beck Theater where he had made his Broadway debut, Sal went into the men's room and encountered James Dean's former friend John Gilmore.

"His hair was very black, and tousled in a Tony Curtis waterfall style," Gilmore noted in his memoir, *Laid Bare*. "He had on a big roll-collar sport shirt and a huge knot in his red tie."

Gilmore hadn't seen Sal since the filming of *Rebel Without a Cause* and thought that Sal "seemed a lot taller than he'd been back then." Surprised to see him, Gilmore asked what he was doing in town. Sal replied, "Hiding out." Gilmore didn't ask why and Sal offered no explanation.

Because of the state of his finances, he was rarely in a position to pick up dinner checks as he'd been able and happy to do even if it wasn't his party in the years when the roller coaster was going up. Now he found that not only was the check paid by the friend who invited him out for a meal or drinks, but the host also discreetly inquired if he could use a little cash to tide him over; a loan, of course, but no hurry about paying it back, either.

Should he go to a disco or a gay bar, there was always someone offering to treat him to a drink or two or three just to be able to brag about having spent some time with a star named Sal Mineo who still had the glow. If the guy buying the drinks happened to be the right type, he might also earn bragging rights about having gone to bed with him.

Sal's "type" was well-built, and preferably English. His ideal was a Michael York or a Courtney Burr III. In *Conversations with My Elders*, Boze Hadleigh wrote of just such a young man whom Hadleigh identified only as "Greg." According to Hadleigh, Sal spotted Greg at Studio One in 1974. He sent a friend to ask if Greg would like to meet Sal Mineo. Greg said he'd never heard of him, but agreed to meet him. They danced and eventually went to Sal's apartment.

"And," Greg said, "we began our affair."

It ended, he said, because Sal was possessive despite "an open arrangement." Greg wanted "to roam, to move on to other relationships, meet more people."

Discos such as Studio One in L.A. and those in New York afforded plenty of choices in partners for dancing or sex who'd be impressed with doing either or both with Sal Mineo. If he wanted to avoid New York club mob-scenes he had his pick of numerous quieter, more intimate, old-style bars, from Julius on Tenth Street in the Village (the oldest gay bar in the city and perhaps the country) and the uptown and downtown Uncle Charlie's, to places that served patrons with tastes in clothing ranging from bikers' leathers to cowboy to the preppie look. If he found himself in the mood to rub elbows with men with more edge, he could put on tight jeans, a muscle shirt, and a black leather jacket and cruise the "rough trade" hustler hangouts all over the town. For a real sense of danger there were the cellar joints and warehouses of the meat-packing district along the Hudson River at the western fringe of the Village.

Because neither Sal nor I were suitably attired for what Sal called "the raunchy scene," he proposed exploring the gay bars on the Upper East Side. As we left the Plaza, he added, "I'd also like to check out the action among the hustlers on Third Avenue."

I joked, "Do you want to see if any of your old customers might still be around?"

"Paulie," he exclaimed, stopping short. "I never charged anybody for it in my life." Then he flashed the grin that Romolo had turned on to light up the screen in *Somebody Up There Likes Me.* "But I could have. Plenty of times."

Sal found the selection of male prostitutes along the east side of Third Avenue between 54th and 52nd Streets that the young men called "the meat rack" limited and unexciting. Nor did he find anyone of interest in a bar on 53rd near Second Avenue. The same proved true in a place farther down Second named "The Last Call," possibly because he was asked if he were Sal Mineo and then wasn't believed. As we left that bar, he said, "Screw this. Suppose we just find some place where we can bullshit the rest of the night away without getting dirty looks if we don't keep on buying drinks. Okay?"

I decided that he was less interested in finding sex than in just having company because he was feeling lonely. I suggested the automat at Third and 42nd.

Most of the hours spent there were more a Sal Mineo monologue than a conversation. He reminisced about Broadway, his movies, Jimmy Dean, his success, and how everything suddenly changed. At one point I said, "If I knew I was going to be hearing Sal Mineo war stories that should be in your biography, I would've brought a tape recorder and notebook."

"What you don't remember you can make up."

"I could only write what's true."

Sal grinned. "What's the fun in that?" Then the smile faded. "Kidding aside," he said, "if I were to drop dead tomorrow and your boss at the radio station told you to write my obituary, how would you start it?"

"C'mon, Sal, that's a terrible thing to ask."

"I know. I'm a prick. So what would you write?"

"Well, first, I'd have to state the cause of your death."

He giggled, "I died at the box office. Then what?"

"Sal Mineo was a two-time Academy Award nominee who—"

"Yeah? Who what?"

"Who was a lovable guy full of self-doubt who had a hell of great time living life to the hilt even when it kicked him in the ass."

"Can you say 'hell' and 'ass' on the radio?"

The dull light of dawn and daytime people were appearing on Third and 42nd.

"I've got a plane to catch to L.A.," Sal said. "Thanks for a great time."

"Hey, I'm always available for a Sal Mineo one-night stand."

As we left the automat, Sal looked around at the tables and the walls with little windows that displayed the selections and said, "I ate in plenty of these between the matinees and evening performances when I was on Broadway . . . a long time ago. A verrrrrry lonnnng time ago."

fourteen

P.S. Your Cat Is Dead

The next time I heard of Sal was in *Variety* on February 5, 1974:

Sal Mineo Will Play
Bob Kennedy Killer

> Ananke Prods has signed Sal Mineo to portray the role
> of the convicted assassin of Senator Robert F. Kennedy,
> Sirhan Bishara Sirhan. According to Donald Freed, au-
> thor of the still-untitled screenplay, the film will dem-
> onstrate the tragic psychological manipulation of Sirhan
> at the hands of a conspiracy.

The subject appealed to Sal because he had come to believe, as
did many other Americans at the time, that the United States government was riddled with sinister people who had plotted and carried out political murders in the 1960s, starting with the
assassination of President John F. Kennedy on the day that John
Ford decided it would be a good time to "kill Saul."

In the parlance of the period, Sal was "an assassination buff" who
had refused to accept the verdict of the Warren Commission investigation that JFK had been shot by a misfit ex-Marine named Lee
Harvey Oswald. In an interview that was meant to deal with *For-*

tune and Men's Eyes, the subject of prison reforms led into a discussion of people who protested against "the system." Sal complained, "They're very fast to get into demonstrations, the fighting for this, the fighting for that, but they avoid the most obvious problem in the history of the United States. To find the men, the people who killed the president."

He asked rhetorically, "How is it the citizens did not have a representative on the Warren Commission? Everybody on the Warren Commission was appointed by President Johnson. The American people should have had an attorney, a representative, on the staff. The Warren Commission Report is totally wrong. The thing is worthless. It's bullshit. We know it wasn't Lee Harvey Oswald alone. There can't be one man shooting from three different angles. It has been proven that there were more shots from different angles. It's on film."

Among the earliest doubters that Oswald acted alone had been Mark Lane, in a 1964 book titled *Rush to Judgment* Lane later coauthored a novelization of a movie, *Executive Action,* which dealt with government-sanctioned assassination of JFK. Lane's collaborator on the novelization had been Donald Freed, screenwriter for the proposed Sirhan Sirhan picture. In addition to playing Sirhan, Sal was to join Freed and researcher Jack Kimbrough in writing the film.

Unfortunately for Sal and the others, the project ran into the objections of Sirhan's mother, Mrs. Mary Sirhan. She claimed that she had not authorized any such film. She feared that her son was going to be exploited. An explanation by Freed that the film would show that Sirhan Sirhan "was not guilty" proved unavailing. The project foundered.

Five and a half years after the JFK assassination Sal became fascinated by a murder case closer to home. On March 23, 1969, a gang had entered the former Benedict Canyon residence of Doris Day's son, film producer Terry Melcher. The house on Cielo Drive was currently occupied by movie star Sharon Tate (pregnant wife of director Roman Polanski), and three guests. The intruders slaughtered them all, and on the way out wrote the word "pig" on the front door in Tate's blood. When a band of female killers led by an ex-con and psychopath named Charles Manson went on trial for what the press called "the Sharon Tate murders" and those of Rosemary and Leno LaBianca, Sal attended the proceedings nearly every day. Manson and his "followers" were found guilty and sentenced to death in the San Quentin gas chamber. They were saved in 1972 when the California legislature abolished the death penalty. Sal had followed the Manson trial with an eye toward writing a film about the case, but more promising projects came up.

With the Sirhan Sirhan film abandoned, Sal found work in television, mostly in the crime and detective series, which were TV's current vogue. He'd been a guest star on *Hawaii Five-O* for a second time on October 10, 1972, and in the test production (a pilot) of *Harry O* starring David Jansen as private eye Harry Orwell, on March 11, 1973. That same year he did *Griff*.

Sal also proved to be a box-office draw in dinner theater. In Jacksonville, Florida, he was in the Alhambra Dinner Theater production of Alan Ayckbourne's *How the Other Half Lives*. He costarred with Marjorie Lord, who'd been Danny Thomas's wife on TV's *Make Room for Daddy*.

The year 1974 provided continuing work in TV's crime wave. On January 2, on *Tenafly* he was in an episode titled "Man Running." The show was unique in that detective Harry Tenafly, played by James McEachlin, was black. The show was one of four rotating elements of NBC's Tuesday/Wednesday mystery movies. On February 26 Sal was on *Police Story,* in an episode called "The Hunters." October 19 he did *Police Surgeon*. While none of these parts presented a challenge to his acting abilities, they paid the rent.

A film called *Dynamite* by a Los Angeles–based Philippine production company was to be shot in Manila. Sal was to double as director and in the role of a footloose hippie. This project, too, never reached fruition.

Television offers continued coming his way. His third appearance on *Hawaii Five-O* was on February 25, 1975, and two nights later he was again on *Harry O*. Four days after that he was in an episode titled "S.W.A.T" on *The Rookies*. The cop show with "hip" young police officers fresh out of college was a hit, and in its third year. "S.W.A.T." proved so successful that it became a series. Sal was a guest star on its 26th show (September 13).

On October 12 he worked with Peter Falk on *Columbo* in an episode in which he was a clerk named Rachman Habib in the L.A. consulate of an Arab kingdom. Duped into staging a fake robbery that was to be blamed on political dissidents, Habib is double-crossed by the chief of the consulate and murdered.

Unfortunately, the script did not include a scene in which Sal would act with the man he'd advised as to how to campaign for an Academy Award. He greatly admired Peter Falk and said of him, "He sustains his acting ability and can break stereotypes."

Sal joked that the writers of the show had missed a great opportunity to present to the *Columbo* audience a pair of "actors who lost the Oscar on the same night, hamming it up and trying to upstage one another."

The guest shot on Falk's program was followed with the role of Johnny Danello in "The Adventure of the Wayward Witness" on the series *The Adventures of Ellery Queen,* broadcast on ABC and starring David Wayne and Jim Hutton as father-and-son sleuths. Sal's appearance was scheduled to air on January 25, 1976.

Eight nights later he would be on an episode of yet another crime show, *Joe Forrester,* starring Lloyd Bridges not as a plainclothes detective but a uniformed cop who'd been pounding the same beat for years.

Although TV was keeping Sal busy and supplying money, movie roles were not forthcoming. But television was not offering him starring roles, or the kinds of parts he desired that would challenge his talents.

In the meantime, he heard about a comedy that was to open in San Francisco following a successful run in New York.

The play was *P.S. Your Cat Is Dead.*

Written by James Kirkwood, it had opened at New York's Golden Theater in April 1975, produced by Richard Barr, Charles Woodward, and Terry Speigel in cooperation with the Buffalo Studio Arena Theater. A two-act, three-scene comedy, it was directed by Vivian Matalon in New York. The two main characters are Jimmy Zoole and Vito Antonucci.

On New Year's Eve Jimmy walks into his New York loft-apartment that in the past few weeks has been repeatedly burglar-ized by Vito. Among the items stolen was the only copy of a manuscript of a novel that took Jimmy a very long time to write.

Kirkwood envisioned Jimmy as a 38-year-old-actor who has not made it, but hasn't given up trying. The playwright's sketch of Jimmy continued, "In his attempts to achieve success he has kept himself as square as possible." Jimmy has jumped through hoops and played "good dog" for "about as long as he can play good dog without turning rabid."

When Jimmy unexpectedly finds his girlfriend, Kate, in the apartment, both are startled—Kate because she is surprised by him coming in, Jimmy because he thought that he'd caught the repeat burglar in the act. Neither knows that the burglar is, indeed, pres-ent and hiding under the bed. He'd entered the loft through a sky-light.

"At twenty-seven," Kirkwood wrote of Vito "he's been through more than his share of scrapes. Humpy, in an off-beat scroungy tom-cattish way, Vito would do and has done anything to get by. Despite a tacky life and his wiseguy toughness, he is an optimist, a part-time romantic and a soft touch. He is also a congenial fuck-up—but with a flair and his own unique style."

Vito also happens to be bisexual.

When Vito is at last discovered by Jimmy, he is made prisoner by the man he has made a career of burglarizing. Quite naturally, Jimmy seeks revenge. He does so by stripping Vito half-naked, tying him up, and strapping him to the sink. That done, Jimmy relishes taunting his captive with offers of chicken and Coca-Cola, snapping his photo and inviting Vito to "make yourself at home." When he puts a hand on Vito's shoulder, Vito jerks away and exclaims, "Don't touch me. My body is a temple."

Jimmy then decides that because Vito has stolen and thrown away Jimmy's novel, Vito must provide material for a new book. Vito is going to give an "in-depth interview" in which Vito will "spill the beans on what it's like to be you."

Jimmy learns that Vito might not be as bad a guy as he seems. Vito sees an opportunity to make a friend, maybe have some sex, and not have to live on the streets.

When the play ran for a month in Buffalo before moving to

Broadway, the audiences took the play for what Kirkwood intended—"an entertainment about two losers who meet at a certain
crucial time in their lives." Will they help each other? Can people
at the midpoint in their lives change directions if the careers they
have been following no longer satisfy them?

New York audiences and critics found more in the play than Kirkwood intended. It was not meant to be a play "proselytizing for
bisexuality," Kirkwood wrote. "Vito, the hustler-burglar, uses his
sexuality as a commodity with which to trade in return for a place
to stay, clothes, food, and, most importantly, companionship."

For the play to work, Kirkland wrote, Jimmy and Vito "must be
warm and vulnerable; if the audience does not have a love affair
with both of them, the play is damaged. Most of all, it is a play to
have fun with and Jimmy and Vito are characters that should touch
the audience."

With the play being brought to San Francisco, the producers
needed a new Vito. Believing the part could have been written with
him in mind, Sal read for the role. The producers and directors
immediately wanted him. Kirkwood had doubts, but he deferred to
their judgment.

They did not regret it.

"Sexy Sal Mineo!" exclaimed theater critic Bob Kiggins. "Mineo
is wonderful as the wisecracking intruder, only to find himself the
victim of sweet revenge and rather bizarre fantasies. In fact, Mineo
all but steals the show with his outlandish, marvelously antic gestures, his facile facial contortions and his robust delivery. Mineo's
nimble, engaging performance calls for a visit to the Montgomery
Playhouse."

Writers on the theater and other newspaper reporters saw Sal as
a good story: The actor who was in a slump and possibly washed
up makes a comeback. When requests for interviews came he gladly
granted them, but made sure that they would be conducted in his
favorite restaurants with the interviewers picking up the check.

Over lunch at Bardelli's, Bob Kiggins (of the rave review) found
Sal less "the anti-hero in person than one might expect after all those
snarling, rebellious, off-beat film roles." Sal came to the table "carefully turned out in a conservative suit and tie" and proved to be "a
polite, articulate, and sensitive man."

Kiggins inquired about Sal's choice of film roles, particularly those that had imposed on him the nickname Switchblade Kid.

"I find that kind of person fascinating," Sal answered. "They exist and they have an effect on us. I like the underdog. People I find attractive do not throw in the towel. Besides, demented roles are the best. You can do the most with them."

Writer Jeremy Hughes of *In Touch* magazine found the star of *P.S. Your Cat Is Dead* to be, as the title of the article stated, "Sal Mineo, the Eternal Original."

Hughes's account of his talk with Sal was unusual because it dealt with an aspect of Sal's character that never found expression in fan magazines. Much of the article dealt with Sal's lifelong interest in fine art. The article began, "Cruising the back alleys of late Renaissance Rome, Baroque artist Michelangelo Merisi da Caravaggio, in search of pretty street boys for models (or whatever) would have found his ideal in an archetypical Sal Mineo: tousled black ringlets, darkly vulnerable eyes, poutily sensual lips, sleekly hairless body. And the present-day Sal Mineo delights in this notion, exclaiming, 'He's one of my favorite artists! I love his work!' "

Sal described having posed nude for painter Harold Stevenson. A gigantic reclining male figure titled "The New Adam" was an oil on canvas in nine sections, eight feet high by 39 feet in length, done in 1962–63. Sal explained that he was in Paris and saw a little painting that he liked. He asked the gallery owner if he had any more of the artist's work. He didn't, but he gave Sal the painter's phone number. "I thought he was going to be French," Sal continued, "but it turned out he was from Oklahoma and was living in Paris. We got to be friends and he asked me to pose for him."

The conversation about art and artists reminded Sal of meeting Salvador Dali at a party. "We talked awhile," he recalled, "and Dali said, 'I must do your eyes. I love your eyes. Could we set up a sitting?' " It never happened, but a couple of years later Sal went to a Dali showing at the Huntington Hartford Gallery in New York and was surprised by people saying to him, "We just love what Dali did with you." Among the paintings on display was one that might have been of Sal, but, he said, "I just don't know for sure."

Hughes's interview and the dinner he was buying were interrupted several times by fans asking for Sal's autograph. During their conversation Sal smoked Kool Filter King cigarettes. His leather shirt had three buttons opened. Knuckle-covering silver rings flashed in the light. From a gold chain around his neck hung a gold pendant watch. Looking at it anxiously and noting that he was due back at the theater, he said, "I gotta go. They'll be freaking."

"Then he shrugged into his long brown leather coat, shook hands warmly, and was gone," Hughes wrote, "followed by many, many eyes."

In *Vito* he played a character who was not far from the Sal Mineo who had found himself scrambling to put a roof over his head, keep up his wardrobe, and eat regularly, while looking for companionship through casual sex. As in L.A. and New York, opportunities to pick up appealing young men abounded in San Francisco's bars. If he was in the mood for sex with overtones of danger he could find partners on streets where rough hustlers plied their trade.

While playing Vito on stage Sal recognized that it was quite possible that if Josephine Mineo had not placed her troublesome son in dancing and acting classes Salvatore Mineo, Jr., could have drifted into a life like Vito Antonucci's. He might well have grown up to be humpy in an offbeat, scroungy, tom-cattish way, doing anything just to survive in a tacky life of wise-guy toughness. Instead of having become a part-time romantic and congenial fuckup with a flair and his own unique style, he was starring in a hit play. The roller coaster was heading up again.

When the producers announced that *P.S. Your Cat Is Dead* would move to Los Angeles, Sal told an interviewer, "My gypsy days will soon be over. I'm finished with traveling the world. On January 10 I'll be 37 years old. Life is short, and I want to feel I've given my all, met it head-on, tackled it full force."

He was feeling optimistic and better about himself than he had in a long time. He was now a hit in a show that was going to the place where everyone who'd written him off would have to grant Sal Mineo all the attention and respect due a star.

fifteen

———

It's a Mystery

Always on the lookout for a property with the potential for a film with an edge to it, Sal had read a novel titled *McCaffrey*. Written by Charles Gorham, it was about a hustler and a prostitute who fall in love with each other. Sal saw in it a story of hope and redemption. As usual, he struggled to raise money to make it. To assist in the effort, he'd formed a partnership with 41-year-old William Belasco. A producer and former talent agent, he'd packaged the TV hit series *Batman* and *The Green Hornet*. Among his clients were Pat Boone, Frankie Avalon, Chuck Connors, and Fabian. As executive producer with Russell Thatcher and Walter Selzer, he'd just completed a film for 20th Century-Fox, *The Last Hard Men*, starring James Coburn.

While Sal was in San Francisco cavorting and wisecracking as Vito every night on the Montgomery Playhouse stage, Bill Belasco had been working in L.A. to line up financing for *McCaffrey*. The deal came together just as *P.S. Your Cat Is Dead* was wrapping up its run in the city by the bay and preparing to move to L.A.'s Westwood Playhouse. On Westwood Boulevard between Wilshire and Sunset, the theater was only a few minutes drive in Sal's secondhand blue Chevelle from his home.

Owned by attorney Marvin Mitchelson, the two-story garden-type apartment complex with a carport for each tenant was just off

Sunset at 8563 Holloway Drive in West Hollywood. It was in the heart of an area favored by gays. Sal had been using it as base of operations, professional and personal, for three years. His one-bedroom was considerably less commodious and inviting than the houses in which he'd thrown parties for the Hollywood A list. While its furnishings were barely a cut above the items he'd rented from Crazy Nate, they were adequate to the needs of a bachelor who spent little time there as he chased roles to fund his day-to-day needs and his projects. The apartment rented for $75 a month.

A photographer who visited it to discuss Sal posing nude in a centerfold and several-page spread for *Playgirl* magazine, Bob Seidman, described the place as funky, warm, and loaded with candles. Because Sal had admired Burt Reynolds's courage for posing naked in *Cosmopolitan*, but with a hand strategically placed to cover his groin, Sal had decide it would be fun to be nude in a magazine that was ostensibly intended to be the women's answer to *Playboy*, yet had become a favorite of gays. Seidman found Sal's apartment "the kind of place where you could put your feet on the coffee table and rap until three in the morning."

Should such a rap session with a young man lead Sal to propose a more intimate activity, there was a king-size bed. While walls of the living room were decorated with Chagall and Dali lithographs and framed posters of Sal Mineo movies, the walls of the bedroom were hung with photographs of good-looking, naked, muscular men and a painting of a young boy who had just slit his wrists. Tables within easy reach of the bed were piled with gay pornographic magazines.

When Sal was in residence there were no parties as in the old days. "There was never any rowdiness," said neighbor Roy Evans. "Sal was always very, very quiet."

If Sal entertained in the apartment, his guest was usually a friend such as Michael Mason or Elliott Mintz. Occasionally there would be dinner for two with an attractive boy prior to a night or perhaps only an hour in the bedroom.

When business was to be discussed over a meal it would be served in a classy restaurant such as Chasen's or The Palm. At the latter on Wednesday, February 11, 1976, Sal dined with Bill Belasco to celebrate closing the deal for financing for *McCaffrey*. Like its parent restaurant at Second Avenue and 45th Street in New York, The Palm on Santa Monica Boulevard offered the finest steaks and lobsters, priced accordingly, in a harried ambience of rushing waiters and people jammed together in close quarters and trying to be heard over the noise of their own combined voices.

In Belasco Sal had at last found someone in the movie business who could see beyond Sal Mineo the actor and discern a film director. Bill's interest in show business was genetic. His father, Leon Belasco, had been an orchestra leader who became a movie actor, and his mother's family owned a chain of theaters in Maryland and Virginia. Bill Belasco had become an agent after he read an article in *Esquire* that told how Leland Hayward had sold his agency to MCA and became a Broadway producer. Bill saw himself carving out a career as a producer by starting as an agent. In rather short order he owned Progressive Management Corp., which he sold in 1968 to become the producer he always wanted to be. Among his most recent movie successes was *They Only Kill Their Masters* with James Garner and Katharine Ross. He was excited about working with Sal.

Sal was happy to finally have a project in the works and pleased to be bringing Vito-the-bisexual-burglar to L.A. and not having to worry about what the movers and shakers in the movie business thought about him being identified by the public as a gay actor. Returning to Holloway Drive after an exhilarating discussion of plans for the film, he looked forward to tomorrow.

He was to dine out again, but not to talk business. He'd be seeing Michael Mason before going to a rehearsal of *P.S. Your Cat Is Dead* in its new venue. If all this were not enough reason to be in a good mood, Courtney Burr was flying to Southern California to move in with Sal during the L.A. run of the play.

Sal was up early, mindful that Thursday, February 12, was the forty-third anniversary of his parents' wedding. It was also the birthday of Abraham Lincoln, the only U.S. President to have had his portrait painted by Sal Mineo.

Had Sal taken the time to look at "On This Date in History" in a newspaper he would have learned that Lincoln and Charles Darwin, proponent of the theory of evolution, had been born on the same day. On February 12, 1554, the heads of Lady Jane Gray and her husband Guilford Dudley had been lopped off at the Tower of London on orders from Jane's cousin, Queen Mary. It was also the day that director Franco Zeffirelli was born (1923), as was the English poet and composer Thomas Campion (1567). And on February 12, 1924, Paul Whiteman's "jazz" orchestra premiered George Gershwin's "Rhapsody in Blue."

How Sal spent most of February 12 is not known, except that at some point he got a call from Michael Mason telling him that he wouldn't be able to keep their dinner date. As a result, Sal showed up at the Westwood Playhouse for rehearsal a little early.

The role of Jimmy was being played by Keir Dullea. In him the producers had found the right actor, although Keir was short of Jimmy's age by seven years. Born on May 20, 1936, in Greenwich Village, he'd been to two colleges before taking up acting in stock and repertory companies. He'd made his New York stage debut in the 1956 production of *Sticks and Bones*. He broke into films as a disturbed juvenile delinquent in 1961 in *The Hoodlum Priest*, and drew critical acclaim as another troubled youth in 1963 in *David and Lisa*. Film stardom came in the role of Dave, an astronaut fighting a computer named HAL in *2001: A Space Odyssey* in 1968. Two years later, Keir debuted on Broadway as a blind man in the comedy *Butterflies Are Free*.

When Sal arrived for rehearsal, Keir found him in "tremendous spirits."

The run-throughs went well and ended a little after 9:00 P.M. Dullea said good night to Sal as Sal got into his Chevelle to go home.

In her bedroom seated at a desk overlooking the carport area when Sal arrived at around 9:30 was nine-year-old Monica Merrem. She heard a man shout, "Oh, no! Oh, my God. No! Help me, please." Looking out the window, she watched a white man running away and guessed that he'd hurt whoever had shouted for help.

Roy Evans also heard someone cry for help in the carport area. He raced from his apartment to the alleyway and found a man on the ground behind a garage. He was on his left side, curled into a fetal position and bleeding. Evans recognized him and gasped, "Sal, my God!"

Turning Sal onto his back, Evans saw the left side of his shirt soaked with blood. Sal's face was ashen. His breathing was shallow and labored. Bending over him, Evans desperately tried artificial respiration by blowing into Sal's mouth.

By now the carport area was filling with people. Security guard Stephen Gustafson saw a white man with dirty blond or brown hair running away like a bat out of hell. Scott Hughes had the impression the man was Italian or Mexican. Hughes watched as the fleeing figure got into what appeared to be a yellow Toyota and sped away with headlights off. Somebody said, urgently, "Call an ambulance." Sal gave a long breath and Evans knew he was beyond the help of anyone.

In the tangle of towns, villages, and neighborhoods that had over the years become inextricably part of the City of Angels, the drawing of lines of jurisdiction between numerous police agencies had resulted in 8563 Holloway Drive falling under the aegis of the Los Angeles County Sheriff's Department. When several of its deputies and a couple of detectives arrived, they found $21 in bills in the left pocket of Sal's jacket. In the right was a yellow metal pocket watch with chain. A white metal ring was on his left index finger. Next to him on the ground were his glasses, a clipboard with notes he'd taken at the rehearsal, a package of cupcakes, and the keys to his car. Coins in the amount of 85 cents were found under his body.

One of the detectives said, "We know it's not robbery. It looks like whoever did it knew precisely what they were doing. It's a mystery."

sixteen

File No. 76-1953

A grim-faced paramedic of the Los Angeles Fire Department noted that Sal Mineo had been pronounced dead at 9:55 P.M., apparently as the result of a single stab wound to the middle of the chest. The case report prepared by the paramedic noted the "homicide" had been committed in an "alley" between carports R7 and R6 at the rear of apartment 1 at 2130 hours (9:30 P.M.) on 2-12-76 by "unknown person(s)."

When Sal's body was removed to the morgue of the Los Angeles County Coroner at 1104 North Mission Road for an autopsy, the case report number was 76-1953. The postmortem performed by Deputy Medical Examiner Dr. Manuel R. Breton found the immediate cause of death to be a "massive hemorrhage" due to "stab wound" to the chest "perforating the heart." The death was certified a homicide. ("Homicide" is the taking of a human life by another human. The word "murder" is a legal one meaning the "unlawful" taking of a human life. The act is charged by a prosecutor and if taken to trial must be proved beyond a reasonable doubt.)

Sal's physical statistics were recorded at autopsy as male Caucasian, medium complexion, 144 pounds, height: 68 inches, black hair, brown eyes, no surgical wounds or tattoos or other deformities, fresh abrasion of the left gluteal region, and a small hemorrhage of the subcutaneous tissue of the scalp. These abrasions were attributed to Sal falling to the ground.

Removed from the body were specimens of kidney, liver, stomach, bile, and urine. Also excised to be preserved was the stab wound of the skin and heart. This was done because the knife used to murder Sal had not been found at the scene. The chief medical examiner at this time was Dr. Thomas Noguchi. In a book dealing with controversial murder cases, *Coroner at Large,* coauthored by Joseph DiMona and published in 1982, he explained, "When a stab wound causes a fatal injury, we always examine that wound for several characteristics such as length, width, thickness, single-edged blade or double, sharp or dull. By surgical procedure we also examine the wound layer by layer. In effect we create what I call a 'negative cast' which is the wound itself and which is preserved in its surrounding tissues in formalin. Our goal is to provide a precise means of identifying the murder weapon, if it is recovered, by matching the wound with the knife."

Dr. Breton's examination also found intramuscular injection sites (right and left gluteal) and in peripheral arteries. The two punctures in Sal's buttocks may be attributed to testosterone shots. According to Michael Mason, two days before the murder he and Sal had gone to their doctor's office for injections of the male hormone to assure they wouldn't suffer from flagging masculinity. "Sal was depressed," Mason said, "because he didn't have it [the sexual energy] to screw around any more."

The presence of injection sites in peripheral arteries suggested that Sal might have been abusing drugs.

Nothing about Sal Mineo's life and death has proven more controversial than the question of his attitude toward illegal drugs.

That he smoked marijuana and had dabbled in LSD is not in dispute. The issue has been whether he regularly took cocaine and/ or heroin because he was an addict. His defenders have been as emphatic in stating that he did not as they have been steadfast in denying that Sal was homosexual, pointing out that he'd had sex with numerous women but overlooking the fact that in the last years of his life he had been only with men.

Others described Sal as a heavy user of cocaine. In *Laid Bare,* John Gilmore wrote that Sal was in a "tailspin" in which the

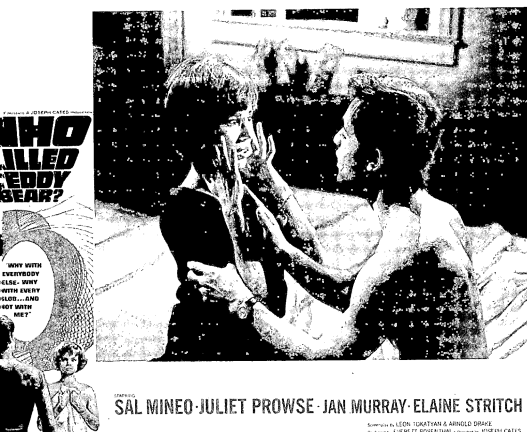

...by card for the controversial and provocative 1965 film *Who Killed Teddy Bear?* Sal
...med that his role as the sexually frustrated busboy who stalks disco dancer Juliet Prowse
...him on Hollywood's "weirdo list." AUTHOR'S COLLECTION/MAGNA PICTURES CORPORATION.

MOE WEISE and PHILLIP GITTELMAN PRESENT
JOHN HERBERT'S

FORTUNE & MEN'S EYES

STARRING
DON JOHNSON

Directed
by
SAL MINEO

CORONET THEATRE · Reservations 65

STAGE 73

KENNETH WAISSMAN and MAXINE FOX present

SAL MINEO'S

FORTUNE
AND
MEN'S
EYES

JOHN HERBERT

with
MICHAEL GREER

MARK   BARTHOLOMEW   JEREMY   JOE
SHANNON   MIRO, Jr.   STOCKWELL   DORSEY

GEORGE RYLAND   JESSE DEANE

Setting and Costumes by   Lighting by
ALAN KIMMEL   KEN BILLINGTON

Production Stage Manager   Special Sound by
GIGI CASCIO   GARY HARRIS

Jimmy:

In memory of your friendship and inspiration,
I dedicate this production to you.

Sal

Playbill covers for the Los
Angeles and New York
productions of *Fortune and
Men's Eyes*, which Sal ded-
icated to James Dean.
AUTHOR'S COLLECTION.

JAMES DEAN
1931–1955

lathering up for a publicity photo promoting the Los Angeles production of *Fortune and n's Eyes,* which plays out its most dramatic moment in a prison shower room.

The cast of the Los Angeles production of *Fortune and Men's Eyes* with (left to right) Don Johnson, Gary Tigerman, Sal Mineo, and Robert Redding. AUTHOR'S COLLECTION.

Sal in director's mode outs[ide] the Coronet Theater in Los Angeles. AUTHOR'S COLLECTIO[N]

Sal and Don Johnson, who would go on to TV stardom in *Miami Vice* and *Nash Bridges*, in the brutally climactic rape scene of *Fortune and Men's Eyes*. AUTHOR'S COLLECTION.

al at the time of his death. In February 1976, the 37-year-old Sal was scheduled to open at Los ngeles's Westwood Playhouse as the bisexual burglar in the comedy *P.S. Your Cat Is Dead* hen he was stabbed in the alleyway behind his West Hollywood apartment. / AUTHOR'S COLLECTION.

L.A. County Sheriff's Department detectives photographing Sal's sheet-covered body at the crime scene.

ıl Mineo Knifed to Death in Hollywood

.LYWOOD, Feb. 13 (UPI)
Mineo, the actor who was
· nominated for Oscars,
abbed to death last night
returned home from re-
·ng for a new play.
·iff's homicide detectives
·oned apartment neigh-
today. One unofficial
; said they were checking
'drug angle" in the case.
Mineo, who was 37 yea⁻
vas felled with a si
thrust to the chest
arport area of
vood apartr
he lived
t Strip.
core
an

Mιı·o in movie ˈ
·ι· a Cause 'Rebel Wiᵗʰ
Dry·
said ι
·s apar.
white n.
ınd wearin₆
·een fleeing t·
·ives questione·.
· hope of gettin.
ption.
Mineo's wallet was ·
on his body, but inve·
; said he could have bee·
resisting a robbery at-

cried out, "Help! help! Oh
·od!" before he died and
·ssa·lant may have fled in
f capture.
   Mineo was returning
the Westwood Playhóuse.
· he was rehearsing for
·lay, "P. S. Your Cat is
" when he apparently was
shed in the garage area.

·roadway Debut at 11

   Mineo made his Broad-
·debut at the age of 11 in
Rose Tattoo" and went on
·opear in more than 20
·s and dozens of television
·s.
   became a teen-agers' idol
·56 when he was seen as
· the switchblade-wielding,
·otic juvenile delinquent in
ames Dean movie, "Rebel
·ut a Cause." Young peo-
: the time seemed to iden-
·ith Plato, and the aura of
·lering, sensuous boyishness
·the then 17-year-old actor
·ht to the role won Mr.
· an Academy Award nom-
·ın.
   was nominated for his
·d Academy Award for best
·rting actor in 1961 for his

---

performance as Dov Landau,
the Nazi concentration camp
survivor turned Zionist terror-
ist In Palestine in "Exodus."

In TV Series

   Mr. Min· recently appeared
in TV ·   of the "Ellery
Queen   Forrester" se-
rie·   last stage
                  San Fran-
                  ·es Kirk-
                  ·r Cat·
                        ·l a
                        ·at

a g·
was d·
school ·
ker. He la
pher Colum·
never receive·

   When he wa·
largely to keep
street, his mother
signed ·him up for ·
class. Two years la·
Broadway producer
Crawford, looking for two ·
ian-American children for Te·
nessee Williams's "The Rose
Tattoo," spotted him in dancing
school and asked him to recite
the line, "The goat is. in the
yard."
   For a year, the boy led a goat
across the stage of the Martin
Beck Theater and recited his
single line. Then he became the
understudy for the young acter
plaving the Prince in "The King
and I" and later succeeded him
in the role.
   Mr. Mineo's first film appearance was ·in "Seven Bridges
to Cross," playing Tony Curtis
as a boy, in 1955. Later movies
included the title role in "The
Gene Krupa Story." "The

Young Don't Cry." "Dino"
(again as a young delinquent),
"Crime in the Streets," "Somebody Up There Likes Me" and
"Giant." He was one of the
major simians in 1971's "Escape
From the Planet of the Apes."

   In 1969, he directed "Fortune
and Men's Eyes," which had ·
successful engagement in Los
Angeles before it began a run
here. The play, concerning prison life and including an onstage nude homosexual rape
scene, led Clive Barnes to comment in this newspaper. "If this

---

does sound like the kind of play
you'd like, you need a psychiatrist a lot more than you need
a theater ticket."
   The play had a successful
run, however, and Mr. Mineo
later directed a screen version
filmed in Canada.
   At the height of his success
in the 1950's, Mr. Mineo bought
his family a $200,000 home in
Mamaroneck, N.Y. from which
his mother directed the answering of some 4,000 letters a
week from Mineo fans. Mr. Mineo, described by a friend yesterday as "a bit of a loner,"
was a bachelor. He is survived
by his mother, a sister, Sarina,
and two brothers, Victor and
Michael.

Seek a Blond Man in Mineo Slaying

INDEX TO FEATURES

·nited Press International reports of Sal Mineo's death in the New York
DAILY NEWS AND NEW YORK TIMES ON FEBRUARY 13, 1976.

SAL MINEO
1939-1976

The July 1976 edition of the magazine *Rona Barret's Hollywood* published a tribute to Sal Mineo. The photograph shows him as the busboy in *Who Killed Teddy Bear?*
AUTHOR'S COLLECTION.

money he'd earned "was funneled into dope." He wrote that Sal told him he thought a lot about suicide, but he was too chicken to do it. Gilmore quoted Sal as having said, "I'm looking for the fast combination [of drugs] that'll do it for me."

A woman who knew Sal as the result of her relationship with Michael Mineo said that in the 1970s Sal "was getting really weird," apparently because of drug use.

The most persuasive evidence that Sal had not become an addict was that he continued to get roles on television shows and that he'd been appearing every night in *P.S. Your Cat Is Dead* in San Francisco, whose producers were bringing him to L.A. to continue the role. Had Sal been abusing drugs, all of this activity would have been most unlikely. Nor was there anything in Sal's life to suggest that he had an addictive personality.

Further evidence that he was not an addict lies in the fact that those who investigated his murder as being possibly drug-related came to a dead end. Sal certainly could not have been a drug pusher, as some suggested. When he died he was living in a $75-a-month apartment, driving a used car, and had 21 bucks in his pocket and roughly $8,000 in the bank.

"If Sal was a drug dealer," said Tom Korman, "he was the poorest one I ever heard of."

Did Sal Mineo occasionally dabble in the "recreational" use of cocaine? Probably. But so did a large number of people in Hollywood and the theater, as well as almost every occupation in the country in a decade when "coke" was fashionable and available everywhere, especially in the discos and bars that were at the heart of the gay world.

Might Sal have owed money to someone who'd supplied him cocaine? If so, whoever that person was would probably have been told to "join the line" of debt collectors. Would a supplier who had been told to "fuck off" be so furious as to plunge a knife into Sal's chest? Maybe, but disgruntled dealers have a strong inclination to settle such disputes with guns.

Could there have been someone else with a reason to kill Sal Mineo adjacent to the carport of his house? When detectives of the L.A. Sheriff's Office looked around Sal's apartment, they thought they'd discovered the motive behind his murder. A glance at the

pictures of naked men on walls and gay pornographic magazines in
the bedroom cried out to them in cop lingo:

"This is a fag murder."

On the night of her 43rd wedding anniversary, Josephine Mineo had
been a widow for two and a half years. When the Mamaroneck
"mansion" had to be given up, she and Big Sal had moved to 83
West Street in Harrison, New York. The member of the Los Angeles
Fire Department who'd been given the terrible task of notifying her
of her youngest son's death reached her there by phone early in the
morning of Friday the 13th.

Remembering that dreadful morning, Victor Mineo said, "I received a phone call from a police officer who told me that Sal was
killed. I just couldn't believe it."

The heartbreaking chore of bringing Sal's body home for a funeral
mass and burial fell to Victor and Michael. The services were scheduled for February 17. When Victor and Michael took off from Los
Angeles International Airport on Sunday evening with their
brother's coffin in the cargo bay, the *Hollywood Reporter* noted in
a story by Gerry Levin that investigators had set up a special phone
number (974-4141) to receive information on the murder.

The article quoted Sheriff's Detective Dan Tankersley. He and his
partner Ed Pia were at the head of the investigation. "We're questioning many people both inside and out of the entertainment industry," he said. "We don't think robbery was a motive because his
wallet didn't have a lot of money in it."

The detectives had descriptions of a possible suspect. At the murder scene they'd been told of a fleeting youth with long blond hair
or that they should be seeking a white man in his twenties, of medium height and build with wavy or curly brown or black hair.

Sal's remains were taken to the O'Neill funeral home in Mamaronek to be prepared for viewing in an open casket, as the family
had done for Big Sal. They apparently didn't know Sal had been
upset by that. More than 20 years after he'd found himself teased
and shunned by neighborhood kids when they learned his father
made coffins, Sal was sensitive on that subject. He told friends that
when the time came for his funeral he did not want a coffin with

an open lid. He wanted no one looking at him dead. "Bury me," he said, "and then have a big party."

His funeral was not exactly the party he'd hoped for. It was more in the style of send-offs that had been given to previous movie stars. There was a mixture of family and friends, and a throng of fans and the morbidly curious. Among the friends were David Cassidy, Desi Arnaz, Jr., Michael Greer, and Nick Ray. Honorary pallbearers were Courtney Burr, Elliott, Mintz, and Michael Mason.

The first night of the wake, there was an unpleasant exchange between Mason and Victor, to whom Mason was a reminder of a part of Sal's life the family had difficulty in accepting. It was as if the family blamed Mason and others for Sal's becoming known as a homosexual and for the estrangement that resulted. When Victor asked about Sal's money, Michael replied angrily, "It's too bad you didn't know him [Sal] well enough to find these answers yourself. But I see why he didn't like you or have anything to do with you in recent years. He had no money. He had nothing. Some clothes, a table, some books, and that's it."

Later, Mason had a bitter conversation with Josephine. Since the collapse of Sal's career that resulted in the loss of the Mamaroneck "mansion" and Sal's financial support of the family, she worked in a health-food store, the Mamaroneck Nutrition Center on the town's main street. When Mason called on her at the store to express his condolences and to talk about Sal, Josephine told him, "You didn't know him. You didn't work with him. You didn't go places with him. You weren't with him. Blood is thicker than water. My son Michael, he suffers. My daughter, Sarina, she suffers. Her brother Victor, he suffers. I work here six days a week. I have to. There are some things better if you don't think about them. I can't talk about it at all."

Rather than a party celebrating Sal's life, his funeral marked the beginning of a struggle for how Sal would be remembered.

For the Mineos he was the "Junior" they carried in their minds and hearts.

For Mason, Elliott Mintz, Courtney Burr III, Joe Bonelli, and others who had populated the world of movies, television, and the stage, he was the Sal Mineo whose name went above the title on theater marquees and screens. He was the Sal who had discovered his sexual nature and then refused to deny it, even if it meant the ruin of his career.

The family that could not accept the Sal Mineo represented by Mason, Mintz, and Burr gave a warm welcome to Jill Haworth. With tears streaking her beautiful face, she leaned into the coffin to hug the handsome young lover she'd known. She found a man whom she could barely recognize. She sobbed, "It doesn't look like you. They did such a terrible makeup job."

When Michael Greer arrived at the church for the funeral service, the actor who'd played Queenie in *Fortune and Men's Eyes* in Los Angeles and New York gazed at the large crowd lining the street. "Well, my God," he gasped, "it looks like Garland or Presley died." he added, "A star is being buried today. It's a standing-room-only smash funeral."

Inside Holy Trinity Roman Catholic where barely three years earlier Sal had given a eulogy for Big Sal sat 250 mourners. The funeral mass was celebrated by the Reverend Gerard DiSenso. Sarina's husband, Charles "Chip" Meyers, eulogized Sal as "a special and rare person, a gentleman" whose sensitivity and understanding affected everyone he met. "It was a happy irony of his life that he was so very different a person than the roles he created," he said. "Those who love him knew he loved life and that he lived with courage, abandon, with humor and grace. His art, what he created, will always stand. Nothing can take it away from him."

Sal was carried from the church in a gleaming brown coffin as a misty rain fell. He was buried beside his father in Gate of Heaven cemetery. In graves around them lay some of the most famous people in the history of sports, show business, journalism, and New York politics. Headstones marked the final resting places of Babe Ruth, Fred Allen, Anna Held, Broadway columnist Dorothy Kilgallen, and a colorful mayor of New York, James J. "Jimmy" Walker.

He probably would have been pleased to note that interred nearby was a genuine 1930s gangster by the name of Dutch Schultz.

Tributes to Sal poured out everywhere.

In the essay "Plato Dies," in *The New Republic*, Roger Rosenblatt saw Sal's death as a fate ordained by his movie roles and as "a bloody, cathartic escape" from having been typecast as The Switch-blade Kid. "Sal Mineo died again, stabbed outside his West Holly-wood apartment house," he wrote. "This time there were no searchlights hailing the American teenager gone berserk—only one man cutting up another in a grown-up world that deals with such realities calmly."

In *Esquire* Peter Bogdanovich sounded the same theme. "That Sal was stabbed to death in an alley was so horribly in keeping with so many of the movie deaths he died that its bitter irony might have amused him. After all, he had a black sense of humor and firm grasp of the absurd—a teenage symbol in his late thirties who never had a childhood. To know that newspapers plastered his murder in a banner headline across the country would probably have made him drop his head to his side and snore: 'A lot of good that does me.' "

If Sal had been able to read these observations, he might have pointed out that in *Rebel Without a Cause, Giant, Cheyenne Autumn, The Longest Day,* and *Who Killed Teddy Bear?* he died from bullets, and that in his last theatrical film, *Escape From the Planet of the Apes,* he'd been strangled by a gorilla.

Keir Dullea said, "I've never been so shocked by this kind of senseless tragedy in my life. It's difficult to describe that night. My initial reaction was that I didn't want to do the play. Then I went to the opposite extreme. I decided that the only way to restore sense to all the senselessness was to pay tribute to this guy. I had never known Sal before but I got so I loved him. He thought this play would be the start of a new career."

Milton Kaselas, director of *P.S. Your Cat Is Dead,* said, "He was always a gentleman, always with a joke, and never balked at direc-tion." Kaselas announced that a replacement would be found to play Vito and the show would go on, dedicated to Sal.

For the benefit of so many of the people who knew Sal in Hol-lywood who were not able to go to the funeral, Sal's partner in *McCaffrey,* Bill Belasco, announced that he would be the host in his home for a memorial service on Sunday, February 22. Scores of A-list people let him know they would attend. The night before, Be-lasco dined with friends at The Palm and recalled having been there with Sal the night before Sal was killed. Feeling shaky from too many drinks, he asked one of the waiters to drive him home. On the way, the waiter lost control of the car. It slammed into a tree. Although the waiter was unhurt, Belasco was seriously injured. He died five days later.

When Elliott Mintz learned of Belasco's death he recalled that during one of Sal's tries at making psychic contact with James Dean, Sal had used a Ouija board. Elliott remembered Sal reporting that Dean told him a friend would die in a traffic accident.

In the motion-picture enclaves in the City of Angels where, as Frank Capra had observed, the governing emotion was nervousness, the murder of Sal Mineo came as the latest in a recent rash of killings of show-business personalities. The previous July, actress Barbara Colby and actor John Kierman had been shot to death as they left a yoga class in Venice. On January 19, popular publicist Robert Yaeger had been found shot to death. Less than two weeks later, Bill Brownell, secretary of the Hollywood Foreign Press Association, which gave out the Golden Globe awards, was murdered. And two days before Sal was killed, Vincent Donahue, assistant executive secretary of Actors Equity, was found stabbed to death in his New York hotel room.

Five days before Sal's death there had been a frightening incident in Beverly Hills. On February 7 while entering their apartment house, a young couple had been robbed at gunpoint by three young thugs.

Now whoever killed Sal Mineo was at large and presumably still in possession of the knife he'd lunged into Sal's chest.

A possibility that was espoused recalled that in doing research for *Fortune and Men's Eyes* Sal had visited prisons. Was it possible that an inmate he'd met had gotten out of jail, looked Sal up, and tried to rob him? It was also remembered that he spent some time with the Hell's Angels; perhaps one of them had killed him. Why not? Everyone knew that the motorcycle group was infamous for being violent.

If none of those theories held up, and because the detectives on the Mineo case had ruled out robbery, what motive remained?

Because Sal was known to be gay and was assumed to have been involved with drugs, a general frisson of anxiety took on a more particular character in two elements of the Hollywood community that the minders of the film capital's reputation did their best to keep out of the public eye. Rumors spread that Sal's murder was drug-related or connected to his sex life, and possibly both.

While not ruling out a narcotics aspect of the murder, after Sheriff's Detectives Tankersley and Pia entered Sal's apartment on February 12 they were certain of the explanation of Sal's murder. "During the investigation that night," Tankersley said, "we found out that he was homosexual. That opened a whole new field. Is this a disgruntled lover? A prostitute he picked up off the street? Was Sal into bringing home strangers?"

This possibility quickly made its way into the press.

Courtney Burr recalled, "The papers went berserk."

To exploit the homosexual-prostitute angle the press dug into the archives for just such a murder of a gay movie actor that had occurred eight years ago. The "Latin Lover" of silent films and talkies, Ramon Novarro, a closeted homosexual who'd made numberless women jealous of Greta Garbo when he romanced her in *Mata Hari* in 1932 and shocked and thrilled audiences of 1927's *Ben Hur* by appearing half-naked and handling a chariot and four horses in the climactic scene in the epic film, had been brutally murdered on October 30, 1968, at age 69 by a pair of brothers whom he welcomed to his house for sex. They were looking for money, but they left with only a few dollars. The implication of dredging up Novarro's death was that Sal could have picked up a Sunset Strip hustler for sex when what the hustler had in mind was theft. When Sal resisted, he was stabbed.

The more popular sex theory was that Sal probably had broken up with one guy in favor of another and the jealous rejected lover had paid Sal back with a knife in his chest.

To the detectives inside Sal's apartment, incontrovertible evidence that Sal Mineo was homosexual was in piles of gay magazines and the pictures of naked men. He lived alone, so they had to be his. And what about the picture of the kid with the slashed wrists? How about all the leather clothing in his closet? Did these things mean that Sal was into S&M?

On Valentine's Day detectives began knocking on the doors of known gays in the movie business to ask what they might know about Sal Mineo's relationships with men. Was he in the habit of cruising the bars? Did he trawl among the available boys who lined the curbs along the Sunset Strip, Santa Monica Boulevard, and Selma Avenue in downtown Hollywood? Might he have broken up with someone lately? Was he into sadomasochism? What sort of guys did he like? Did he go for ones with long blond hair or curly brown or black? Did Sal pay for sex?

One of those questioned mentioned he knew Sal as a regular at Studio One. "Sometimes he went alone and got lucky," he said, "but he never bought it."

When Elliott Mintz was questioned about his friend's private life, he answered, "He spent a lot of time at home in bed reading books, mostly to find promising ideas for movies or plays."

Asked by a reporter which theory the detectives considered the most promising, the lieutenant in charge of the investigation, Phil Bullington, was noncommittal. He replied, "We can make a logical argument for a variety of motives."

Disgusted by the lurid stories about Sal's debauched lifestyle, Mike Mineo rallied to defend his younger brother. "All his life, no matter what Sal did, people drummed up stories," he said, "He was an innocent, straight person. All he was doing was fighting to be an artist."

On the night of the murder one of the detectives at the scene had said, "It's a mystery."

When Mike's plea on behalf of Sal's reputation was published in *People* on November 8, nine months after Sal cried for help in the alley behind Holloway Drive, it still was.

seventeen

"This Is a Big Deal"

If a character such as Sal Mineo had been created by Richard Levinson, William Link, and Peter Fisher, the brilliant team who had turned Sal's friend Peter Falk into disheveled, cigar-smoking, L.A.P.D. homicide sleuth, Lieutenant Columbo would have solved his murder in two hours, including breaks for commercials. The basic rule of television detective programs requires that the killer be caught and all loose ends tied up. No killer may ever stump the police. Another rule is that the murderer be so impressed with the skill of his or her adversary that he or she is more than happy to confess. This is why detective shows are classified as entertainment. Except on *Columbo,* where the audience is shown the murderer doing the deed, these dramas are a popular constant on television because they ask "Who done it?" and guarantee the viewers that they will be told who did it just in time for a final commercial.

Very few real-life murders are genuine mysteries, and even fewer present detectives with the kind of puzzle that Sal Mineo's murder became for the sleuths who worked the case for the Los Angeles County Sheriff's Office, headed by Peter Pitchess. A general rule in real-life murders is: "If the case isn't cracked within 48 hours it probably will never be solved."

A belief among gays everywhere is that if a killing seems to have the aspects of a "fag murder," the police will be less motivated to solve it than if the victim were heterosexual.

Law enforcement officers vehemently deny the accusation.

Another belief among many serious students of police procedures is that once a theory of a murder has been settled upon, often in the first few minutes of an investigation, the investigators turn a blind eye to possible alternatives. They follow the original view of the crime so implacably that a murder can go unsolved.

This allegation is bitterly rejected by police.

In the case of Sal Mineo, Sheriff Pitchess's stymied investigators found themselves on the receiving end of both allegations. They'd failed to solve Sal's murder, it was said, because they had made up their minds on the night of February 12 that the motive was not robbery and that Sal was the victim of a fag killing. They then refused to consider any other reason.

There is yet another verity in murder cases. If a celebrity is the victim, the public is intensely interested. The story dominates front pages of newspapers and leads the evening news on television. But the longer the case goes unsolved, the faster public interest wanes. The murder slips to inside pages and lower in the newscasts. Eventually it disappears. The effect of this loss of press and public interest results in eased pressure on the authorities. As the case cools, resources assigned to it are shifted to more promising, cost-effective avenues. Eventually, the murder goes into a "cold case" file. Many stay there forever.

When "the Mineo murder," as it was called by press and public, seemed headed in that direction, Sheriff Pitches stated that the investigation remained "active" and had taken his investigators to Nevada, Arizona, Washington, New York, and Florida. Why they had ranged so far and wide was not explained. Part of the problem for lead detective Lt. Phil Bullington and his team in advancing the case was a paucity of information. Witnesses were contradictory. Some said the man running away was white with long, blond hair. Others saw bushy or curly hair.

Most agreed that the man who'd fled the murder scene had gotten into a yellow car, possibly a Toyota.

The announcement of a special phone number set up to collect information had prompted numerous leads. All were pursued. They led nowhere.

Frustrated and angry at the apparent lack of progress, Michael Mason set out to investigate on his own. He and other friends of Sal tried to raise $10,000 to offer as a reward for information. They collected only a few hundred dollars.

Peter Bogdanovich thought he knew why so little was contributed. "In this racket when you're not hot anymore, or when you're cold, you're dead anyway," he said, "so a lot of folks had turned the page on Sal's murder and shrugged. He wasn't up for any picture."

To borrow and paraphrase the passage from the magazine *in* describing gay life in L.A., from the snowy ski slopes of Mt. Baldy to the sunny surf of Santa Monica, from the automated delights of Disneyland to the desert farmlands of San Fernando Valley, from the drag bars of Main Street to the sailor bars of Long Beach, and from the tuxedoed glamour of the Music Center to the hip hangouts of the Sunset Strip, Sal Mineo's murder was yesterday's sensation and there was no reason to be nervous. When fears that somebody might be bent on launching a killing spree either among druggies or in the gay community proved unfounded, the A list breathed a sigh of relief and turned its attention to making deals and sometimes movies.

Whoever stabbed Sal Mineo to death had nothing to do with Hollywood. Yet Sal had been one of them. He'd put a lot of asses into seats. At some point, perhaps, someone might try to raise enough money to sponsor a star for him on the Walk of Fame. There might even be a proposal floated that Sal be honored at the next Academy Awards in some manner. Not with a special Oscar, of course; he hadn't been important enough for that. A commemorative moment might be part of the TV show, perhaps with Natalie Wood or Paul Newman or Brian Keith presenting clips from Sal's movies: *Rebel Without a Cause, Giant, Dino,* and *The Gene Krupa Story,* probably.

Neither the star nor the on-air memorial at the Oscars happened.

A year after Sal had parked his Chevelle in his carport and been met by a man wielding a knife, the killer apparently had gotten away with it. That was too bad. If he had been caught, the murder of Sal Mineo might have made a pretty good TV movie of the week.

*   *   *

At the L.A. Sheriff's Office in May 1977 the investigation of Sal
Mineo's murder was as cold as the unsolved murder of the director
William Desmond Taylor in 1922, the unexplained 1935 death of
actress Thelma Todd, the Beverly Hills rubout of Bugsy Seigel in
1947, and in the same year the torture and butcher-slaying of beautiful would-be film star Elizabeth Short, known as "The Black
Dahlia." The whole-court press to solve the Mineo case was a thing
of the past. Men who'd been assigned to it full-time in February and
March 1976 were eventually needed on more promising cases in the
spring of '77.

If the Mineo case were to come alive, there'd have to be a break
of some kind, perhaps a confession blurted out by someone who'd
been arrested for some other crime, which would be a miracle. More
likely would be a pitch by some guy who'd been collared and was
looking to cut a deal with the district attorney by ratting out someone. Such a thing was possible if Mineo had been killed because of
a drug deal that went bad and the man who'd settled the matter
with a stab to the heart let it slip out to one his pals. There were
also cases on record in which a witness suddenly recalled something.
And it was not out of the question that someone who knew who
killed Sal Mineo would get so troubled about keeping silent that he
had to get it off his chest.

It happened in the Mineo case in May 1977, but the person who
decided to come forward was a woman. Her name was Theresa
Williams. Her husband was Lionel Raymond Williams, a former
pizza deliveryman. The night of February 12 last year, Theresa told
a sheriff's detective, her husband had come home with blood on his
shirt. He explained that he'd just stabbed someone.

As they were watching the news on TV, they heard the report of
the murder of Sal Mineo. According to Theresa, Lionel pointed at
the picture of the movie star on the screen and blurted, "That's the
dude I killed."

In the minds of the detectives cautionary alarms went off. They
wondered why Theresa had waited more than a year to tell her
story. They asked themselves if Theresa had decided to make trouble
for her husband. Such things were not unheard of. If so, why would

she pick a year-old murder to pin on him? Why not a more recent crime?

More puzzling, however, was that in a case in which witnesses had described a white man running from the scene, Lionel Williams was black.

Leery of Theresa's accusation, the detectives asked for more details of Lionel's confession to her that he'd killed Mineo. She answered that her husband told her he'd used a hunting knife that he'd just bought for $5.28. She told them that Lionel had carried it when pulling a string of robberies on the west side.

A check of the criminal files confirmed that there was, indeed, a Lionel Williams. He was 21 years old and had a light complexion. He had a lengthy criminal record. It indicated that his most recent arrest had been in April in Inglewood. He'd been picked up there on several traffic warrants. Routine checking of wanted notices and warrants from the L.A. area and around the country turned up another in Michigan. Williams was wanted for passing a bad check in the sum of $174. He'd been shipped off to the Midwest to face the charge.

Further examination of Williams's rap sheet persuaded sheriffs detectives that Theresa was married to a very bad guy. His record contained a report that he and a male companion had been stopped in a Buick that matched the description of a car that had cut off and stopped another. One of the two men in the Buick had used a ball peen hammer to smash the terrified other driver's windshield and demand money. The men had fled with cash and credit cards. When Williams and his partner were stopped 20 minutes later by police, the officers searched their car and found the credit cards and the hammer. The men were arrested but released. The incident had occurred on February 26, 1976, two weeks after Sal's murder.

Before being released from the L.A. County Jail, Williams had approached a deputy and said, "I want to talk to someone about the Mineo case."

He told a deputy that he'd been in "a dope shooting gallery" and had heard some "blood dudes" talking about having been paid $1,500 to carry out a contract on Sal Mineo because he'd burned them in a drug deal.

Williams's story had been listened to with both skepticism and a suspicion that he might have been involved in the Mineo murder and was laying the groundwork to point to someone else if he were ever accused of it. A deputy was sent to Williams's house to ascertain his whereabouts on the night of February 12, 1976. Williams's mother said that to the best of her recollection her son had been home watching TV. For a brief time Williams had been kept under surveillance, but nothing linked him to the murder beyond the tale he'd told the deputy about having heard talk about a drug dealer's contract on Mineo. The surveillance ended.

With no other evidence that Sal's murder had been drug-related, and certain that robbery wasn't the motive, the investigators had continued in their belief that they had "a fag killing." Theresa Williams's story notwithstanding, they clung to their original theory, hoping, perhaps, that a homosexual version of Theresa would show up one day in a disgruntled mood or suffering from pangs of conscience and spin a story about how a jilted lover or a robbery-minded Sunset Strip hustler had killed Sal Mineo. Or maybe they'd hear how Sal had invited home a starstruck boy to "discover" and put a move on him, only to find that the kid was straight and carried a knife, as little Sal Mineo had carried a fake gun to scare off queers.

Theresa's story had turned up the heat under the Mineo case, but with nothing more to go on to connect Lionel Raymond Williams to the murder the investigation was again relegated to the back burner. Should something come up to rekindle interest in Williams as a suspect, he wasn't going anywhere. He'd been convicted of the bad-check charge and sentenced to ten months. He would be locked up in Michigan's Calhoun County Jail until January 18, 1978.

When Sal visited San Quentin and Riker's Island to find out about men in prison in order to make *Fortune and Men's Eyes* authentic, he learned what it takes to survive as an inmate. He heard about how imperative it was for a new man to quickly establish a reputation as a guy who'd better not be fucked around with, literally and figuratively. For men in prison, as with males of every species on earth, dominance had to be asserted. If a man failed to demonstrate that he was willing and able to defend himself, he would soon find himself pushed around and even enslaved. Short of actually re-sorting to violence, toughness was most easily asserted by pointing to what one did on the outside. By bragging, truthfully or not, of one's toughness on the other side of the walls, a man sent a message that he wasn't to be trifled with on this side. It's called "jailhouse talk."

In October in the Calhoun County Jail, Lionel Williams engaged in it with his cellmate. "I killed a dude a while back," he said. "An actor by the name of Sal Mineo."

The boast was overheard by Deputy Sheriff Ronald Peek. Later, another guard, Albert Lemkuhl, observed similar bragging by Wil-liams. Although the remarks were regarded as jailhouse braggado-cio, they were conveyed to Los Angeles. Sheriff Pitchess responded with a request that a court order be obtained allowing a listening device to be secreted in Williams's cell.

The Mineo murder was taken off the back burner.

With a suspect, at last, Pitchess reconstituted the investigative team to probe every aspect of Lionel Raymond Williams. What they quickly learned was that Williams was an armed robber who had no qualms about resorting to violence. Digging into reports of strong-arm stickups in the West L.A. and Beverly Hills areas, detec-tives followed up on the couple who had been accosted by gunmen as they entered their apartment in February 1976. Shown a mug shot of Williams, they identified him. Victims of other robberies before and after Sal's murder also fingered him. The theory that Sal had been killed because he was gay was abandoned.

Many years later, Detective Dan Tankersley said, "In retrospect, I think, why didn't I pursue the robbery angle more? We might have solved it a lot sooner."

To Sal's friends and the Hollywood gay community, the reason the robbery angle hadn't been pursued was that Tankersley and oth-ers had made up their minds that Sal died because he was a queer.

A lot of people in America in 1976 would have said Sal got what he deserved, because everybody who'd ever seen a movie with a queer in it knew that the fairy had to die.

However, overheard jailhouse talk and the uncorroborated story of a wife who might have had her own agenda were not proof that Lionel Raymond Williams had murdered a queer movie star. To claim success, the detectives would have to develop evidence that would enable a district attorney to present a case of murder to a jury and prove it beyond a reasonable doubt.

The prosecutor assigned to the case was Deputy District Attorney Burton S. Katz. It was not his first high-profile murder case. In the Charles Manson case he had obtained convictions of two male Manson followers, Bobby Beausoleil and Steve "Clem" Grogan, for the slayings of two other targets of Charlie Manson's madness, Gary Hinman and Donald "Shorty" Shea.

Katz's first tasks in the Williams case were to charge him with the murder and seek his extradition from Michigan to Los Angeles. Having done the first, and with Williams under arrest and being detained in Michigan, he was assisted in the second when Williams waived his right to resist being returned to California. But Williams insisted he was not guilty.

Exclaimed Sheriff Pitches to a throng of reporters in his office on January 4, 1978, "The sheriff's bulldogs have done it again."

Why the bulldogs had needed almost two years to "have done it again" was not explained, nor that the arrest of Williams hadn't been the result of sleuthing by his bulldogs, but had come about because of a disgruntled wife and jailhouse bragging that was first overheard by guards and then picked up by a concealed microphone. Neither did Sheriff Pitches note that all of this was circumstantial evidence, some of which might fall into the category of inadmissible hearsay when the case went to trial. While Pitches and D.A. Katz had a suspect in custody, they had nothing in the way of corroborating evidence, such as the murder weapon.

Pitchess did have a new theory of the murder. Sal Mineo hadn't been a chance victim.

"Our belief is that it was a premeditated murder," he declared, "because as you will recall, Mineo was returning from the rehearsal of a play and came directly there to his place of residence and had just left his car when he was attacked."

In positing the theory that Williams had been waiting for Sal in order to rob him but had been scared off of robbing him by Sal's cries for help, the sheriff provided a basis for the charge of murder while "lying in wait." This made Williams, if convicted, eligible for the death penalty.

Pitchess also held open the possibility that Williams knew Sal Mineo, but he gave no indication he had evidence of a relationship between them.

On the basis of Theresa Williams's story that Lionel had recently bought a hunting knife, Pitches told the press that such a knife had been the murder weapon. He did not state at the press conference that his detectives were in the process of finding a duplicate of the knife Williams was believed to have used. They began by asking Theresa Williams to describe the knife and whether she knew where her husband had bought it. The best she could do was point them to stores that sold such knives and which she knew Lionel patronized.

Their purpose in finding the place where Williams bought the knife was to get an identical one. They'd been told what to look for by the L.A. County Medical Examiner Dr. Noguchi. He showed detectives the "negative cast" of the fatal wound to Sal's chest. Examination of its width and depth provided the dimensions of the knife. Combined with Theresa's description of its color, shape, and the price Lionel had paid made finding a twin relatively easy. They presented a duplicate to Noguchi's office.

"Normally, we don't insert an allegedly matching knife into a wound during an autopsy because it would distort the incision," he wrote in a chapter on the Mineo murder in his book. "But now, because the tissues had been fixed in formalin for storage, we could do so without such distortion. We inserted the blade of this knife into the wound, and it matched perfectly."

The detectives next set out to find the car Williams drove on the night of the murder. The witnesses at the scene thought it was a yellow Toyota. Legwork by investigators determined that on February 12, 1976, Williams had borrowed a light-colored 1971 Dodge Colt from a Lincoln-Mercury dealer. Proof that he'd done so was found in the firm's files. It was a loan agreement that Williams had signed. In the opinion of the detectives, a Dodge Colt could easily be mistaken for a Toyota. They swore to this in a report that D.A. Katz incorporated in a sworn declaration of "information and belief" that enabled him to lodge a charge of murder against Williams and bring him back from Michigan to be arraigned.

Upon his arrival Williams was interviewed by detectives. He denied the charge. But as he was being interrogated, one of the questioners noticed a fresh tattoo on Williams's arm. It was a knife. Asked about it, Williams said, "I had it done while I was back in Michigan." In the opinion of the detective and others it was a picture of the kind of knife Williams had bought, that they'd found a duplicate of, and that on the night of Lincoln's birthday and the 43rd anniversary of the wedding of Salvatore and Josephine Mineo had been plunged into their beloved youngest son's chest, perforating his heart and causing him to bleed to death in an alley behind a $75-dollar-a-month apartment littered with gay magazines and pictures of naked men.

On January 17, 1978, seven days after what would have been Sal Mineo's 39th birthday, 22-year-old Lionel Raymond Williams stood before Judge Andrew J. Weitz in Beverly Hills Municipal Court for a pretrial hearing on whether Deputy D.A. Burton J. Katz had sufficient evidence to hold Williams for trial. Wearing L.A. County Jail fatigues and slippers, he was asked to enter a plea to ten counts of robbery, one attempted robbery, and first-degree murder.

He answered, "Not guilty."

Bail was set at half a million dollars.

Asked by a reporter if he believed he'd beat the rap, Williams said, "Yeah, man. I'm cool."

Leaving in shackles to be returned to jail, he looked at a courtroom jammed with people who'd put their asses in seats to see the man who'd killed Sal Mineo.

Williams grinned and said to a deputy, "This is a big deal, ain't it?"

eighteen

_____

Who Would You Cast?

With Lionel Williams bound over for trial, Deputy D.A. Burton Katz could proceed with the case either with a hearing in which Williams through his lawyer could challenge each piece of evidence in open court or a presentation to a grand jury in which Katz would be in control of what the jurors heard. He declared that he wished to avoid "a circus" and chose the latter route. To no one's surprise Williams was indicted on the ten counts of robbery, the attempted robbery of Sal Mineo, and first-degree murder.

The court-appointed lawyer representing Williams at this stage of the proceedings was Robert Harris. He wasted no time in complaining about Katz's tactics. "Had the case gone to a preliminary hearing," he said, "witnesses would have been exposed to vigorous cross-examination and evidence helpful to the defense would have been presented. The prosecution obviously does not want that."

Harris continued, "One thing I know for sure is that Mr. Williams's mother, who says Williams was with her the night of the murder, was not even summoned to appear."

Katz said he'd also chosen the grand jury route "for the protection of witnesses, some of whom fear for their lives. We've already lost one of our witnesses." He declined to elaborate. He may have meant the person who first implicated Lionel. After going to detectives with

a story about her husband's bloody shirt and admission of murder-
ing Sal Mineo with a hunting knife, Theresa Williams had shot herself in the head.

With Lionel indicted, the prosecution now passed from Katz into
the hands of Deputy D.A. Michael Genelin. Confident of the evidence amassed against Williams, he referred to the tattooed knife
on the defendant's arm as "the mark of Cain."

He defined the man he would prosecute as "a strange breed of
cat, totally unconcerned with any human being. He doesn't give a
damn who he hurts. He told his girlfriend that when he felt bad he
had to go out and hurt someone."

Part of the evidence that Genelin would present to a jury was
testimony by 26-year-old Allwyn Price Williams. Nicknamed Rock,
he was not a relative of Lionel, but he had participated in an armed
robbery with Lionel in 1976. Allwyn was in jail on a kidnapping-
robbery charge unrelated to Lionel's activities. Allwyn stepped forward looking to cut a deal for immunity from prosecution for
testifying against Lionel.

He informed prosecutors that on the date of the Mineo murder
he'd been employed as a civilian warehousemen in a U.S. Army-
operated club in Germany. Before that he'd been in the Army. In
both occupations he'd trafficked in heroin. He said he'd flown to
Los Angeles in March 1976 to deliver a package of heroin to Lionel
in North Hollywood, for which Lionel paid $2,500. Lionel invited
him to go along on a robbery on March 7. They and a confederate
held up four people in Beverly Hills. Allwyn then flew back to Germany. Asked why he'd taken part in the robbery that netted him
little in the way of money ($200) compared to his heroin proceeds,
he said, "I did it for the hell of it."

Before returning to Germany, Allwyn said, Lionel had told him
about killing Sal Mineo. Allwyn, Lionel, a cousin of Lionel's (Perry
Ross), and two or three other men had been "drinking and taking
drugs" and bragging about their criminal exploits. Allwyn said that
Lionel claimed to have killed someone famous. When asked who it
was, Lionel had replied, "Sal Mineo."

According to Allwyn, Lionel said he had been driving around in
Hollywood below Sunset looking for someone to rob. He'd spotted
Mineo getting out of his car, accosted him, and stabbed Mineo with

a pearl-handled knife. Because Mineo had yelled, Lionel left him on the ground with his money and valuables untouched and fled in a Lincoln Continental.

Word that Allwyn had been talking to prosecutors reached Lionel. Furious about this, he wrote a note to a visitor. It asked for the aid of someone named Big Perry and said, "The Rock is trying to kill me. I want to do something to Rock right away. He can kill me. So do something about him. He is against me all the way. Important. He is in high power."

The note was intercepted. "Lionel Williams knew that Allwyn had finked on him and could send him to the gas chamber," a member of the prosecution said, "so he apparently was soliciting his murder—or at least bodily harm—in the county jail."

Yet no matter what Lionel Williams might have said about killing Sal, the testimony of Allwyn Williams and other jail inmates did not prove that Lionel Williams thrust a knife through Sal Mineo's heart. The only person who could put a knife in Williams's hand in the alleyway after Sal parked his car on the night of February 12, 1976, would have to have been an eyewitness. But there was no such individual.

This was the main point that would be made in Lionel Williams's defense at trial. His new lawyer, Mort Herbert, would also emphasize that neither was an alleged duplicate of the murder knife conclusive evidence against Lionel. Nor did the word of a medical examiner that the knife presented by the police fit the preserved stab wound mean that Lionel Williams held one just like it in the alley where Sal Mineo was found bleeding to death—from which, according to witnesses in the alley minutes later, a *white* man had fled.

The only eyewitnesses to crimes attributed to Lionel Williams in the indictment were the people who'd looked him in the face when he robbed them. In that aspect of the trial the attorney for State of California had a strong position.

Mort Herbert felt that the case for convicting Lionel Williams of the first-degree murder of Sal Mineo was riddled with reasonable doubt.

A routine petition to Superior Court Judge William Ritzi to dismiss the indictment was routinely denied on March 3, 1978. The trial was scheduled for May 25. Legal maneuvering by both sides delayed the date into the next year.

*   *   *

Before the proceedings against Lionel Williams went on hold, Susan
Braudy, a freelance journalist who'd written on the subjects of
crimes and films for *The New York Times* and *The Atlantic
Monthly,* published an article about Sal's life and murder. Titled
"The Slow Fade," it ran in the March 1978 issue (actually published
in February) of *Crawdaddy.* A magazine for the hip generation, its
cover featured a picture of Gilda Radner with John Travolta to hype
an article by them entitled "Looking for the Heart of Saturday
Night." Promoting the Braudy piece, a small blurb said, "Sal Mineo:
End of a Hollywood Dream." The article ran nine pages. A teaser
headline above a head-and-neck photo of a mature, long-haired Sal
said, "Sal Mineo peaked at 20 and died two years ago this month
at 37. His world was the darker side of Hollywood. Even James
Dean couldn't save him." The article covered Sal's career and life
through his funeral.

    Braudy reported that her attempt to interview Courtney Burr III
about his relationship with Sal had proved unavailing. Noting that
Burr had been the beneficiary of Sal's Screen Actors Guild insurance
policy, she wrote that Burr had told her, "I can't talk about him.
People have always talked about me, because of my association with
him. No, I can't talk about myself apart from him. He taught me
so much. He is one quarter of my life. I owe him a great deal."

    Braudy's article discussed what she'd learned of Burr's acting ca-
reer, that he apparently gave Sal money, had used an inheritance to
finance their stay in England, and "reports of sexual jealousy on
both men's parts."

    The article would not be the last time Susan Braudy would be
heard from on the subject of the life and death of Sal Mineo.

The day before Sal's 40th birthday and nearly three years since the
murder, six men and six women assumed seats in the jury box to
hear opening arguments by prosecutors and defense counsel. Their
sworn duty was to listen to witnesses, weigh the evidence, follow
the law as defined for them by Judge Ronnie Lee Martin, and then
deliberate and decide whether 23-year-old Lionel Raymond Williams was, in fact, "a strange breed of cat, totally unconcerned with

any human being" who didn't give a damn who he hurt in pulling a series of robberies and had incidentally killed Sal Mineo.

Knowing the weakness of evidence to support the first-degree murder charge, prosecutor Genelin adopted a strategy he called "connect the dots." If jurors made a dot on a piece of paper representing each fact and coincidence in the Mineo murder and then drew lines between the dots they would see that they'd drawn a picture of the face of Lionel Williams.

The state would be asking the jury to make a leap from overwhelming evidence that Lionel Williams was a violent predator to say that he *probably* also murdered Sal Mineo.

Defense attorney Herbert's strategy was to show that if just one of Genelin's dots was out of place, it represented reasonable doubt. It was not acceptable with a man's life at stake to come back and say "He *probably* did it!" or "It's *very likely* he's the killer."

Herbert hoped to undercut the state's case through witnesses' descriptions of the figure observed running away from the murder scene.

Scott Hughes took the stand to relate having seen a man with curly hair who looked Italian or Mexican jump into a yellow Toyota and speed off.

Stephen Gustafson described a white man with a long nose, high cheekbones, and dirty blond or brown hair.

Monica Merrem, now 12 years old, told of looking through her window and seeing a man wearing a black leather jacket. She said he had dark curly hair and was "very white."

Genelin countered with a police photo of Williams taken after the killing when he was booked for the robbery of the man whose windshield he'd smashed with a hammer. The mug shot was of a black man with light complexion and long bleached hair.

When Genelin presented Allwyn Williams, the star witness appeared in the uniform of a private in the U.S. Marine Corps. His deal with the L.A. District Attorney's office, he told the jury in cross-examination by Herbert, was a reduction of the kidnap-robbery charge and a one-year suspended sentence. Since then he'd joined the Marines.

Herbert extracted from Allwyn the information that in the story he'd given prosecutors to get his deal he had lied twice. Allwyn admitted he'd made up the pearl-handled knife and Lincoln Continental getaway car. "I was hoping to get out of jail," he said. "I told them [about the knife and car] because I felt my prior statements were not strong enough."

"Would you lie again if it was absolutely necessary to get off the hook?"

Allwyn replied, "I guess so, sir."

Still pursuing the deal struck between Allwyn Williams and the D.A., Herbert called to the witness stand the man who'd approved it. Burton Katz, now a municipal judge in Beverly Hills, defended the bargain, notwithstanding Allwyn's admission that he lied on two key points.

To further undermine Allwyn's credibility, Herbert put on the stand one of the men whom Allwyn had named as participating in the bragging session during which, according to Allwyn, Lionel had admitted killing Sal Mineo. A cousin of Lionel, Perry (Chick) Ross III said it hadn't happened. When cross-examined by D.A. Genelin, Ross was forced to admit that he'd lied when he said he'd never been arrested. Genelin showed he'd been arrested for assault with a deadly weapon, marijuana possession, and hit-and-run driving. So much for a cousin's credibility!

On January 31, 1979, in the fourth week of trial, both sides rested. Granting them one day to prepare their closing arguments, Judge Martin told them to be back in court February 2.

Summing up the case against Williams, Genelin connected the dots. The knife that fit the wound. The tattoo. The bragging. The robberies. The yellow car Williams had borrowed on that day. The area he favored for his muggings. The police mug shot in which Williams had long hair and could have passed for white in a dimly lit alleyway. The image Genelin found by connecting the dots was a portrait of "a predator."

This was a progressive process with him.

"These were not just street robberies but one incident after another where he inflicted pain and enjoyed it.

"He is a sadist, a man who wants the world to know how tough he is."

Why else would he brag about killing a dude who turned out to be a movie star?

Having gotten rid of the murder weapon, why not get a tattoo on his arm of the knife he'd used and show it off as a mark of how mean he was?

"He is a night marauder who would kill you if he had to—even if he didn't have to."

Connect the dots of coincidence, ladies and gentlemen of the jury, and a face will emerge, "and that face is the face of the defendant."

Mort Herbert's summation on behalf of Lionel Williams went directly to the question of the race of the man seen running from the spot where dying Sal Mineo curled into a fetal position as his blood formed a widening pool around himself, his glasses, clipboard, cupcakes, and car keys. He was keenly aware that the jurors before him were equally alert to the fact that the victim had been a famous actor. A movie star who was in *Rebel Without a Cause* with James Dean. He was the kid who fought for the Jews in *Exodus* beside Paul Newman. He'd gotten two Academy Award nominations. He'd been on *Columbo.*

In a movie or TV show called *Who Killed Sal Mineo?* who should play the murderer?

On the basis of descriptions provided by the witnesses who had testified about seeing the killer running from the scene of the crime, what kind of actor should a casting director look for?

"I want him to have large curls," said Herbert. "I want him to look like an Italian. And I want him to have large cheekbones. I want him to have a long nose. I want him to be about five feet ten inches tall. And I want him to be *white.*"

Herbert stepped out of the way of the jurors' view of the crowded court. "Look around the room and point out who is the *last person in the world* that you would cast for this part," he said, "and I submit to you that he is sitting at the end of the counsel table."

The jurors' eyes went to the defendant.

"Whether Lionel Raymond Williams is a saint or scum or someplace in between," Herbert said, "you are to judge him by the standards of reasonable doubt and your own conscience—and nothing else."

No connecting imaginary dots. No jumping to the conclusion that because Lionel Williams had been a very nasty mugger marauding through the plush pickings of Beverly Hills, he'd turned his car off Sunset Boulevard and parked near the very modest apartment house on Holloway Drive to lie in wait until he saw a young man who looked like an easy target.

No thinking that Lionel Williams *probably* did just what the prosecution contended.

In the law books of the Golden State and in a criminal court in the City of Angels where the charge was murder, *probably* required a verdict of *not* guilty.

As the jurors filed out to begin deliberating, Lionel Williams, who knew nothing about the movies or casting actors but who was very familiar with the looks on jurors' faces, whispered to Mort Herbert, "My God, they're going to convict me on every one of these things."

Not quite. On Valentine's Day they came back to court and said they had found him not guilty of the attempted robbery of Sal Mineo and guilty of murder in only the second degree, thus sparing him from the death penalty.

Williams's reaction was to unwrap a stick of chewing gum and pop it into his mouth.

Mort Herbert was disappointed but not surprised by the verdict.

He offered a tribute to Michael Genelin. "Whenever the state has a weak case," he told reporters who had covered the trial, "they use their strongest prosecutor."

On March 16, 1979, as Williams appeared before Judge Martin, he was not as generous to his lawyer. Noting that Herbert had been appointed by the court, he said to the judge, "He wasn't in my corner. I didn't want him, but you put him on me. I asked you to get rid of the man twice but you didn't do it. I fault you for my going to the penitentiary."

Martin gave him the maximum: 11 consecutive sentences amounting to 51 years to life. She said she did this because Williams's criminal record began when he was 14 years old. "I don't think he's susceptible to rehabilitation," she said, "considering his escalating conduct of committing more and more serious crimes, with more and more violence."

Under California's new set-term law, legal experts estimated that

Williams would serve about 14 years. With good behavior he would be eligible for parole in nine years. In 1981 an appeal based on a claim that he had been wrongly convicted was denied by the California Supreme Court. He made parole in the early 1990s but was soon back in prison, still proclaiming he didn't kill Sal Mineo.

Many of Sal's friends believed him. They were convinced that those who were involved in the Mineo case saw in a mugger against whom the evidence in ten robberies was overwhelming an easy way to close the file and end the embarrassment of not solving the murder sooner because they'd assumed it was a fag killing.

Mort Herbert said only, "Basically, this was a case of ten brutal robberies with Mineo tacked on. It was ironic that Mineo became a very minor part of the trial."

Did Lionel Williams kill Sal Mineo? Because I believe the prosecution presented a very shaky case founded on circumstantial evidence, were I a juror I would have been left with more than a reasonable doubt that the charge was proved. Lacking hard evidence to show me that *only* Williams could have killed Sal Mineo, I would have voted to acquit and wished that we in the United States had the option of jurors in Scotland who can come back to court with a verdict of "not proven." The jurors in Sal's case connected all the dots and as far as the law was concerned, the case was over. If Lionel Williams didn't kill Sal, who did? In 25 years, there has been no other plausible suspect or motive proposed.

Because Sal's life was cut off in a moment of promise, his murder was an offense against all of us who'd learned from movies that lives of good people deserve happy endings. That is why the universal reaction to Sal's murder was bewilderment. When I heard of his death on the radio in my house in Huntington Beach, I was one of the millions who asked, "Who would kill Sal Mineo? Who *could* kill Sal Mineo?"

The answer is that the man who plunged a knife into Sal's chest *didn't know* he was killing Sal Mineo. Sal died because of bad luck. If he had chatted a little longer with Keir Dullea . . . if his second-hand Chevelle had had a flat tire . . . if only he had stopped for a drink in a gay bar . . .

epilogue

Plato Lives!

When Samuel French, Inc., a publisher of plays, printed the script of *P.S. Your Cat Is Dead* in 1979, the author, James Kirkwood, wrote in Author's Note that "this play is dedicated to Sal Mineo, who was a perfect Vito in San Francisco and who was rehearsing again for the Los Angeles production at the time of his tragic death. He is greatly missed."

In the same year a brief account of Sal's life and murder was published in a profusely illustrated book about celebrities who met untimely deaths. Written by Patricia Fox-Sheinwold, *Too Young to Die* contained brief biographies of Sal and 30 others presented chronologically from Valentino to Elvis. Sal's filled ten pages. One of the photos was a publicity picture taken at the time of *Fortune and Men's Eyes* when Sal and the cast had posed naked in a gymnasium shower room. Lathering himself with soap, he's shown from head to just above the pubic hair.

While the Fox-Sheinwold compendium on the too-soon demises of famous people was in the process of publication, the woman who'd written about Sal's life and death for *Crawdaddy* in March 1978 had become fascinated by the circumstances of Sal's murder and the fact that many observers of the trial doubted Lionel Williams's guilt. Susan Braudy wondered: if Williams didn't murder Sal Mineo, who might have? Her theory of the crime took the form of fiction.

Published in 1982 by Wyndham Books, a division of Simon & Schuster, Braudy's 318-page novel's title asked *Who Killed Sal Mineo?*

It carried a disclaimer, "Any references to historical events; to real people, living or dead; or to real locales are intended only to give the fiction a setting in historical reality. Other names, characters, places, and incidents either are the product of the author's imagination or are used fictitiously, and their resemblance, if any, to real-life counterparts is entirely coincidental."

The book's cover was a photo of a teenage Sal Mineo superimposed on a picture of part of the Sunset Strip. Flap copy noted, "Mineo's real-life murder in the late 1970s is the spark that ignites Susan Braudy's novel into a spellbinding investigation of the violence and 360-degree sexuality that are part of Hollywood's secret life."

Laudatory blurbs on the jacket were provided by some heavyweight names in the field of book-writing. Novelist Robin Cook found "all the ingredients of a great tale," including show business, celebrities, sex, and "a fascinating look at the psychosexual cauldron of Los Angeles." An author of true-crime books, Peter Maas, said, "It's the best novel about the kinky Hollywood scene I've read in a long time . . . In the tradition of Nathaniel West, and of Raymond Chandler, had he had a female operative."

The novel built on, expanded upon, and interpreted the facts of Sal's life and career that Braudy presented in the *Crawdaddy* article, but the novel weaves a story depicting Sal as a homosexual sadomasochist deeply involved in drugs. Assigned by a newspaper to write a follow-up story on the Mineo murder, investigative reporter Sarah Martin digs into it and quickly becomes convinced that the solution of Sal's death will unlock the dark consequences of Hollywood's narcissism and its habit of instant gratification.

Who killed Sal Mineo?

In the novel, Sal's boyfriend has stolen cocaine from a woman, who wants it back. She believes Sal has the stuff. Sal confronts her, threatening trouble if she doesn't leave his lover alone. She sends an associate to see Sal and settle the matter. He is supposed to scare Sal but things get out of hand.

The novel generally received good reviews and fared well in bookstores.

Other authors became interested in writing about Sal's life and violent and mysterious death, but they produced true-crime books in which Sal's murder would be one chapter, as it had been in *Too Young to Die*. In 1983 one of the most prolific true-crime writers, Jay Robert Nash, published *Murder Among the Rich and Famous*. Its cases encompassed a century (1872 to 1980). The nine-and-a-half-page chapter devoted to Sal was subtitled "The Murder of a Rebel."

The year after Nash's hardcover book, Jeff Rovin published a paperback, *TV Babylon*. It dealt not only with celebrity murders but also scandals. "Sal Mineo: 'Stabbed' " summarized Sal's career in two paragraphs and devoted the rest of its three-and-a-half pages to the murder and trial.

In 1985 Boze Hadleigh brought out *Conversations with My Elders*. It was mainly transcripts of interviews—Hadleigh called them "encounters"—with famous homosexuals: Luchino Visconti, Cecil Beaton, George Cukor, Rainer Werner Fassbinder, Rock Hudson, and Sal. The "encounter" with Sal was the first in the book. Hadleigh recalled Sal's trip to Santa Barbara in 1972 when Sal had expressed admiration for Michael York by calling him "a hunk." The text of the interview ranged from Sal's films to his thoughts on bi- and homosexuality. (Eight years after the book was published, Hadleigh was himself interviewed by Ronald Milton on the subject of "Sal Mineo Remembered" for the June 1993 issue of a gay magazine, *Mandate*.)

St. Martin's Press in 1987 published Michael Munn's *The Hollywood Murder Casebook* (a paperback edition came out the next year). "Case 12" was "Sal Mineo: 'The Switchblade Kid.' " It ran nine pages. On the last page Munn wrote, "He died before he was ready, before he had done the things he wanted to. And what he wanted was to be *someone* again."

A Pinnacle True Crime paperback edited by Art Crockett, *Celebrity Murders* (1990), had a recap of the murder and lengthy account of the case against Williams. Written by Chris Edwards, it was titled "Day of Reckoning for Sal Mineo's Murderer."

An oversize, lavishly illustrated *Dead Before Their Time*, co-authored by Diana Karanikas and Jackson Harvey, was published in 1996. The introduction was accompanied by a page-and-a-half photo of Natalie Wood stroking Sal's hair as he and James Dean look at each other lovingly in the scene in the deserted mansion in *Rebel*. The title page for chapter two, "Dial M for Murder," is again a page-and-half photo with Sal. It's of Plato with his eyes shut tight as he fires the pistol at Jim Stark. The passage devoted to Sal was accompanied by a color head-and-shoulders portrait. He wears a red sweater over a navy-blue knit shirt with its open collar revealing a gold necklace on which he wore his Christopher medal.

In 1992 William Morrow Co. published the third of Roddy McDowall's *Double Exposure* books in which a McDowall photo of a star was accompanied by an essay by another star. Sal's was written by Dennis Hopper. He recalled using Sal "as a shill" to distract Natalie Wood's tutor on *Rebel* "so that I could get Natalie out of the trailer." He remembered Sal's "beautiful brown eyes, his innocence, and how proud he looked in his uniform" as Angel Obregon II in *Giant*. Inexplicably, Hopper wrote and an editor failed to catch an erroneous statement that Sal had been stabbed 58 times "by a crazed killer."

Among these books, the one that disturbed Sal Mineo fans was Susan Braudy's novel. They were outraged by the portrait she'd presented of him. The book also added to the pain of the Mineo family, already anguished by what his murder and a renewal of interest in him during the Lionel Williams trial had exposed about his sex life.

Having faced a parent's worst heartache—the death of a child—Josephine Mineo had to go through it again on June 28, 1984. Michael died of a heart attack at the age of 47. He was buried next to Sal and their father at Gate of Heaven cemetery.

For a few years Michael had lived with a young woman who had met Sal while browsing in a store in Hollywood that specialized in motion-picture collectibles. Her name was Trevina. They began a friendship. After Sal's murder, she moved to New York and took a job as a magazine reporter. While researching an article on Sal, she contacted Michael. They fell in love, became a couple, and opened the health-food store in Mamaronek where Josephine pitched in to help out by handling the checkout counter.

Devastated by Michael's sudden death, Trevina went back to L.A.

She began writing a play about Sal and his idol, James Dean. Because the site of Dean's death was near a bridge over a creek near the town of Cholame, the play was given the awkward title *Occurrence Near the Cholame Creek Bridge*.

In 1994 a young actor auditioned to portray Sal. Born in Buffalo, New York, he'd acted at the drama school of the Studio Arena Theater where *P.S. Your Cat Is Dead* was first staged. From Buffalo he went to Toronto to train with Wayne Thomas, who'd mentored Michael J. Fox and Jason Priestley. He then went to Hollywood and gained parts in several film, TV, and theatrical productions. His name was Brandon Slater. He bore a remarkable resemblance to Sal. However, because of irreconcilable creative differences among the production staff and Trevina about how the play was to be presented, the show did not go on.

In preparing for the role of Sal Mineo, Slater studied Sal's life and death and became convinced that Lionel Williams had been framed and that investigators of his murder knew who the real killer was. Having been a conspiracy buff concerning the Kennedy assassination, Sal would no doubt have been interested in the idea that the truth about his own murder had been covered up by the government.

He probably would also have been intrigued that his murder had caught the attention of so many writers, and that so long after he was stabbed to death in Boys Town he could still fascinate the gay world. As an example he might have pointed to the September 1985 issue of the magazine *Playguy*. Along with numerous photos of sexually aroused young men and gay fiction titled "A Space Orgy," "In the Line of Duty," and "A Cock Like a Garden Hose," the readers of the magazine were offered a serious, non-pornographic article by Bill Baumer with the simple title "Sal Mineo."

Baumer began by recalling hearing the news on the radio on February 13, 1976, that Sal had been murdered. He wrote, "I didn't know that some people thought he was murdered by an ex-boyfriend or a hustler. I didn't know, either, that living in a West Hollywood apartment complex just below the Sunset Strip 'meant something.' I didn't know he was gay. What I did know was a sense of loss; I felt as if he and I had shared a little secret. We met at two A.M. across the screen of my portable black-and-white television. He did something for me by helping me understand a little bit more about myself."

When asked to do a "life and works" piece about Sal, Baumer was hesitant.

"Chronicling his career wouldn't be difficult," he wrote, "but I was apprehensive about discovering the 'real' Sal Mineo. Would I uncover a Hollywood 'star' whose love for the trappings of Tinsel Town outstripped his talent? Would my image of him as an intense yet vulnerable man be shattered? Would I come up with a portrait of a bitter man who had been at the top of his profession, but who was later saddled with the label of 'has been'?"

The Sal discovered during his research and talking to people who knew him, Baumer wrote, was "a good actor, a somewhat confused and self-doubting man, generous to others, wonderfully self-mocking, totally inept in handling his finances, and a fighter determined to break the mold Hollywood had cast for him."

It was a concise and accurate portrait.

Four years after Baumer's article was published, the tiny, effervescent, optimistic, loving woman who had worried what would become of her beautiful third son; had grabbed a chance to keep him on the right path in life by enrolling him in dancing class; had seen him attain wealth, fame, and popularity as a star of TV, stage, and screen; and had suffered with him when it all came crashing down was reunited with him in the Gate of Heaven cemetery. No son was ever loved more by, or owed more to his mother.

In 1998 there appeared on a means of communication that had not existed when Sal Mineo lay dying in an alley of Boys Town in 1976 the following message: PLATO LIVES!

The exclamation of immortality showed up on an Internet chat room dedicated to keeping alive the memory of Sal Mineo. Created by a devoted fan, Kimberley Hartman, the "tribute" to Sal contained a "biography" with the awkward title, "Pretty Boys Make Graves." Through its message board Sal's other fans, whether longtime or having just found Sal through one of his movies on television, were able to express their feelings for him.

A man named Deke wrote of having "recently discovered" him by renting *Rebel Without a Cause* "more or less at random." He became "an instant fan."

On the 22nd anniversary of Sal's murder, the following messages were posted:

"Let us remember him in the many facets of what he was and all the good he did. God love our Sal."

"What a wonderful person to cherish."

"I think Sal is HOT."

"The more I learn about Sal Mineo's life the more fascinated I become."

Six weeks before these messages were posted, "Norma" had discovered the site as she surfed the World Wide Web. She wrote, "I was a 9 year old girl when my older sister had to take me to the movies with her. We went to see 'The Young Don't Cry,' and I discovered Sal Mineo. He became my life's obsession until his death 17 years later. I abandoned him and his memory in anger and disappointment when aspersions were cast on his character."

When Norma learned that Sal preferred to make love to men, she was crushed. She had entertained the same fantasy as millions of girls that one day she would meet Sal, he would fall in love with her, and they'd marry and live happily ever after. Heartsick, Norma destroyed a collection of Sal Mineo photographs and other items that she had lovingly assembled. But suddenly in 1998 she found herself again opening her heart to him and collecting Sal Mineo memorabilia.

The result of Norma Harding's rekindled affection was a collaboration with two other Sal Mineo fans, John Seger and Karen Hardcastle, in the Web page, "Sal Mineo Tribute." Found at the World Wide Web address Salmineo.com, it offered a filmography, Sal's TV schedule (listing which of his films or TV shows were running on what dates and times), a picture gallery, and a means of posting thoughts about Sal in a "guestbook" for others to read. In January 2000 they launched a campaign to raise money to finance a Sal Mineo star they believed was long overdue on the Walk of Fame.

One means by which Norma and other fans collected Mineo memorabilia, films, and other collectibles was through Internet auction sites, especially eBay. On most days scores of Sal Mineo items were offered, ranging from programs for *The King and I* when Sal was appearing as the prince and the playbill for *Fortune and Men's Eyes,* a computer mouse pad with his photograph, a Sal Mineo Fan Club membership pin, and genuine posters and lobby cards for his movies, to vintage 45s and the LP made by Sal during his brief stint as a recording artist.

Mineo films were also available on video through services such as Amazon and Barnes and Noble. The recently released CD containing Sal's performance and other songs from the TV production of Cole Porter's *Aladdin* could also be purchased.

Occasionally in the 1990s various film appreciation societies screened Sal's films. Several presented *Rebel Without a Cause* to mark the 40th anniversary of its making. A group of film enthusiasts gathered in June 1996 at the Castro Theater in the very heart of San Francisco's gay community to watch *Who Killed Teddy Bear?* It was also screened in August 1996 at the Cinefest Film Theater in Atlanta and at New York's Film Forum in March 2000.

In a January 30, 1998, edition of the online magazine *Lavender,* columnist David Blanco asked, "Who was Sal Mineo?" He answered the question by summarizing Sal's life and career in an article titled, "From Teen Idol to the Planet of the Apes." Discussing *Rebel,* he noted, "The character of Plato is significant in gay filmography because he was the first gay teenager in Hollywood history." He continued, "Like many gay characters in films of that era, Plato died a violent death at the movie's end, while Jim went on to a heterosexual future with Judy."

In late 1999 the E! cable TV program *Mysteries and Scandals* presented a half-hour show on Sal's life and career with the emphasis on how he met his death. Around the same time, the A&E cable network's *Biography* offered a one-hour program that emphasized his work as an actor whose career went into decline and his struggle to make a comeback in theater, only to have his dream snuffed out by a man with knife. Both programs were repeated early in 2000.

By the time these documentaries were shown and perhaps introduced Sal Mineo to a new generation of Americans, Sal's most memorable film was regarded as a milestone in the history of motion pictures and a defining moment in the creation of the youth culture that had been cited by Elia Kazan in the 1950s as a distinct demographic power.

Many people who admired *Rebel Without a Cause* had come to believe in a *Rebel* "curse." Since the film's completion in 1955, violent death had overshadowed it:

James Dean, killed at dusk speeding along a California highway four days before the film's premiere in New York;

Nick Adams, dead at age 37 of an overdose of drugs and in a mood of despair over the failure of his marriage and the decline of his career;

Nicholas Ray, dead after a long and painful struggle against lung cancer;

Natalie Wood, accidentally drowned; .

Sal Mineo, murdered.

All were gone before they reached the age of 50.

These bizarre deaths, especially Dean's, enshrined Sal and Natalie in a *Rebel Without a Cause* cult that a half-century after the picture was made shows no sign of waning in its appeal to each new generation of teenagers who find it on television or home video.

Some students of film consider it great because it captured the essence of adolescence. It is seen as an ageless story of growing up.

Film historian Parker Tyler, in *Screening the Sexes,* disagreed. He wrote that *Rebel* "matters not in the least" as a serious work of fiction.

"By far its greatest interest is Dean and Mineo," he continued, "as they play out the game of displaced sex: the senior master type and the junior slave type irresistibly, if subconsciously, drawn to each other."

Nine months after somebody wielded a knife in an alley in Boys Town, Sal Mineo spoke for the last time of the actor who was the idol and first and lasting love of his life. Sal had been interviewed for an article for *New York* magazine that was published on November 8, 1976.

Sal said, "I realize now, twenty years later, that from the moment I met Jimmy my whole life took on a completely different meaning. Where I am as a person today goes with the time I was developing, when I didn't realize what was happening. It was only years later that I understood I was incredibly in love with him. But at the time, that feeling was something else. I never found men sexually attractive. No way. But I realized later that I was homosexually attracted to him. When he showed love to me, when he said it, that did it. The very last time I saw him, I had a feeling. I was sad and yet vibrant. I mean, those are feelings I can understand, but I just knew that I was feeling something that I didn't feel with anything or anybody else."

When Dean died, Sal spent the rest of his life hoping to find that feeling again.

The admirable, lovable thing about him is that he never gave up believing in love and in his talents.

Not once on his roller-coaster ride, whether he was going up, at the crest, or plummeting into disgrace with fortune and men, did Sal Mineo raise those dreamy brown eyes, shake a fist, and lift his "wop from the Bronx" voice to trouble deaf heaven and beweep his outcast fate.

Author's Note

When I began thinking about writing the biography of Sal Mineo, I wondered how many people besides myself would remember or care about an actor who'd been dead for nearly one-quarter of a century. I discovered that everyone to whom I mentioned him said, "Sal Mineo! I remember him." Why the name rang a bell was a puzzle to some. But when I said, "Plato in *Rebel Without a Cause*," eyes lit up and smiles appeared. "Yes, of course," was the general response, "he was wonderful in that." Older friends had seen *Rebel* in a movie theater. Younger ones had watched it on television or on home video. I never spoke of *Exodus* to a Jewish friend who did not immediately recall Sal's portrayal of Dov Landau.

I was amazed that no one had done a book. His life had all the elements of a great story: the poor kid with glowing charm and natural ability to entertain gets discovered by a producer. Breaks into the movies. Instantly becomes a star and heartthrob of millions of teenage girls. Gains the approval of peers in the form of *two* Academy Award nominations before he's old enough to vote. Then he hits the skids, goes broke, can't get work. But he refuses to give up. He's on the road to a stunning comeback when some guy steps out of the shadows of an alley and sticks a knife in him.

And what ironies! A father who made coffins told him to grab life and enjoy it because one day he'd be fitted for just such a box. The night he was murdered was his parents' wedding anniversary. It was also the birthday of an American president whose portrait he'd painted. Ironies and coincidences don't stop there. Not long before his murder he'd been a guest star on three TV dramas whose titles foreshadowed events that unfolded as police looked for his killer: "Marked for Murder," "Man Running," and "The Hunters."

His family was notified of his death on Friday the 13th. The trial of the man charged with his murder began the day before his 40th birthday. At the start of his movie career the nickname bestowed on him by film critics and audiences had been "Switchblade Kid," and he was stabbed to death.

Added to all this drama was the fact that after Sal Mineo discovered he preferred to make love to men, he not only refused to conceal his preference, he proclaimed it by producing a play with an onstage homosexual rape. He followed that with another show with a gay theme. Then he played a bisexual burglar. It was a role he expected to put him back on the Hollywood A list.

In undertaking the writing of the life, career, murder, and mystery of Sal Mineo I faced the daunting task of learning everything about him. I'd done two biographical studies of Theodore Roosevelt and one of President Grover Cleveland, for both of whom there exists an abundance of material in the form of public record, their letters and diaries, voluminous coverage by the press, and biographies. No such convenient archive existed for Sal Mineo.

In wondering where to find him I recalled the great English architect Christopher Wren who built and is entombed in London's St. Paul's Cathedral.

"If you seek his monument," someone had said, "look around."

Another actor who'd been a hit in movies in his youth, Robby Benson, once said to me, "Every frame of a movie is eternal." To begin my search for Sal Mineo I had a unique record in his movies and TV shows and in articles in newspapers and magazines that followed his career step by step from "The goat is in the yard" to a humpy, wisecracking, bisexual burglar telling his captive, "Don't touch me. My body is a temple."

Early in my quest, I tapped into the mystifying but marvelous World Wide Web and found a treasure trove of data. I also discovered Sal Mineo collectibles for sale on auction sites such as eBay. These told me that people were interested enough in Sal Mineo to want things connected to him and to compete fiercely with one another to obtain them.

Material related to his television roles was available by a mouse-click from the Library of Congress and in other archives. Copies of most of his movies could be bought on video. Critical summaries

of some of his films were available via the Internet. Sal Mineo fil-
mographies were also found with all the credits of people associated
with making them, from the director to the assistant sound man.
There were commentaries and analyses of the films. Magazines had
done contemporary profiles of him.

As I ventured into cyberspace looking for information on a long-
dead movie actor, I met people for whom Sal was still alive. Soon I
was engaged in almost daily e-mail conversations about him with
fans and Mineo collectors. Eventually, I found myself in contact
with people who had known him and worked with him. They were
willing to put me in touch with others who were happy to enlighten
me further. For example, because I'd become acquainted with
Norma Harding when we found ourselves repeatedly competing to
buy Sal Mineo items online, and because she later helped create a
Sal Mineo Tribute Web page, I found Joe Bonelli. Because Joe was
associated with *Fortune and Men's Eyes* in L.A. and New York
longer than anyone but Sal and the show's producers, he provided
valuable insights regarding *Fortune* that were available nowhere
else. Through Joe I observed Sal casting, directing, promoting the
play by showing up at a movie premiere handcuffed to the cast, and
giving house seats to a guy who'd slapped him with a summons. Joe
also told me about Sal looking at himself with James Dean in *Rebel
Without a Cause* on the Joey Bishop TV show and then admitting
he'd let the whole world see his soul for ten seconds.

Not everyone was willing to dip into memories that could be
painful. It didn't matter. I found an enormous amount of information. In scores of newspapers and magazines from *The Saturday
Evening Post* and *Life* to *Modern Screen*, *TV Guide*, and
publications for gays, Sal gave interviews that were amazingly frank
and revealing. During his meteoric ascent to stardom, his mother,
sister, and brothers also happily shared their experiences with reporters and interviewers. What they said rang with an authenticity
that my research corroborated.

Pieces of the Sal Mineo puzzle were found in numerous volumes
on the movie business and in memoirs and biographies of people
who worked with him. In books related to the period in which Sal
was a significant figure in Hollywood it was rare not to find his
name in the indexes. As noted in the epilogue of this book, his mur-

der and the trial of Lionel Williams were included in true-crime books. They afforded me viewpoints of other authors and allowed me to check and double-check my data as I wrote. Having been a newsman for more than 30 years before I took up book-writing full-time, I concur with the old aphorism that journalism is the first draft of history. Accordingly, I turned to press coverage of Sal's murder in newspapers in Los Angeles and elsewhere and in trade papers such as *Variety* and *The Hollywood Reporter*.

The process of writing a biography is very much like making a movie. A film is images shot out of sequence and put together in an editing room. When it's finished, no matter how many people worked on it, the responsibility lies with a director. This biography was also a collaborative effort. To those who helped me re-create Sal's life I extend my gratitude. Any errors are mine.

When Sal and I talked from time to time in the last seven years of his life about me writing his biography, we agreed that the best way to remember him would be to watch his films.

If you seek his monument, see them.

Sal Mineo's Credits

Feature Films

1955   SIX BRIDGES TO CROSS. Universal-International.
        THE PRIVATE WAR OF MAJOR BENSON. Universal-International.
        REBEL WITHOUT A CAUSE. Warner Bros.
1956   CRIME IN THE STREETS. Allied Artists.
        SOMEBODY UP THERE LIKES ME. MGM.
        GIANT. Stevens & Gilsberg, Warner Bros.
1957   DINO. Block-Kamansky Productions.
        THE YOUNG DON'T CRY. Columbia.
        ROCK PRETTY BABY. Universal-International.
1959   TONKA. Disney, Buena Vista.
        A PRIVATE'S AFFAIR. 20th Century-Fox.
        THE GENE KRUPA STORY. Columbia.
1960   EXODUS. Otto Preminger.
1962   ESCAPE FROM ZAHRAIN. Paramount.
        THE LONGEST DAY. 20th Century-Fox.
1964   CHEYENNE AUTUMN. Warner Bros.
1965   THE GREATEST STORY EVER TOLD. George Stevens/United Artists.
        WHO KILLED TEDDY BEAR? Magna.
1969   80 STEPS TO JONAH. Warner Bros.
        KRAKATOA, EAST OF JAVA. Cinerama.
1971   ESCAPE FROM THE PLANET OF THE APES. 20th Century-Fox.

Television

PROGRAM	EPISODE TITLE	DATE
HALLMARK HALL OF FAME	"A Woman for the Ages"	5/5/52
OMNIBUS	"The Capital of the World"	12/6/53
JANET DEAN, REGISTERED NURSE	"Jose Garcia"(Syndicated)	1954
BIG TOWN	"Juvenile Gangs"	11/1/55
OMNIBUS	"William Saroyan"	10/16/55
PHILCO TELEVISION PLAYHOUSE	"The Trees"	12/4/55
FRONTIERS OF FAITH	"The Man on the 6:02"	12/25/55
STUDIO ONE	"Dino"	1/2/56
LOOK UP AND LIVE	"Nothing to Do"	1/15/56
SCREEN DIRECTORS PLAYHOUSE	"The Dream"	5/16/56
ALCOA HOUR	"The Magic Horn"	6/10/56
CLIMAX	"Island in the City"	10/4/56
PERSON TO PERSON	Interviewed by Edward R. Murrow	12/14/56
KRAFT TELEVISION THEATER	"Drummer Man"	5/1/57
KRAFT TELEVISION THEATER	"Barefoot Soldier"	10/2/57
DUPONT SHOW OF THE MONTH	"Aladdin"	2/21/58
PURSUIT	"The Vengeance"	10/22/58
JANET DEAN, REGISTERED NURSE	Untitled (Syndicated)	1959
ANN SOTHERN SHOW	"The Sal Mineo Story"	11/2/59
CRY VENGEANCE	NBC-TV special	2/21/61
DUPONT SHOW OF THE WEEK	"A Sound of Hunting"	5/20/62
GREATEST SHOW ON EARTH	"The Loser"	10/22/63
DR. KILDARE	"Tomorrow is a Fickle Girl"	3/19/64
KRAFT SUSPENSE THEATER	"The World I Want"	10/1/64
COMBAT	"The Hard Road Back"	10/24/64
PATTY DUKE SHOW	"Patty Meets a Celebrity"	1/20/65
BURKE'S LAW	"Who Killed the Rabbit's Husband?"	4/14/65
MONA MCLUSKEY	Untitled	1/27/66
COMBAT	"Nothing to Lose"	2/1/66

RUN FOR YOUR LIFE	"Sequenstro"	3/14/66
		3/21/66
COURT-MARTIAL	"The House Where He Lived"	4/29/66
COMBAT	"The Brothers"	10/4/66
THE DANGEROUS DAYS OF KIOWA JONES (MOVIE)		12/25/66
BOB HOPE CHRYSLER THEATER	"A Song Called Revenge"	3/1/67
STRANGER ON THE RUN (MOVIE)		10/31/67
HAWAII FIVE-O	"Tiger by the Tail"	10/10/68
THE CHALLENGERS (MOVIE)		3/28/69
NAME OF THE GAME	"A Hard Case of the Blues"	9/26/69
NAME OF THE GAME	"So Long Baby, and Amen"	9/18/70
MISSION: IMPOSSIBLE	"Flip Side"	9/26/70
MY THREE SONS	"The Liberty Bell"	1/2/71
THE IMMORTAL	"Sanctuary"	1/7/71
DAN AUGUST	"The Worst of the Game"	2/11/71
IN SEARCH OF AMERICA (MOVIE)		3/23/71
HOW TO STEAL AN AIRPLANE (MOVIE)		12/10/71
THE FAMILY RICO (MOVIE)		9/12/72
HAWAII FIVE-O	Untitled	10/10/72
HARRY O	Untitled (pilot)	3/11/73
GRIFF	"Marked for Murder"	10/27/73
TENAFLY	"Man Running"	1/2/74
POLICE STORY	"The Hunters"	2/26/74
POLICE SURGEON	Untitled	10/19/74
HAWAII FIVE-O	"Hit Gun for Sale"	2/25/75
HARRY O	"Elegy for a Cop"	2/27/75
THE ROOKIES	"S.W.A.T."	3/3/75
S.W.A.T.	"Deadly Tide"	9/13/75
COLUMBO	"Case of Immunity"	10/12/75
POLICE STORY	"The Test of Brotherhood"	11/14/75
ELLERY QUEEN	"Adventure of the Wary Witness"	1/25/76
JOE FORRESTER	"The Answer"	2/2/76

Theater
Broadway

1951–52	THE ROSE TATTOO	"Salvatore"
1952	DINOSAUR WHARF	Shoeshine boy
	(four performances)	
1952–53	THE KING AND I	"Prince Chulalongkorn"
1964	SOMETHING ABOUT A SOLDIER	Recruit
	(12 performances)	

Off-Broadway

1969	FORTUNE AND MEN'S EYES	Director
1969	THE CHILDREN'S MASS	Director

Los Angeles

1969	FORTUNE AND MEN'S EYES	"Rocky" and Director

San Francisco

1976	P.S. YOUR CAT IS DEAD	"Vito"

Awards

1955 Academy Award nomination, Supporting Actor, *Rebel Without a Cause.*

1956 Emmy nomination, *Dino.*

1960 Academy Award nomination, Supporting Actor, *Exodus.*
Golden Globe, Supporting Actor, *Exodus.*

Also, *Modern Screen* magazine poll, Favorite Actor; *Film Daily* Survey, best actor; *Motion Picture Herald* Award for Achievement; *Independent Film Journal* award; Exhibitors Laurel Award as one of the top ten personalities of 1956–57.

Index

Index

Shannon, Mark, 139
Shea, Donald "Shorty," 192
Sheldon, Sidney, 127
Short, Elizabeth, unsolved murder of, 188
Shulman, Irving, 23, 24, 33
Siegel, Donald, 53
Silk Hats gang, 67, 68
Silver Chalice, The, 25, 51
Simenon, Georges, 150
Simmons, Jack, 28, 29
Simoni, Dario, 90
Sinatra, Frank, 45, 99
Sirhan Bishara Sirhan, 162, 163
Six Bridges to Cross, xi, xiii, 16-18, 23, 28, 48, 82, 218
Skir, Leo, 157
Skolsky, Sidney, 28
Slater, Brandon, 208
Sloan, Everett, 51
"Slow Fade, The," 198
"So Long Baby, and Amen," television, 147, 220
Somebody Up There Likes Me, xi, xiii, 44, 50-53, 160, 218
Somebody Up There Likes Me (book), 39, 45, 50
Something About a Soldier, stage play, 105, 221
Sons and Lovers, 95
Spartacus, 95, 97
Speigel, Terry, 165
St. Catherine's Military School, 19
Stack, Robert, 80
Stage 73, xii, 137-138, 139, 142
Stapleton, Maureen, 7, 9, 27-28, 46
Steiger, Rod, 105
Steinbeck, John, 21
Stern, Stewart, 24, 25, 30, 32-33, 43, 87
Stevens, George
  as director, 37, 39
  Giant, 36, 38
  The Greatest Story Ever Told, 124

Stevenson, Harold, 168
Stewart, James, 84, 108, 110
Sticks and Bones, stage play, 173
Stone, Harold J., 51
Stonewall Rebellion, xi, 138-139, 142, 157-158
Stranger on the Run, television movie, 128
Strasberg, Lee, 44
Strip, Sunset Boulevard, 119, 120, 125
Stritch, Elaine, 46, 115-118
Studio One, disco, 158, 159
Studio One, 21, 46-47, 219
Such Dust As Dreams Are Made On, television, 150
Sundowners, The, 95, 97
"Switchblade Kid," xiii, 55, 60, 66, 180-181
  shedding the image, 69, 72, 97
"*S.W.A.T.*," television series, 164, 220

T

Tankersley, Dan, murder investigator, 178, 191
Tate, Sharon, 163-164
Taylor, Elizabeth, 36, 112
Taylor, William Desmond, unsolved murder of, 188
Ted Steele Show, The, early performances on, 6
Teenagers, as movie audience, 48-49, 55, 59, 76-77
"Telephone psychotic, the," 116
Television
  Hollywood shows on, 80
  James Dean, 21
  Sal Mineo, 13-15, 21, 46-47, 57, 58, 60, 107, 128, 147, 150, 164-165
Temple, Shirley, 112
Ten Commandments, The, 89
Tenafly, television series, 164, 220
That Certain Feeling, 86

The Method, 44, 45
They Only Kill Their Masters, 172
This Property is Condemned, stage
     play, 7
Thomas Crown Affair, The (1968), 51
Thomas, Wayne, 208
"Tiger by the Tail," television, 128,
     220
To Hell and Back, 67
Todd, Thelma, unsolved murder of,
     188
Tokatyan, Leon, 115
Ton Ombre est la Mienne, 101
Tonka, xiii, 69-70, 218
Too Young to Die (book), 204, 205
Tracey, Spencer, 45, 61, 79
Travanti, Daniel J., 115, 116
Treasury Men in Action, television, 21
"Trees, The," television, 15, 219
Trevina, 207-208
Troup, Bobby, 74
Trumbo, Dalton, 85
"Tube, The," 48
Turner, Lana, discovery of, 17, 84
TV Babylon (book), 205
TV dinner, invention of, 61
2001: A Space Odyssey, 173
Tyler, Parker, 145, 212

U

Untouchables, The, television series,
     80, 107, 112
Uris, Leon, 24, 83, 92
U. S. Steel Hour, James Dean, 21
Ustinov, Peter, 95, 97

V

Valentino, Rudolph, 18-19
van Druten, John, 2
Van Fleet, Jo, 39, 150

Vidal, Gore, 29
Visconti, Luchino, 206

W

Wagner, Edward A., 78
Wagner, Robert, 62, 99, 105
Wagon Train, television series, 128
Walk of Fame, The, 111, 210
Wallach, Eli, 7, 9, 27-28
Walsh, Raoul, 72
Warden, Jack, 107
Warfield, Donald, 154
Warner, Jack L., 49
Warren Commission, Kennedy assassi-
     nation, 162-163
Watch on the Rhine, stage play, 7
Waterskiing, 14-15, 114
Waxman, Joseph, 77
Waxman, Philip A., 73
Wayne, David, 165
Wayne, John, 105
Webb, James R., 108
Weis, Don, 73, 127
Weise, Moe, 133
Weitz, Judge Andrew J., 194
Weld, Tuesday, 80
Welles, Orson, 7
Werker, Alfred L., 56
West, Nathaniel, 205
West Side Story, 106
Whiteman, Paul, 173
Whitmore, James, 53, 56
Who Killed Sal Mineo? (book),
     205
Who Killed Teddy Bear?, xiii, 115-
     119, 181, 211, 218
Widmark, Richard, 108
Wilcox, Collin, 60
Wild Angels, 146
Wilkes, Bobby Jack, 128
Williams, Allwyn Price, testimony of,
     196-197, 199-200

About the Author

H. Paul Jeffers has published 40 books. His nonfiction includes *An Honest President, The Life and Presidencies of Grover Cleveland,* three books on Theodore Roosevelt, two studies of the FBI, and a history of Scotland Yard. A member of the Sherlock Holmes society The Baker Street Irregulars, he is the author of 14 mystery novels. For part of his 33 years as a broadcast journalist before devoting himself full-time to writing books, he worked as a theater and movie critic. He lives in Manhattan.